Beautiful Twentysomethings

Marek Hłasko. Warsaw, 1955.

Beautiful Twentysomethings

Marek Hłasko

Translated by Ross Ufberg

Foreword by Jaroslaw Anders

NIU PRESS / DeKALB, IL

© 2013 by Northern Illinois University Press

Published by the Northern Illinois University Press, DeKalb, Illinois 60115

Manufactured in the United States using acid-free paper

All Rights Reserved

Design by Shaun Allshouse

Library of Congress Cataloging-in-Publication Data

Hlasko, Marek.

Beautiful Twentysomethings / by Marek Hłasko ; translated by Ross
Ufberg ; foreword by Jaroslaw Anders.

pages cm

ISBN 978-0-87580-477-4 (cloth : acid-free paper)

ISBN 978-0-87580-697-0 (pbk : acid-free paper)

ISBN 978-1-60909-095-1 (e-book)

1. Hłasko, Marek. 2. Authors, Polish—20th century—Biography. I.
Ufberg, Ross, translator. II. Title.

PG7158.H552A3 2013

891.8'537—dc23

[B]

2013017701

Frontispiece: Marek Hłasko. Warsaw, 1955. [Courtesy of Archive MH.]

Support for this publication was generously provided by the Kosciuszko
Foundation, the American Center of Polish Culture, Promoting Educa-
tional and Cultural Exchanges and Relations between the United States
and Poland since 1925.

Generous support was also given by the Department of Slavic Languages
and Literatures of Columbia University.

Contents

An Introduction to Marek Hłasko

Jaroslaw Anders

Every generation of Polish writers that had to live and create under the communist regime can be described as a "lost generation." But the generation born in the 1930s was probably the most ill-fated of them all. It was a profoundly tragic generation that also happens to be one of the least well known to Western audiences.

Members of this generation, of which Marek Hłasko was to become the most celebrated icon, lived through World War II as children. They witnessed the unprecedented eruption of evil, experienced fear and brutalization of human relations, from the perspective of passive, helpless victims. Having survived this nightmare, they grew up and made their first attempts at adult life in the stifling, menacing years of Stalinism. Unlike their older colleagues—the generations of Czesław Miłosz, Tadeusz Różewicz, Zbigniew Herbert, or Wisława Szymborska—they lacked any memory of a different reality, knowledge of a different culture capable of sustaining a semblance of faith in history and in humanity. As Hłasko reminisces in *Beautiful Twentysomethings*, during their school years Soviet propaganda and socialist realist drivel were the only reading available and Western authors were practically unknown.

The relative and short-lived liberalization of political and cultural life after Stalin's death seemed to open new opportunities for this generation. The few years in the mid-1950s that constituted the Polish version of Khrushchev's "thaw" did witness a series of brilliant literary debuts. Apart from Marek Hłasko, the group included such names as poets Andrzej Bursa, Stanisław Grochowiak, Jerzy Harasymowicz, and Halina Poświatowska, short story writer Marek Nowakowski, and dramatist Ireneusz Iredyński, to be followed by slightly younger adepts of literary lost-ness, such as the poet, prose writer, and lyricist Edward Stachura and the poet Rafał Wojaczek.

The second half of the 1950s was also a heyday of literary cabarets and politically progressive theater—places like the Students' Satirical Theater (STS) in Warsaw, the Cellar under the Rams in Kraków, or Little Theater Bim-Bom in Gdańsk, led by another generational icon, actor Zbigniew Cybulski. It was a time when jazz came to Poland in a big way, mostly influenced by American "cool," with the leader of the Polish jazz scene Krzysztof Komeda giving it a distinctively local character. New ideas were also transforming Polish cinema, although the creators of what later became known as the "Polish School" of cinematic art—Andrzej Wajda, Kazimierz Kutz, Andrzej Munk, Jerzy Kawalerowicz, and others—belonged to a slightly older generation. Hłasko's contemporaries in film, such as directors Roman Polański or Jerzy Skolimowski, had to wait for their screen debuts until the 1960s.

Many of these people knew one other and collaborated artistically, forming a new bohemian community that also included a fair number of "characters," eccentrics known less for their own artistic creativity than for their wit, unconventional lifestyles, and usually dark, slightly menacing charm, like the rich playboy and aspiring actor Wojciech Frykowski, who would die in Roman Polański's villa at the hands of the Manson gang; the mysterious stonecutter, amateur actor, and prose writer Jan Himilsbach; or Jerzy Kosiński, whose literary career would take off only in America.

There was quite a bit of playacting, mystification, and showmanship that characterized both the lives and the work of many members of this generation. They liked to embellish their biographies with invented heroic or scandalous incidents, style their clothes and demeanor after Western cultural icons (Hłasko's famous photo with ruffled hair and a cigarette dangling from his lips is pure James Dean), and stage little real-life performances to provoke or confuse innocent bystanders. But there was also something dark and extreme in much of their artistic production—a fascination with ugliness and violence, a proclivity to depict the seemingly inevitable debasement of everything noble and lofty in what they saw as a thoroughly corrupt and degraded world. Perhaps prevented from clearly articulating the source of their anger, they lashed out against everything that smacked of normality, convention, and decorum. The setting of their stories is often the milieu of big-city riffraff, the impoverished, perennially drunk, semicriminal world, the last, sad expression of "real life" surviving in the crevices of the socialist Potemkin village. Ireneusz Iredyński spoke for many of his colleagues when he said: "I'm interested in extremes. They are the best reflection of the main tendencies of our time. A certain world is dying right in front of our eyes, our future is obscured."

The turbulence, brutality, and degradation they depicted in their work often spilled into their lives, as if in order to remain creative and true to themselves they had to imitate the existence of their forlorn protagonists. They wasted themselves in drunkenness, drugs, sexual excess, and run-ins with the law, and there were an unusual number of untimely, tragic, and mysterious deaths among this small group of friends and companions.

Against this backdrop, Marek Hłasko's life looks like a perfect example of his generation's promises, triumphs, and failures. He was born in 1934—the only child of a civil servant father and a mother with artistic and intellectual ambitions. His parents divorced when he was three, and his father died in 1939, a few days after the outbreak of World War II. During the German occupation his mother supported herself and her son by running a food stall in Warsaw, until they lost everything in the failed Warsaw Uprising of 1944. Forced to leave the city with the rest of its civilian population, they moved to Częstochowa, where they witnessed the brutal "liberation" of their country by the Red Army. Later, Hłasko would say that the hunger and terror of the war accounted for what he called "the intellectual poverty" of his stories. "I simply cannot make up a story that wouldn't end in death, a catastrophe, a suicide, or prison."

After typical postwar peregrinations, Hłasko's mother, her new life companion, and Marek settled down in Wrocław. Undisciplined and aggressive, he was expelled from one school after another, first in Wrocław, and later in Warsaw. For a while he studied at the Warsaw High School of Theater Arts, which trained future backstage professionals but also offered acting workshops and other "creative" subjects. He ended his formal education at sixteen and started earning his living as a truck driver, although he was unable to keep any job for more than a few months.

It appears that from his early years Marek kept some sort of a diary and displayed a writing talent. It is hard to tell, however, what pushed this unruly and poorly educated young man to try his hand as a "professional" writer. But he started writing in earnest in 1951, around the same time he was recruited as a "people's reporter" for the Communist Party organ *Trybuna Ludu*. He was working on a novel about the tough Warsaw neighborhood of Marymont and sent fragments of his work to Polish writer Bohdan Czeszko. Encouraged by his response and advice, Marek decided to turn the material into several short stories. In 1953, thanks to another writer and a family friend, he received a three-month literary stipend that allowed him to leave his job and spend some time finishing his first pieces. His stories started appearing in Polish newspapers in 1954. His true debut, however, was a collection of short stories, *Pierwszy krok w chmurach* (*A First Step in the Clouds*). Published in 1956, it established both Hłasko's style and his favorite themes. Written in economic, understated language with minimalist descriptions and terse dialogue, the stories treated seemingly tough and jaded but in fact sensitive, predominantly male, young outsiders trapped in the circle of hopelessness and despair of their gray, disadvantaged existence. They harbor vague dreams of something beautiful and liberating that seems within their reach— usually represented by romantic love for a woman. But the degraded, claustrophobic reality inevitably frustrates those dreams, leaving them even more hopeless and cynical. The title story of the collection tells about an attempt at tender lovemaking by a young couple in a public park, brutally interrupted by the vulgar jeering of drunken gawkers. At the end, the story leaves the humiliated and disgusted lovers and focuses on their tormentors, who seem in equal measure satisfied and saddened by the lesson of "real life"—the only one they know—they had just taught the young romantics.

This pessimistic picture of the life of the Polish working class, which Hłasko claimed to know from experience, was in direct contradiction to the official communist propaganda. Some critics pointed out that Hłasko exploited the conventions of socialist realist fiction by putting them on their head—that he simply replaced one facile formula with another. While in proscribed socialist realist writing everything was to be good and uplifting, in Hłasko's world everything had to be bad, relentlessly bad, and discouraging. But after the years of Stalinist cant, this reversal of signs seemed fresh and revelatory, and expressed some form of truth that all suspected but were afraid to call by its name.

In 1955–57, in the heyday of the Polish "liberalization," Hłasko quickly became a literary celebrity and a symbol of his ascending, rebellious generation. He became a prose editor and columnist in an important political and cultural magazine, *Po Prostu* (*Simply Speaking*), which tried to carry the banner of post-Stalinist "renewal." A trio of graduating students of the Polish Film Academy in Lodz produced the film *Koniec nocy* (*Night's End*) based on Hłasko's screenplay, with Zbigniew Cybulski and Roman Polański playing the main roles. His novella *Ósmy dzień tygodnia* (published in English as *The Eighth Day of the Week*), about a young woman who deliberately destroys her love for a former political prisoner (played, again, by Cybulski), was being adapted for the screen by director Aleksander Ford in an ambitious Polish–West German coproduction with an eye on international distribution. Another novella, *Następny do raju* (available in English as *Next Stop—Paradise*), and a story "Pętla" ("The Noose") were also being put on screen. Hłasko was treated with fatherly indulgence by political rulers, celebrated by critics as the most talented Polish prose writer, and idolized by the masses for his bohemian, rebellious lifestyle. He was making good money, mainly from his movie contracts, although he continued to live like a poor bohemian artist.

His disheveled good looks made him the object of desire of many women and quite a few men in Polish cultural circles.

But the political skies soon started to darken, and censorship started to tighten again. Publishers, so enthusiastic not long ago, were reluctant to publish his new work, especially *Next Stop—Paradise*, the story of a group of former criminals hauling timber in the mountains on rickety, unsafe rigs (its film version, *Baza ludzi umarłych—The Depot of the Dead*—was given a more optimistic meaning against Hłasko's protests), and *Cmentarze* (available in English as *The Graveyard*), a Kafkaesque story of a loyal Communist Party member who through a series of mishaps ends up expelled from the party and blacklisted, losing his job and his family. *The Eighth Day of the Week* was still in production, but Hłasko hated Ford's prettified version (which would not save the film from a twenty-five-year-long ban in Poland). The signs were clear enough: Hłasko's career, as well as the fate of his whole generation, was again in the hands of political puppet masters. The period of relative creative freedom was coming to an end.

In 1958, still enjoying the support of his colleagues in the Polish Writers' Union, the author received a literary stipend to travel to Paris with a group of Polish writers that included the future Nobel Prize winner Wisława Szymborska. He always claimed that he had every intention of returning to Poland, but he made contact with the Literary Institute in Maisons-Laffitte near Paris, a respected Polish émigré publishing house, and offered it his *Graveyard* and *Next Stop—Paradise* for publication. That almost instantly made him *persona non grata* in Poland. He kept trying to extend his passport, but was rebuked by Polish authorities. He had to return to Poland immediately, facing the prospect of never traveling abroad from then on, or stay abroad with little chance of seeing his country again.

In the meantime, his literary reputation in Poland and his political problems at home attracted the attention of Western publishers and the media. Several of his books were translated and published throughout Europe, and there was talk about new movie deals. Throughout the storm of his first years in the West, Hłasko remained close to the Literary Institute; he published in its periodical, *Kultura*, and even lived for a while in Maisons-Laffitte. But the attempts by the institute's head, Jerzy Giedroyc to "manage" Hłasko's career in the West proved futile. The Polish author behaved like the public celebrity he believed he was, gave interviews to disreputable publications, hung out with the wrong crowd, drank to excess, got into fights, and wasted money. He quickly antagonized many of his friends and burned a lot of bridges.

In Paris, Hłasko established an unfortunate self-destructive pattern. Having spent his early career navigating the difficult waters of cultural life under communist rule, he was completely unprepared, and also probably unwilling, to navigate the very different but equally treacherous waters of literary life in the West. He believed in his star power and expected to achieve success—by which he meant not only literary recognition, but also money and fame—on the strength of his talent and charisma, without much effort. He refused to master the art of marketing, publicity, and image building. Failing to receive what he thought was his due, he grew angry and contemptuous, eventually ending up marginalized and alone.

Hłasko continued writing and publishing short stories and novellas, but his life, already marked by depression and alcoholism, was clearly falling apart. Its details were also becoming increasingly murky and often contradictory, with much of the gossip probably perpetuated by the author himself. He had to support himself doing menial work. He apparently was imprisoned for disorderly conduct, spent some time in mental institutions, and attempted to commit suicide twice. He traveled to West Germany and Italy, and spent a year in Israel, where he worked, again, as a laborer. His four novellas and several short stories set in Israel, including *Brudne czyny* (*Dirty Deeds*), *Wszyscy byli odwróceni* (*All Backs Were Turned*), *Drugie zabicie psa* (*Killing the Second Dog*), *Nawrócony w Jaffie* (*Converted in Jaffa*), "Opowiem wam o Esther" ("Let Me Tell You about Esther"), and "W dzień śmierci Jego" ("The Day of His Death"), are considered some of his best, and also darkest, among his prose works. (*All Backs Were Turned* and *Killing the Second Dog* are also available in English.) He settled for a while in West Germany, marrying a popular German actress, Sonja Ziemann, who played the heroine of *The Eighth Day of the*

Week, and he entertained some prospects of working on a German movie, but a romantic scandal ended both his marriage and his German artistic plans.

In 1966 he went to America on the invitation of Roman Polański, who was just working on his *Rosemary's Baby*. His acquaintance with Polański and with Krzysztof Komeda, who was composing music to Polański's films, gave him access to Hollywood studios, but the expected new break in his career never materialized. He tried his hand as a Hollywood screenwriter but was discouraged by the lack of production offers. He was approached by CBS, which wanted to try him as a TV series writer, but he apparently failed to follow up on the offer. He continued writing in Polish, and *Kultura* published his series of articles "Letters from America." He was also taking flying lessons and working on his "American" novel about a mysterious pilot from behind the Iron Curtain, published posthumously in 1985 as *Palcie ryż każdego dnia* (*Rice Burners*). But, as before, he had to support himself by hard manual labor and in his free time was visiting Los Angeles bars with his Polish pals Krzysztof Komeda, Wojciech Frykowski, and Polish-born Hollywood photographer Marek Niziński.

In December 1968, Hłasko went with Komeda for a late night walk in the Hollywood hills. They were both seriously drunk, and neither of them was later able, or willing, to explain what really happened. But Komeda ended up unconscious with a bleeding head, at the bottom of a ditch. Hłasko tried to carry him out, but dropped him and tumbled down himself, probably aggravating Komeda's injuries. He eventually managed to get his friend to a hospital, and Komeda quickly recovered. But a few months later he fell ill and went into a coma. A blood clot was discovered in his brain, which might have been related to his fall. Running out of money, Komeda's wife took him back to Poland, where the composer died in April 1969.

Komeda's death devastated Hłasko. It is possible he blamed himself for it. "If Krzysio goes, I will go with him," a friend remembers him saying during Komeda's final illness. He left America for West Germany, talking about plans to start a movie collaboration with his estranged wife. On June 14, 1969, at age thirty-five, he was found dead in his apartment in Wiesbaden with a deadly mixture of alcohol and sleeping pills in his blood. It is not certain whether it was suicide or an accidental overdose.

Beautiful Twentysomethings, written before Hłasko's American trip and published in 1966 by the Literary Institute, has often been described as the author's attempt at autobiography, as his life credo, as his political and cultural commentary about life under communism, and also as a kind of manifesto of his whole generation. In a sense it is all of the above, but its main value consists in its unique portrayal of the writer's tormented psyche—his dreams, hopes, disappointments, his anger, his particular mixture of self-aggrandizement and self-depreciation. Despite its tone of a picaresque adventure story—with a strong dose of posturing and machismo—it is also a sad tale of decline and failure, of helplessness and loss shared by Hłasko with so many brilliant people of his generation.

Attempting to grasp the factors that shaped him, the narrator moves back and forth between his life in Poland, as a young rebel chafing under the ideological yoke, and his years in the West, as a down-and-out "free man." He reaches back to his horrifying wartime childhood and to his often frustrating literary beginnings. His invariably vitriolic portraits of Polish cultural personalities of the late 1950s—his literary mentors and artistic collaborators—are often unfair but always witty and perceptive. He declares his love for Dostoevsky and for American pulp fiction; he writes about his disappointment with the seemingly liberal *Po Prostu* and about his surprisingly positive reception in the party organ *Trybuna Ludu*. He also comments on the main political event of his generation, a series of protests in 1956 known as the "Polish October," which ushered in a seemingly more liberal communist regime. He declares his conviction that "books are only worth writing after you cross the outermost boundary of shame," and he tells, often in bragging terms, about his drunken escapades and his conflicts with the law in France, West Germany, and Israel. (His claim that he sometimes earned his living as a pimp and a gigolo should probably be taken with a grain of salt.) He notes bitterly that only prominent communist apparatchiks defecting to the West were greeted with open arms, book contracts, and teaching positions, while average, decent defectors were "greeted by years of misery, humiliation, waiting on a visa: years of emptiness and despair." He skewers both East Europeans, for their shameless peddling of their victimhood, and gullible Westerners, for their endless reservoirs of compassion, especially when it does not require any sacrifice on their part.

Most importantly, however, *Beautiful Twentysomethings* captures the fundamental paradox of Hłasko's generation. Tormented and oppressed by the political environment of their youth, they were also, in a sense, its product and its expression. They could not function outside its confines as creative individuals. The world into which they were born both destroyed and inspired them. Those who chose emigration lost not only their favorite subject, but sometimes also the very locus of their existence. They grew silent and resentful, or tried to recreate and relive the familiar oppressiveness, squalor, and paranoia in Paris, New York, Jaffa, or Hollywood. The exercise proved often more deadly than when they were facing communist censorship and secret police.

Hłasko and his generation continue to fascinate just as the period they lived in and described is receding into history. In his native Poland, Hłasko has experienced several posthumous returns, and one seems to be going on right now. The author may be right when he says that "there weren't any masterpieces made" in his time. His own literary output, as well as the output of many of his colleagues, is often uneven, and there is something sadly fragmentary and unfinished about it. But as Hłasko puts it in *Beautiful Twentysomethings*, they gave "evidence of the powerlessness of a person living in a nightmare who doesn't have the inner strength to recognize it as such." They were the first to challenge the monster and carried the scars of combat throughout their short or long lives. Brought up in an all-encompassing lie, they were desperately searching for "truth" and "authenticity" in the darkest, most dangerous regions of experience. Their somber vision and rough poetics purified Polish literary language and imagination, preparing the ground for future generations and future battles.

Preface

Marek Hłasko was one of the first Polish writers to capture my imagination. His writing was so fresh, so bold, so unlike anything I'd read before, that I was hooked. I shared what was available in translation with others, and when I exhausted the supply, I undertook one myself. *Beautiful Twentysomethings* is the fruit of those labors.

The first and largest debt of gratitude, which I can never hope to pay back though I will keep trying, is to Professor Anna Frajlich-Zając, Senior Lecturer in Polish at Columbia University. Professor Frajlich—poet, mentor, teacher, friend—sat with me for many hours in many places discussing Polish literature in general and my translation in specific, literally line by line. In fact, I should rather call this "our" translation, for without Professor Frajlich it would never have seen the light of day.

I want to acknowledge the East Central European Center at Columbia University, and Director Alan H. Timberlake, for financial and moral support of this translation. In addition, I'm incredibly thankful to the Harriman Institute and the Slavic Department of Columbia University, and the Kosciuszko Foundation and its president, Mr. Alex Storozynski, for various grants during the course of this project, without which I'd never have had resources to complete what I'd started.

Thanks also to Mr. Andrzej Czyżewski, executor of Marek Hłasko's literary estate, who, in addition to granting permission to translate and publish this book, also shared the photographs seen between these covers. Jarosław Anders, a gentleman always, contributed the lovely "Introduction to Marek Hłasko," and my hat is off to him.

Finally, I'd be remiss if I didn't acknowledge Amy Farranto, my editor (twice now) at NIUP and always a ray of light, no matter the skies. Amy is kind and smart and full of insight; she owns a royal sense of humor, and working with her has been a rare pleasure. Max Ufberg helped me trim the semicolons; Stefanie Halpern, who humbles with her brilliance, helped smooth out the translation. To Danielle Golden, my wife, who tolerated my final midnight rounds of editing, gratitude is what I can offer, though it is not nearly enough.

Translating Hłasko was an education in language, literary style, and culture, both Polish and American. He often misquotes from American films or literature, either archly or in error, and I've been faithful to his words. I have also tried to stay true to the film noir tone of the original, even if at times it seems foreign to today's vernacular. Marek Hłasko wrote hard-boiled prose, and I didn't want to cook the English translation sunny-side up. All errors are mine, and mine alone. The success this book may enjoy, however, rests on a multitude of glorious shoulders.

—R.U.

Beautiful Twentysomethings

CHAPTER ONE

Belt, Shoelaces, Tie, If You Don't Mind

In February 1958, I disembarked at Orly Airport from an airplane that had taken off in Warsaw. I had eight dollars on me. I was twenty-four years old. I was the author of a published volume of short stories and two books that had been refused publication. I was also the recipient of the Publishers' Prize, which I'd received a few weeks before my departure from Warsaw. And one more thing: I was known as a finished man, and it was taken as a given, beyond any doubt, that I'd never write anything again. As I said, I was twenty-four years old. Those who'd buried me so quickly with the skill of career gravediggers were older than me by thirty years or more. Adolf Rudnicki once wrote that the most fashionable trend in Polish literature is carving others into mincemeat. That same Adolf Rudnicki, when I published my first story, asked me:

"Are your colleagues already saying you're a finished man?"

"Why?" I asked him.

"Well," said Rudnicki, "when I wrote *Rats*, my first book, I met Karol Irzykowski, and Irzykowski asked, 'Are your colleagues already saying you're a finished man?'"

Disembarking from the plane at Orly Airport, I thought I'd be back in Warsaw in no more than a year. Today, I know I'll never return to Poland. I also know, writing this, I wish I were wrong. I haven't spoken Polish for many years. My wife is German, all of my friends are either American or Swiss, and I notice with horror that I've begun to think in a foreign language and translate it for myself into Polish. I know this spells the end for me; the gravediggers from Warsaw weren't wrong. In their line of work, people are rarely mistaken.

I've never told anyone of the motives that induced me to stay behind in the West. When journalists used to ask me, I'd answer as stupidly as I knew how. Finally they backed off. I couldn't tell them why I abandoned my country, because I never *did* abandon it. But I'm going to try to write about why I live in a different country, or rather, in different countries: I've already lived in England and Spain, in Germany, in Switzerland, France, Austria, Denmark, Israel, and a few other places.

I began writing when I was eighteen. The fault is my mother's, who used to give me books to read—so much that it became another addiction for me. I didn't finish school, partly as a result of family complications, partly because my teachers diagnosed me as a moron. To this day I'm not sure if there's a difference between physics, algebra, math, and chemistry, and I'll never find out. I don't know if fortynine is divisible by anything. If, by some miracle, the problem can be solved, it certainly won't be by me. I pushed through elementary school thanks only to the fact that my math teacher was the same teacher who taught Polish language. In the war years, I went to a school run by the nuns on Tamka Street, where there was a practice of pinning huge paper donkey ears on the worst pupil; I wore them the entire time. After the war, "when a new Poland erupted," my situation improved somewhat. I didn't have to wear the donkey ears. I just stood in the corner, facing the wall. Under such conditions, it was difficult to learn anything at all, but until eighth grade I skated by on the strength of my compositions.

Then the hell began. I went to School Number Two, a comprehensive school that was first named after La Guardia, then renamed for Maria Konopnicka. I was kicked out of there on account of stupidity. On the suggestion of the superintendent, I was sent to a psychometric clinic. I'm not sure if I'm recalling the term correctly. They made me arrange building blocks, ordered me to fill in the missing words to some idiotic text, asked shocking questions about my parents and relatives. Finally, they had me undress completely and found me unfit for studying in a school with a focus on the humanities. They sent me to a vocational school in Wrocław, or rather, a cooperative-vocational school, based on the premise that idiots are indispensable to trade. Maybe they were thinking about the welfare of the buyer. I don't know.

My career ended after a few math classes. At that time in Warsaw the theater production school was opened. My brother Józef and I went there together. For three months my brother did my assignments in math, chemistry, and algebra, but then on account of a family feud he stopped. I was kicked out again. It was a good school, housed in the YMCA building in Warsaw, and we had a swimming pool. The director of the school, as far as I can remember, was the bearded Żmigrodzki, an impressive fellow who could have played the part of the captain of the ship in an adaptation of Conrad's *The End of the Tether*. And it was there I met Basia Świdzińska, a lovely little Rubens angel, and I fell hard for her. But it didn't go both ways.

I returned to Wrocław, where I began to work and at the same time attend trade school at night. I can't remember why I got thrown out of there anymore. Then I started playing center forward for the soccer team. I wasn't very talented, but I was a brute on the field. Like in that Čapek short story, before every match the coach would call me over and say, "Hłasko, if you don't take out at least two guys, you're cut from the team for bad behavior." I learned how to play poker while on the team, and I also met Tadek Mazur, who was the "nephew" of a certain writer indifferent to even the greatest of female charms. Tadek tried writing himself. Sometimes I'd go to see him, and that's how I met his "admirer." He was the first person I'd ever met who wrote. I also met KP there, another schoolmate, who was our left winger and knew how to kick an opponent in the shin and then, once the guy was on his way down, in the face, too. KP stood for "kick the opposing player" with either foot, whichever was facing out. He would try to kick so the referees wouldn't notice. On top of that he was extremely polite: he always helped the players up and bowed to the referees. Later I came across a similar guy: he was a lightweight boxer, Debisz from Lodz, the "Gentleman of the Ring": he would try to land a lightning shot below the belt while getting in an elbow to the forehead.

Meanwhile, he'd bow to the referees in contrition. He won 90 percent of his fights by TKO.

Tadek, KP, and I went to Century Hall in Wrocław every week, where the boxing matches took place. Since we didn't have any money, we got in through the roof, at risk to our lives. The manager of the hall was a referee named Mikula. He was heavyset but athletic, and he used to kick us out. Later, though, he came to like us for our fanaticism and let us in without tickets. Our idol then was Ryszard Waluga, from the sports club in Wrocław, I think: a good fighter who packed a heavy punch and had splendid technique. Later everyone went nuts for Janusz "The Doll" Kasperczak, our first postwar European champion. Attending the matches, I recognized—from afar—two different writers. One of them was Staś Dygat, who always sat in the first row with a disapproving look on his face, and during the Polish Championships in 1949 I saw "Terrible Józ" Prutkowski. That's when I saw the most beautiful fight of my life: Antkiewicz vs. Bazarnik, in the featherweight division. But our idol was "Tolek." The three of us traveled without tickets from Wrocław to Warsaw to see the fight between Tolek and the Czechoslovak Torma. We made it into the fight without tickets, and we traveled back to Warsaw without tickets.

We all—Tadek, KP, and I—lived off of poker, playing for RGO food stamps. Slowly our affairs started to go sour. We were thrown out of the club for gambling. Tadek went to jail, and KP and I became petty thieves. We pulled off our first real job in the school for commerce. "Drake," our friend from the club, told us about the opportunity. Drake "accidentally" broke a window in the school cloakroom that led out onto the neighboring street. The next day KP was already waiting there, and I went with the other students to the cloakroom and hid behind the coats. I had a briefcase with me. Back then I was a small young man with an honest Slavic face, the kind that always lies. Classes began, the school janitor locked the door, and I picked out the valuables from the cloakroom and gave them to KP, then I went through the window myself. An hour later and we'd already sold everything on Bishop Nanker Square, where the black market used to operate. One day we found out there was going to be a school party in High School Number Two, on Stalin Street. A lieutenant from the

UB, the Ministry of Public Security, who was in love with one of the students, was going to be there, too. We were positive that the lieutenant would leave his pistol in the cloakroom, where I'd already be waiting. The weapon came in handy a couple of times. Then KP got sauced, lost the pistol, and we dissolved our partnership.

I turned sixteen, and the law was, since I wasn't in school, I had to find a job. I worked as a driver's helper for the Public Building Trust, then for a company called Paged, at the Bystrzyca Kłodzka depot. I wrote a book about it. Years later, in an article called "Sainted Youngsters," Krzysztof Toeplitz called it a story about people as little Mareczek (that was me) imagined them. People have often asked if it was really that way, how I wrote it. No, it wasn't. It was much worse: We woke up at four in the morning, and at ten at night we finished unloading at the station. Then we had to drive another forty kilometers home, which, along mountain roads in an automobile like a GMC with a manual transmission, took about two hours. We'd still have to get ourselves something to eat, and only then would we lie down to sleep. There were no weekends or holidays. At the end of the month the depot director at Bystrzyca Kłodzka would announce we'd met about 40, sometimes 45 percent of the norm. I worked there relatively briefly. I left because they threatened me with prison for government sabotage. While I was there, I saw two fatal accidents and one accident that ended with a broken back. I guess that guy died, too, in the hospital, since we were in no condition to transport him right away. Our trucks were modified for log hauling, so it wasn't possible to lay him down flat. I was making around seven hundred zlotys a month.

Tadeusz Konwicki once said to me, "This isn't a book, it's a Western." He was right. I never could grasp why Polish literature had such bad luck. Looking at it logically, there are few nations who have so many chances for good literature as we, the Poles, do. We've got everything: misfortune, political assassinations, eternal occupation, informers, mystery, despair, drunkenness. By God, what else could you ask for? When I was in Israel, I lived with the scum of the earth, but still I never met people as desperate, detestable, and unhappy as in Poland. The genesis of the Western is an obsession with justice: the solitary man who must destroy evil and violence. Never mind the tons of trashy books. Jesse James, Wyatt Earp, and other fast hands are fully formed characters. The communist could be such a figure: a person who brings order and peace into a suffocating country amidst a nation depraved by misfortune, if only the commies had wanted it that way. In the tons of rubbish I've read about commies, I've never met a character like that, from the books. Jerzy Andrzejewski was the only one to really show what a communist is: Podgórski in *Ashes and Diamonds*. Podgórski passes judgment on a person who was a capo in a camp, but still wins the first round. He remains a real human being; two years later and he probably would have been a police major in a "masterpiece" by Andrzej Mandalian. Or Prosecutor Gletkin from Koestler. Or most likely Rubashov, who prosecutes Gletkin.

As for me, I don't have anything against the commies. As long as they keep acting like such pigs, and I can keep writing about it, it's all right by me. I'm only a witness to the prosecution; the case makes no difference, just so long as the trial is interesting. That's all. The life I've been given is only a story, but how I tell it—that's already my business. That's my only concern.

As I was writing this, I asked a friend if I was right in saying that we, the Poles, have got everything necessary to write good stuff. He said no. Poles are too tired and dull; we're too resigned. But I don't understand that: Does a surgeon have the right to be tired if they bring him somebody who needs an operation? I don't know. I remember standing in a bar one time with Paweł Hertz and complaining to him about my troubles, about having no money, about difficulties with my editors. Hertz looked at me with distaste. He said, "As far as I understand, you want to write. That's not a pleasant activity—not for you, and not for the people who'll read you. What are you expecting?" He turned away, already shrugging his shoulders. The conversation was over.

So I left the backwoods and returned to Warsaw. I began to work at a company called Metrobuild. I worked as a loader, then after a while I began working in the supply unit. It was a great job. I just went around the city to different enterprises with orders for car parts, and they'd give me a stamp that said PARTS LACKING. Then I'd go to the so-called "socialized sector"—that is, to small workshops. The only difference between the public sector and the socialized sector was that the public sector gave me a stamp that said PARTS LACK-ING and in the socialized sector it just said NO PARTS. That was it. Then, a report would be drawn up about the importance of the purchase, and the director of supplies, the director of the work coun-cil, and the party secretary, plus the driver of the immobilized car as well as the director of the garage, would have to sign. I'd take a bottle of vodka and head over to a certain warehouse manager from a dif-ferent firm, who would give me the missing part. Then I'd go to the commission shop on Chmielna Street, where I'd leave the part. My partner would come by in an hour to buy it, and a little party would be organized. It was my personal system: I'd learned how to think big.

One day a nasty old hag showed up, and the director of the depot called me in to his office.

"Do you belong to the party?"

"No."

"To the Polish-Soviet Friendship Society?"

"No."

"To a trade union?"

"No."

"Then you'll be our worker correspondent."

The nasty old hag was from *Trybuna Ludu*. *Trybuna Ludu* had its own local correspondents who wrote about the setbacks and achieve-ments of the workplace. So I started writing about how there were al-ways missing parts, or how far too many cars were simply idle because there weren't nearly enough gas pumps, which, on top of it all, weren't automatic, and things like that.

One day they called me into *Trybuna Ludu* and gave me a prize: a novel by Anatoly Rybakov called *The Drivers*. I'll never forget it. It was the first socialist realist novel I'd read. I have to admit, I was struck dumb. So idiotic, I said to myself, even I can do it. So I started.

I was fired from Metrobuild. I couldn't find work. There were too many drivers, too few trucks. *Trybuna Ludu* sent me to an organiza-tion known as the Warsaw Provisions Cooperative. By the time I real-ized I'd become a police informer, it was already too late.

The work at the Cooperative was very hard. The warehouse was located on Sokołowska Street. I lived close by in Marymont. At four in the morning I had to be "on premises," as they said. I often woke up at two and marched through the Powązki Cemetery. I'd walk, still fast asleep. It's actually possible. Then the real hell began. The engine didn't want to catch; you had to put petrol under the crankcase with a lighted lamp because the hot water the night drivers had heated for us helped us as much as saying prayers helps a jumping man with no parachute. Finally we'd drive out to the vegetable market. The farmers, peddling their vegetables after driving their carts through the night, were already waiting for us. Warsaw had to have its vegetables by seven in the morning. There were always four of us when we drove: me, my helper, an escort, and the loader. The escort paid the yokels with cash. The vegetables were divided into three categories. The first category was the most expensive one: the escort wrote the farmer a receipt for the first category and paid him for the third. The farmer didn't have a choice. Our escorts from the Warsaw Provisions Cooperative had an agreement with the escorts from the City Retail Organization, the organization that oversaw businesses. If the yokel didn't want to sell, our escort wouldn't buy anything, and the farmer would have to return home and throw out the vegetables. Nobody broke the agreement: neither our guys from the Cooperative, nor those from City Retail. To do a thing like that risked what the newspapers called a trial by knife. A very apt name.

We made a little something on the side, and when we'd get back to the warehouse around seven, there'd be police waiting to check if we were drunk or not. They could nab you for that. The whole practice was ridiculous since the drivers from the Cooperative didn't have the right to be sober, as the farmers liked to say. So they'd give a bottle of vodka to the policeman waiting at the gates. That's how we did it, the drivers from the vegetable market. The drivers from Ząbkowska, the state liquor concern, had their own first-rate method. Vodka was hard to steal, because when the bottle was damaged, you had to present the neck with the cap intact and attach a damage report. It was a waste of time. Instead, they had a medical syringe with a needle meant for intramuscular injections; they would extract a shot of vodka from each bottle and refill it with water.

I was transferred from the vegetable market to the slaughterhouse. It was harder to steal there, but we stole. When we'd pull up onto the scale, the director of the slaughterhouse would write down the weight of the truck, and then we'd ride to the market on a roundabout route. I'd pull over and tell the assistant, "Zdzisiek, drain some fluids." The assistant climbed under the truck and unscrewed the truck's radiator cap and let out some twenty kilos of weight, and we picked up the difference in meat. Then, when we were outside the slaughterhouse gates, we'd pour the water back in again. Finally the people from the slaughterhouse got smart to us, so then we started letting out gasoline. Where those twenty kilos of meat would disappear to will remain my secret.

For the drivers from the Provisions Cooperative, the bane of our existence was the so-called "potato campaign." In those days we had to travel to the countryside for potatoes, though there was nobody to sell them to. We, the Warsaw drivers, found a con. We'd go "campaigning" with a dozen or so trucks; the better vehicles would pull the weaker ones. The odometer ticked off the kilometers, and then we sold the gasoline to private taxi drivers. I was eighteen years old then. Today, I'm not ashamed of it. Let those who forced me into it be ashamed. Working fourteen hours a day, including weekends and holidays, I made about seven hundred zlotys a month. I didn't have an apartment; I lived in a hallway. I bought my first suit at the age of twenty-two. Today I don't even need a suit. I've got nowhere to go.

The strength of the commies depends on the cheapness of their ideology. A German worker can count on the fact that from the moment when the fortunes of the Thyssens or the Krupps become socialized, his income will grow by a thousand percent. The strength of the commies depends on the sheer fantasy of such a phenomenon. Were I to tell a German worker that if I worked twenty hours a month, I could buy myself a pair of shoes, he'd throw up his arms and walk away. And now, if I were to tell my assistant, "Zdzisiek, a German driver can buy himself a car in the course of a year; four suits from his monthly salary; he can travel to Italy on vacation"—I'd get it in the teeth like I've never gotten it before. German journalists always used to say to me about the Soviets, "But you have to remember, they were the first ones to make it into space." I'm not an engineer, but it seems like technological success can only be discussed when you know the cost of the investment. If, at the cost of a thousand trees, you produce a thousand toothpicks, then it's all just a ruse. Kennedy or Johnson has to debate with Congress over every penny that goes into space exploration. The American people know all the numbers from the papers and from television. Over the years they've had their laughs, sitting in front of the television and watching the rockets fall after three seconds of flight. I don't know how many people were tortured and liquidated just so Gagarin could show his face to the world. I don't know how many unsuccessful attempts there were. And if I ever found out, I wouldn't be able to enjoy the successes of my whimsical brothers.

But then, in 1952, I wasn't thinking about that yet. I was thinking about something else entirely on the day I stood in Mostowski Palace and the policeman on duty said to me:

"Belt, shoelaces, tie, if you don't mind."

"I don't wear a tie," I said, and signed the inventory statement.

The idol of my youth wasn't Hemingway or Jerzy Andrzejewski. It was Tadeusz Barwiński, an officer in the UB. As I said, I worked as a driver at the Warsaw Provisions Cooperative under the authority of the editor of the local news department at *Trybuna Ludu*. That was in 1952. In those days there was a so-called "Independent Military Bureau" in every big enterprise. At one point it had a different name: the Independent Defense Bureau. It had other names as well. It was a division of the Department of Security. Each agent, an "Independent"—that was how the security officers were called—had his stool pigeons among the workers of a particular department, who would give him information about people. The agent knew how to handle things from there.

One day around 7:00 p.m., when I pulled in to the depot, the dispatcher said to me, "You've got to see the Independent."

"Are you working here overnight?" I asked him.

"Yeah. Till six."

"If I don't come back, tell my mother."

"If you weren't coming back, they would have nabbed you from home," he said.

If I'd been reading Hemingway in those days, I would have told him, "It is one of the things you can never know." But all I said was, "Only God knows."

I made my way over. A small guy in glasses was sitting there; the doors were upholstered in leather to invoke a mood of terror into the investigation. Everything was like a lousy detective film. I saw one of those films once, or maybe it was from a book I'd read. It went like this:

"Do you know what this is?" asked Sean, taking hold of the teaspoon lying on the table.

"Silver," said Jack. "You bought it from Harry the Horse. From that place on Seventy-Seventh Street. It's used for stirring tea. You serve pretty lousy tea, Sean. Is this what your people drink in Dublin?"

"Not only," uttered Sean, with a crooked smile. "You can find good tea at a joint they call Dirty Dick's. And the teaspoon—well, it's also good for plucking out an eyeball."

Treppengelander would never forget that scream.

Or like this:

The shot from the .45 rang out like a howl, and I aimed right for her stomach. I was thinking, "Mickey, your kid is sitting right there." But I had to do it; Jesus Christ, honest, I had to. That's what I was thinking when Nick took a seat on the armchair, about how we'd shaved his neat little head, because the electrodes work better that way. If not for Nick, I could've done things different. But I couldn't. I leaned on her, and I saw a light dying in her eyes.

"How could you?" she whispered.

I went quiet for a minute. Then I said, "It wasn't all that hard."

Maybe I'm not quoting exactly, but that's beside the point. My case wasn't as entertaining. The Independent ordered me to sit down.

"State your name."

"Marek Hłasko."

"Date of birth."

"Fourteen January. Thirty-four."

"Location."

"Warsaw."

"Father."

"Maciej."

"Profession."

"Lawyer."

The Independent was surprised.

"Lawyer?"

"Lawyer."

"Living?"

"No."

"Mother?"

And so on and so forth. Finally he said, "Are you still employed by *Trybuna*

Ludu?"

"Yes."

"As a local correspondent?"

"Yes."

"Why did you stop writing?"

"I work fourteen hours a day. I don't have the time."

"You don't have to keep writing," said the Independent. "You can just tell me

everything."

"About what?"

And then the Mike Hammer business began. Or anyhow, *Lord Lister, or The Strange Secret.* In all those pulp books popular in Poland back then, there was always an "or." *Lord Lister, or The Strange Secret. Ken Maynard, or The Lone Avenger. Jerzy Rolicz, or A Sixteen-Year-Old Boy among Thugs.* But Lister was the best. My mother, who forced me to read, tried to get me to read Żeromski once, when I was ten years old. I read a sentence: "The dreamer plunged the ravenous glance of his pupils into her soul." I felt relieved of any obligation to ever read him again. I grabbed the entire set of the Mortkowicz edition of Żeromski and took off for Ciepła Street, where there was a place that mended dolls and sold old books all in one shop. I traded the set for *Lord Lister* and a second book, the one where the guy always says, "I never shake hands with a lefty. It's saved my life more than once." I can't remember anymore what the fast hand was called. I really got it from my mother for that, and she used a belt that had once been my grandfather's. My grandfather had been a captain in the Central Warsaw Fire Department, and as everybody knows, firefighter belts are the widest and have the most copper buckles.

The Independent, or "Mike Hammer," took out his pistol.

"You know what this is?"

"Yeah, I know."

"What?"

"A Soviet TT pistol."

"How do you know?"

"I saw one in a film with Pavel Kadochnikov."

Pavel Kadochnikov had played a Soviet agent who had to kill a German spy. He'd pull out his pistol and say, "By the power and law vested in me by the fatherland . . ."

The Independent interrupted me:

"Have you got a fiancée?"

"I do."

"What's her name?"

I told him. And so we jawed on for two hours. He went out and left his pistol on the table. He came back, then left again. It was a psychological investigation. In the end I signed a statement saying I had a fiancée named Wanda, and that the TT pistol was known to me only through films; that I'd played forward on a soccer team and so on and so forth. It doesn't seem real today, as I'm writing this, even to me. But back then, when I was signing the statement, I thought to myself, "Just you wait, pal. I'll find out one way or another what they called you at your christening." The statement had to be signed by the interrogated and the interrogator. His name was Tadeusz Barwiński.

I was arrested a few days later for refusal to cooperate. The argument the police officers used—this was in Mostowski Palace—was simple: since I worked at a firm widely known for stealing, I had to know what was going on there. And since I was refusing to cooperate, thereby preventing the discovery of details of government sabotage, I was subject to punishment under such-and-such an article, and so on . . . It was there that I really did take off my belt, tie, and shoelaces. The Poles love euphemisms, and I can't do anything about it. Nobody asked me for advice when they founded Poland.

Prison's always cheerful if you arrive the right way. Everyone's always innocent; everything's a mistake that's going to be worked out soon. In prison in Palermo I met a man who'd killed his fiancée and her mother. He expected to be let out in a few days. In prison in Munich I served time with a fellow who'd committed seventeen robberies. He expected to be let out in a few days. In prison in Jaffa I made friends with a man who'd been smuggling narcotics since the founding of the State of Israel. He expected to be let out in a few days.

In general, it's not that bad, so long as the only thing you put your trust in is madness. When I lived in Warsaw, I was a regular guest at the police station on Bednarska Street, on account of drunkenness and public brawling. After some time I already had friends among the police officers, and I used to spend the night not on the hard floor, but in the guard booth. In the morning they'd drive me home. It was the friendliest police station in Warsaw. All the fashionable diners returning from the Kameralna and Krokodyl restaurants landed there.

The Youth Festival took place in 1955. The Bim-Bom Theater, with Zbyszek Cybulski, came to town. I met Roman Polański at the entrance to the theater. Romek had a ticket, but they didn't want to let him in, because a heap of people from the public had already snuck in without tickets and the hall was overflowing. Polański protested for so long to be let in, showing his ticket the whole time, that two policemen from the First Precinct finally picked him up. But these were new policemen, and they didn't know me. They led Polański off between them, and I followed behind.

Romek was locked up, and I walked up to my sergeant, the one who always confiscated my belt.

"Let him go," I said.

"He your buddy?"

"Yeah."

They let Polański go. We got ahold of a liter of vodka, and together with Romek, his girlfriend, and the same policemen who had arrested him ten minutes before, we headed to the nearest rubble pile, aiming to drink it all. Then we got our hands on two more bottles. I don't know why I got the urge to start reciting from the Apocalypse. The policemen looked at me, and every once in a while they'd say, "Please,

Marek, be careful, be careful . . ." They had conflicting feelings: on the one hand, they wanted to keep having fun; on the other, they didn't know if the Apocalypse was a hostile text or not. That situation, in which an innocent man was released on the word of an alcoholic, was a first for me, and that's why I mention it.

As I said, madness is the only thing that can be trusted. In Italy I was arrested for a shooting. In a swell of madness I'd tried to shoot a man who told me that they don't kill six million people without a reason. We'd been talking about the Jews. The next day the investigator asked me, "Were you trying to kill him?"

"Yes," I said. I wanted to see an Italian judge who would sentence me for wanting to defend the memory of six million martyred people.

He looked at me for a long time. Gave me back my things. Looked at me again and gave me back my weapon. I don't know if my Italian investigator was a counterpoint to our Rzecki, the idealist from Prus's novel *The Doll*. I only know that he destroyed my file.

I didn't sit long in Mostowski Palace. I thought to myself, "They'll hold you until the investigation, and then you'll get your five years. It doesn't matter that nobody will know what you've been in jail for. The administration of justice doesn't depend on the question of who's really guilty and who's not. It's all about finding a guilty party."

I hadn't read Koestler yet, where the chief investigator carries on long, cordial conversations with the guy he's trying to liquidate. I hadn't read Orwell yet, either, where Big Brother has a squinty-eyed scowl; I hadn't even read Krywicki. Books are only worth writing after you cross the outermost boundary of shame. Writing is something more intimate than the birds and the bees, at least for me. The commies crossed that boundary. When Yezhov liquidated Yagoda, he told the gathered members of the Soviet Political Directorate how he knew for certain Yagoda had worked for Tsarist secret police. Nobody protested. Back when the Tsarist secret police was still in existence, Yagoda had been twelve years old. There were certainly people in the Directorate who had fought against Kołczak, Denikin, and Piłsudski, and at one time they must have been courageous, but nobody stood up, nobody pointed out that any child given a choice between talking with secret police or riding a scooter, is going to choose the latter. The commies crossed a boundary. They created an imaginary world that was impossible to believe in. That was their strength.

Back then, in Mostowski Palace, I thought to myself, "Balzac won't help you; neither will Żeromski, but Lord Lister will." That's how I became a police informer with the code name "Wanda." Wanda was my girlfriend's name, which I figured would be an amusing touch. I was let out.

I went to my dispatcher at the depot.

"Transfer me out of the vegetable market," I said.

"Why?"

"I don't want to know anything."

"You want to go to the slaughterhouse?"

"No. I know the slaughterhouse."

"To the liquor concern?"

"I know that place, too."

We were alone.

"Did they try to get you to talk?"

"Yeah."

"Wait," he said. "I'll transfer you to the Opel Blitz 167, a truck that heads out of the city every day. I'll tell the guys there you're a leftist."

"Tell them."

My Opel Blitz never failed me. Once outside the gates, the clutch would break down. The next day—the carburetor. I went to the garage, where the boss understood everything. We left the carburetor for repairs, which lasted a month; then there was a switch that didn't work; later, the clutch. It was guzzling three times the amount of gasoline it should have, so we sent it to an expert. I hung around at the depot and didn't want to know a thing.

From time to time these two fellows would show up at my place. They looked like spooks from the movies. I guess I'll never know if characters in movies look like people in real life, or if people in real life look like characters from the movies.

When I used to go to the gym in London, I saw professional middleweights in training. There were two managers who looked just like the guys from *The Champ* and *Golden Boy*. They wore bowler hats and waistcoats and smoked cigars. Every so often, one would say to the other, "Harry's over the hill." Then he'd spit, and the second one would say the same thing.

My two secret agents used to say, "Oh, you don't want to get us sore, now . . ." They never said anything more. So began the greatest fun of my life.

One only had to cross that boundary of shame. My assistant once invited me to his sister's name day party. It was boring, and in the middle of the party we stole the record player, brought it upstairs, and came back down. Then, together with the other guests, we undertook a fruitless search for it.

The police transferred me from the Cooperative to the City Business Bureau. I began to write, thinking with my head in the clouds that I was the only informant in the world à rebours. I wrote that people who belonged to the party were two-faced, they yearned to return to a capitalist system; I wrote that people who bad-mouthed the government were sincere democrats who loved Dear Uncle Joe, and so on. I wrote a lot of denunciations. I'd call headquarters and give them my code name and ask them to put me through to Lieutenant Janek, who was one of my secret agents. I caused them a lot of aggravation, and they never caught anybody. But don't blame me. They asked for it.

At that time I'd already begun writing. One time I ran into Tadek Mazur, who incidentally had just gotten out of jail, and I told him I'd started writing something. Tadek told me to show it to him. He grabbed it and went to see his gay lover. The queer said I should try writing something longer. But back then I didn't have anywhere to write. I asked my mother to clear out the kitchen, and in three nights I wrote a two hundred–page novel. Bohdan Czeszko read the novel and wrote me a letter. He told me the book didn't amount to anything, but he felt I ought to keep trying. He pointed out a lot of things to me. Personally, I cherished him; I thought he was very wise. I have that letter till today. Bohdan pointed out that I was overusing vulgar words, and he really discouraged me. Then I got to know him personally. He looked like a bear, and he moved like a strong, dangerous animal. When he spoke, it was difficult for him to use ordinary words.

I remember him saying to a waitress once, "Fuck it all to hell, can I please have some water? I'm drunk as a cunt." That was the shortest thing he ever managed to say, yet *me* he reprimanded. None of us, still more or less youngsters, could ever succeed in writing in such beautiful language as this teddy bear. His story "The Lament" I can read, finish, and start again. He's the only writer of the young generation who from the beginning found his own voice and remained faithful to himself. Neither Brycht, nor Nowakowski, nor I, managed to do that.

I basically copied Rybakov's book *The Drivers*, put my name on it, called it "Sokolowski Depot," and brought it to the Writers' Union. After a while, Igor Newerly, who was the supervisor for the Young Writers' Circle, summoned me for a conversation. Newerly helped me a lot. He asked me about my situation, told me about the flaws in "Sokolowski Depot," and gave me one piece of advice, the wisest advice I've ever heard from a writer: "If you want to write something, you have to tell it first. To everyone. It doesn't matter if people understand you or not. You have to talk: every time you're telling your story, you have to construct it from beginning to end. After a while you'll understand which elements are important and which aren't. The point is to be able to tell it out loud." And so I started to talk about it. Talked about it to people in Poland, in Israel. I told it to stern Germans; I told it to Artur Sandauer, who interrupted me every minute to say, "What are you getting at?"

I don't know. The whole point is, I don't know. I only know that I'm going to run the entire race, and I'll be talking the whole time.

CHAPTER TWO

Wrocław, Obory, Rose Island

Igor Newerly arranged a three-month stipend for me from the Polish Writers' Union. Since I had no place to live in Warsaw, I left for Wrocław.

Newerly helped me a lot. Back then, he was at the height of his success. His novel *A Souvenir from Cellulose* was regarded as a masterpiece. There wasn't a week he wasn't being written about; people walked up to him on their hind legs; dozens came to visit him, and he had almost no time for writing. But Newerly never got too big for his britches. He was modest and couldn't stand flatterers. I remember, when I told him I liked his book better than Gorky's *The Life of Matvei Kozhemiakin*, Newerly bristled. It was unpleasant for him. Finally he said, "I'd like for my book to survive just one five-year plan, that's all." I know he was being sincere.

Cellulose is an excellent book, and I've read it many times. I don't know why Newerly wrote so little. The last time I saw him was twelve years ago, when he severed ties with me. I had behaved unbearably, and he finally lost patience. It seemed to me that everybody was losing patience. On the other hand, I gained a lot of other things. It's like that story about two Jews who went into business together. One of them had money; the other, experience. After some time, the first one gained experience; the other, money.

Newerly would sometimes tell me about himself. He was a character straight out of the pages of London's stories. He'd had dozens of jobs. At one point he'd been Janusz Korczak's secretary. He always told me, during every conversation, that the most dangerous thing for me in my situation would be to arrive too early at being a professional writer. "You should stay up nights reading the books you simply have to read, but which you haven't yet. And you'll learn many things necessary for writing, sooner than you think. Other people will help you. But, by God, don't make it a career. That you can do when you're around forty. Look at all these young people. Ask them how much a kilo of sugar costs. None of them can tell you. Sure, they know that concrete is a construction material, but they learned it from books. In general, write as little as possible. Do whatever you want, but please, write as little as possible."

I returned from Wrocław to Warsaw a year later and told Newerly about an idea I had. He looked at me and said, "You're a sick man." I don't know if Newerly remembers our conversation. I remember.

So I went to Wrocław, where I lived with my uncle. I had a three-month stipend and a little money I'd gotten from *Sztandar Młodych* for my story "Sokolowski Depot." It was a beautiful time: I was finally alone; I could read, write, go to the theater, but I didn't know what I was supposed to do first. When I'd start writing, I'd think I was supposed to be reading, because it would help me to write. When I was reading, I'd tear myself away and run around the city, because it seemed I needed to observe people. I would talk with people and then again it would seem I was wasting time on conversation, and that I needed to be writing. "Jesus Christ," I thought, "I'll lose my mind." One day I'd read Bohdan "Teddy Bear" Czeszko; the next, Balzac. Then I'd wrench myself away from Dostoevsky to read the Linde dictionary. At night I'd go out and look for my alcoholic uncle, and again I'd come back to my books. I don't know how many books I read that year in Wrocław. Several hundred, I imagine. And with each day, I knew less. With each day, I despaired more and more that I'd never read what it was I needed to. Finally, somebody gave me Gombrowicz, and after that I came completely unhinged.

It's not true, what Gombrowicz writes about himself in one of his *Diaries*, that his writing was appreciated too late. There was some connection with an article Sandauer wrote. I don't know what he said. I do know, though, that Gombrowicz was revered by young and old. I borrowed *Ferdydurke* myself, although I had to put down my watch as collateral, because the book's owner didn't trust me. And rightly so. The edition of *Ferdydurke* I was reading in 1953 had already passed through hundreds of hands. The pages were stuck together, stained. The same thing with *Memoirs of a Time of Immaturity*. Such books were impossible to buy; you could borrow them for a day, sometimes for half a day. Gombrowicz couldn't have known this. But I was there and I saw it.

I didn't feel right in Wrocław. I'm a real Warsaw boy, and I couldn't live without it. When I used to work at the company called Paged, my colleagues all hailed from Warsaw, and I decided to head there. At the very least so I could talk in my Warsaw idiom, a language that no Polish actor, not even Adolf Dymsza, is able to imitate.

I tracked them down and got a reception that was colder than cold. I couldn't figure out why. Finally somebody told me: it was all because my story had been published in *Sztandar Młodych*. In their minds I was no longer a worker; instead, I'd become a mouthpiece for the slave drivers. There were some people, though, who were overly polite and friendly. But they weren't the same people; they weren't the ones that I'd slept next to, broken bread with, and worked alongside.

Just three years earlier we used to cross the border together to make ourselves a little money. We'd bring liquor and bacon, and we'd take back stockings and imitation jewelry from Czechoslovakia. The ground around the border was neatly combed in places, but higher up, in the mountains, it was possible to get through, because we knew the mountains better than the soldiers in the border patrol did. We'd hide several cats inside our coats, and when we'd hear the barking of the patrolman's guard dog, we'd let one of the cats loose. No matter how well trained the dog was, he'd chase after the cat. Others wrapped their legs in petroleum-smeared rags, but it wasn't a surefire system. One funny thing is that the Czechs themselves never crossed over to our side. They were afraid. After a while, somebody squealed about the cats, and people got to be interested in where all these animal-lovers in the area were coming from. It became impossible to cross over into Czechoslovakia anymore.

Our colleagues from another depot hit upon a much better idea, which produced more opportunities for the efficient transit of goods. Living close to the border, they used to set fire to certain wooden shacks, and the Polish fire unit being pretty far away, they'd run on foot to a border patrolman and tell him about the blaze. The soldier would telephone the Czech fire unit. The Czechs would already have loaded up their stockings and trinkets, and our guys would toss them liquor and bacon in exchange, since they were difficult to get ahold of in Czechoslovakia then. Some dozen or so cottages went up in flames, but I suppose it all evened out. I was a witness to a similar situation as a guest of the Bavarian justice system. Every Sunday a *Wachtmeister* came to our cell to ask how many takers there were for the *Gottesdienst*. I'd never thought the Christian faith was so strong and deep-rooted. Everybody reported at once: thieves, blackmailers, polygamists, and pimps. And so we went to church, where we bartered with fellows from the infirmary. The sick inmates didn't have the chance to smoke and stroll, so their only opportunity to exchange goods was in church, at Mass.

I went back to Wrocław and tried to write again. I didn't know anybody in Wrocław except for Stefan Łoś and Tadeusz Zelenay. Stefan Łoś had just been let out of jail. He'd been there for about a year, after which he was told a little mistake had been made, and he was released. He died shortly after. When I talked with one of his doctors, I found out his death had been caused by abuse and inhumane treatment in jail. He was already in weak health, and that sealed his fate. I never learned anything from Łoś himself about what happened. He had known me since I was a child, but still he was scared. He told me briefly that before he was let out of jail, he wrote a declaration stating he wouldn't discuss the topic with anybody, and in the event he started telling stories, he'd enjoy another stay in jail, only this time there wouldn't be any mistake.

I know from other people, though, what they did to Łoś. In accounts of torture at the hands of the UB, of course, it's never clear what is and isn't true. It's a fact, though, that things couldn't have been too cheery if rumor had it the security officers beat people at night with their ramrods, spit on them, and pissed on their faces, among other things, not to mention the simple methods, like beating a person until he's unconscious. Łoś was kept in solitary confinement, up to his waist in ice water, which gave him time for contemplation and reminiscences about his childhood. Then they'd send him to his next interrogation. Colonel Jacek Różański took a hearty interest in Łoś. Łoś, to the final moments of my last visit with him, never mentioned the name Różański. Mister Borejsza's brother, he'd say. The very name Różański would drive him to hysterics.

Speaking of Łoś, I want to say a few words about Colonel Różański, whom I'd met two or three years prior. I'd always been interested in hangmen. I was interested in how they looked, these people who ripped out people's fingernails and hair and broke their ribs. A meeting was arranged, and I went to his house. He looked like a fanatic, and he knew it. He had an interesting way of speaking, and he was a good actor. If I had to compare him with another actor, it would be Marlon Brando, who also speaks slowly, ineptly, as if he's in pain in the middle of the dialogue, which gives the impression that Brando isn't pronouncing a text that was already written by some Jewish writer named Rappaport or something, but instead is searching for the precise words and exact formulations. And it was like that with Różański. There were a few of us there, and Różański started talking.

Różański said, "What do *you* know of revolution? You write about it, there are a few good pieces about it, but what do you *know* about it? I had a subordinate in the Partisans whom I loved like a son. A brave soldier, ideological, intelligent. After the war, I took him into the security apparatus and made a major out of him. One time, he was interrogating a saboteur. The saboteur was just a dumb kid, but during the interrogation he behaved insolently and provoked the interrogator. That boy of mine was such a bundle of nerves—he hadn't slept in two days—that at a certain moment he lost it and punched the kid in the kisser."

"So?" we asked.

"I had to give him five years," Różański said. "He was a major in the security agency, and it's forbidden to strike someone during an interrogation. But that isn't what I wanted to tell you. Do you know what the saboteur got? Two years. He was a village idiot. He didn't know what he was doing, so we had to consider extenuating circumstances. But for a member of the security apparatus who broke the constitution he was appointed to uphold . . . Well, there was no consideration of extenuating circumstances. And *that* is revolution."

Then he told us another anecdote: While transporting a young woman from Lodz to Warsaw, he had to yield to her request and stop the car so the young woman could step into the woods by herself. Colonel Różański asked for her word of honor that she wouldn't try to run away so he wouldn't have to send a guard with her, which might embarrass her while she was fulfilling nature's call. The young woman gave her word of honor, and naturally, she returned.

I remember walking out onto the street, and one of my friends said to me:

"Now, there's a strong man. The idea of it: what her word of honor could have cost him—"

"He didn't risk anything," somebody interrupted him. "There's nowhere to run."

Różański also told me that for many years he wasn't able to shake off a feeling of fear, since he knew there were lots of people who wanted to kill him. This was during the first years after the war, when the remains of political organizations fighting against the regime were still active. To overcome the feeling of fear within himself, he gave up the bodyguard who was assigned to him and took to going to work every day on foot. I remember the story about the saboteur and the unlucky major, as well as the one about the young woman who valued her word of honor above her own freedom, likely for the sole reason that the man who told the stories was known as the absolute cruelest agent in the security apparatus. The idea of dedicating a few mawkish words to him just came to me as I'm writing about Stefan Łoś, who was afraid until the day he died to utter that man's name.

Łoś was an unlucky chap. Before the war he wrote a pretty brainless young adult book called *The Watchtower*. I think it was a story about courageous soldiers in the Border Protection Corps who rout some Bolshevik agents. After the war they didn't publish him, and the poor fellow was starving. They used to call him "Cousin Pons" because he always showed up at friends' places during mealtimes.

People helped him out when they could. Tadeusz Schmidt, our most handsome leading man, always invited Łoś to his house under different pretexts in order to feed him. But his time in jail made it hard for him to earn a living. He wrote me a letter from the hospital before his death. The letter didn't get to me for a while, and when I wanted to write back, I found out that the poor guy was no longer living.

The second writer I met in Wrocław was Tadeusz Zelenay. He was a peculiar man with a strange limp on his left side. I remember, somebody had died, and I went to the funeral out of boredom, to watch the widow throw herself into the grave of her beloved husband. We all stood in the rain, listening to the lineup of speakers. Suddenly Zelenay ran up huffing and puffing and handed the speechless widow a box of chocolates. "I couldn't get ahold of any flowers," he declared. Several years later, looking at old issues of the journal *Przekrój*, I saw an identical tale, and to this day I don't know whether Zelenay stole his practical joke from that journal's editor, the genius Marian Eile, or if it was something they both did.

Writing didn't go very well for me in Wrocław. Never before had I had so much time to myself. Now that I could read, I remember the feeling of despair deepening in me day by day. I realized life isn't long enough to read everything I wanted to know. I had a three-month stipend. But I didn't want to give up. I resolved to work overtime, and some doctor acquaintances of mine gave me a concoction with bennies so I wouldn't fall asleep. I was able to work day and night. I was afraid I would stand before Newerly empty-handed and have to go back to work, and then it would be lights out for my writing.

It's hard for me to say today which of the books I read then made an impression on me and which didn't. But first of all, I didn't know how to read. When I'd read an article in the old journals *Odrodzenie* or *Kuźnica*, I wouldn't understand half of what was being said, and there wasn't anybody to ask because in Wrocław there wasn't any so-called literary milieu or whatnot. I had to have a dictionary on hand at all times, but sometimes it didn't help, because in the middle of the article I'd have to put the journal down and search for a book the author had just mentioned in making his point. And I tried to understand the problem of typicality in literature, what it consisted of.

I think I was the one fool in Poland who tried to understand by this method. I'm not saying this tongue in cheek.

Since everybody babbled on about typicality in literature in those days and it was absolutely impossible to understand anything, I decided to approach it in my own way. I went to the city library and searched for everything that was written about *Ashes and Diamonds*, and I learned the opinions of all the wise men regarding my favorite book. After that I fell into a daze.

The critics, though, had fallen into rapture, but at the same time they made accusations against Andrzejewski, saying that the communists in his book weren't as strong as Maciek Chełmicki, or as the negative characters. Again, I'm not being ironic. Professor Stefan Żółkiewski wrote, "We recognize the character of Szczuka from the most conventional point of view: the moral point of view." Szczuka, a tired man, a man without illusions, a man who didn't believe in the possibility of the swift victory of the revolution: he didn't seem an authentic character to the Marxist critics.

These same accusations were leveled at Podgórski, the other communist in *Ashes and Diamonds*. Podgórski loses his first showdown with the new reality: his system of moral and ethical values crumbles the moment it comes into contact with the real world, and Podgórski resigns himself to the possibility of jailing a man who served as a capo in a concentration camp. Podgórski tries to judge the man, but a man can only judge another based on his own personal experiences: Podgórski has never been in a concentration camp, and he hasn't lived through what the idol of his youth had to. He doesn't feel it's in his power to punish a man who was put to such a difficult test. So he lets him go free. That's what makes the beauty of the situation, and it's what the Marxist critics were using to accuse Andrzejewski. That's when I realized that wisdom can't be replaced by knowing how one is supposed to think.

After the war everyone was wild about Borowski's book *This Way to the Gas Chambers, Ladies and Gentlemen*, myself included. But something was missing, and I thought about it for a long time. I couldn't formulate it. I understood it many years later when I was reading, by chance, a letter from one of our greatest writers to a friend of mine:

what really irritated him, he said, especially in Polish postwar literature, was the absence of the feeling of envy. "That's just what's missing in Borowski," I thought to myself: the absence of envy on the part of the beaten. And the fact that those who are beaten always wish they were the ones doing the beating. Those who are beaten dream about giving beatings, both the good and the bad victims. The five-volume edition of Borowski's work should be obligatory reading for aspiring writers in Poland. Borowski started off as an angel of wrath and ended up a sellout. He started out trying to show the truth and only the truth; he ended up calling Faulkner a fascist, a scum, a cheerleader for the atom bomb and biological warfare. Faulkner, whose books he most likely never read. Faulkner, whose obsession was man's relationship with his fellow man.

In 1954, I attended the Youth Conference in Obory. I don't remember much about the conference. Once again, there was a lot of talk about the problem of typicality in literature. My friend Bernstein and I took turns dozing: he'd take five minutes, then I'd have five minutes. From afar it looked good: one of us, hands over his face, lost in deep contemplation. The second would sit rigidly with staring eyes, as Good Soldier *Švejk* put it, like a tomcat shitting in the chaff. After that we'd switch: one would wake the other, and he in turn would start with the gaping eyes, while the second hid his face in his hands. After the final debates Bernstein and I went on our night escapades.

There was a girl there whose name I can't recall. I only remember that she was exceptionally pretty. One day she read a fragment of her prose to us. It was a story about security officers. These agents, after several long and sincere conversations, convince the prisoners in their care that they've acted improperly, and the prisoners bow and scrape, sobbing, proclaiming their contrition and promising to set themselves straight. That's all I remember from the conference: there were lots of commies there, but even they were struck into embarrassed silence. Looking at the beautiful face of the girl who was reading, I thought to myself: "Why couldn't she have just remained a whore? Why did she have to go and write, too?"

After that my friend Bernstein and I went to Masuria. Edward was handsome, like a young god, and I think of him whenever I read *Demons*. While I went thrashing through life, he was supremely and frightfully calm. On top of that he was a champion barroom brawler, endowed with unusual physical strength. Sometime before, he'd boxed. Whenever things came to a head, Edward would set up his opponent like a photographer setting up his models before snapping a shot, and then he'd land one to the jaw. He never had to hit twice, because the victim would sink into sleep, be knocked into the void. Even in a brawl he kept frightfully and impossibly calm. In Orzysz once some stool pigeon, a pistol in his left hand, gave me a punch in the mouth. Edward walked up to him calmly, paying no attention to the weapon, and creamed him in the skull.

He was and is my closest friend. In Masuria he told me about the books he'd read, but which I, not knowing German or English, didn't know about. We lived in a little place, a village, called Rose Island, and for company we had four fishermen who'd been thrown out of the Deep Sea Fishing Cooperative on account of drunkenness and brawling. But one of them had a wife, and they had a kid they wanted to baptize. He acquired a handsome piglet and announced a feast. Every day we were antsy, and we kept track of whether the pig had reached a weight that would accord with our appetites. In those days it wasn't easy to get meat: Edward and I used to eat the eels he expertly prepared. During the day we lay around the island and tried to write. At night we got together to have a good time, because the Deep Sea people were equally devoted to the Polish liquor concern.

I can't remember anymore if it was Edward or me who came up with the idea of inviting Wilhelm Mach to the baptism. In any case, Mach wrote back that he was coming, and indeed the fateful morning arrived, as they say in the newspapers. Mach showed up and headed off to bed after a sleepless night, while we all got busy with preparations for the piglet, whom I'd deprived of life that morning with one terrible blow of the knife. The Deep Sea group was on edge: a bender was waiting for them, and they were looking forward to female company, which they'd been lacking for months. I should add that the closest city was about twenty kilometers away, so we'd always talk and sing at night about how nasty and perverted women were. Finally the guests showed up: there was only one girl, but she was pretty. She was seated on Wilhelm Mach's right. The knife-wielding Deep Sea guys had taken to calling Mach "Professor," no doubt thanks to his dignified appearance. I should make it clear that women didn't interest Wilhelm in any significant way, which was surprising given his highly developed family instinct: I have in mind all his "nephews." During the feast I noticed spasms of terror and revulsion on Mach's face, and I figured out that the young woman was making quite forward advances on him. The knife-wielders from Deep Sea noticed, too, and they'd been licking their chops over the young woman's visit. I overheard them talking about getting even with the Professor. And of course, around midnight, the attempted slaughter began. Wilhelm and I hid ourselves upstairs while they raced around the entire Rose Island armed with fish-gutting knives. I don't know what would have happened to us if not for my friend Bernstein, who had maintained neutrality toward the aggressors until their screams deprived him, as the poet so splendidly says, "of the possibility of a well-deserved rest." Then he lifted his head from sleep and, with the straightforwardness of a nobleman, knocked them all unconscious, one after the other. The next day a terrified Mach, older by twenty years, abandoned Rose Island.

I headed back to Warsaw again and lost contact with Edward. A while later I looked for him again, but because Bernstein and I both found ourselves in constant conflict with authorities clamoring for justice, we didn't have a permanent address and it wasn't easy to find each other. Finally I ran into an acquaintance who'd just finished film school and gotten married. He knew Edward, too. We were sitting on the terrace of a café, where he was waiting to meet his wife. He heard me out, then he said:

"There's a very easy way you can find him. If a woman tells you she's read *Demons* and she's mesmerized by it, it means she's Edward's girlfriend. And she can give you his address."

A few minutes later his wife, whom he'd been waiting for, showed up. We were introduced, and the young girl said:

"I just read *Demons*. What do you think of it?"

My acquaintance went ghostly pale. I paid the check straightaway and left. His idea was simple but not without difficulties. The circle of Dostoevsky admirers turned out to be quite wide, and it didn't set me on the right track.

At that point, my secret snoops turned up again. I explained to them in vain that I lived alone and that the most I could do would be to write a denunciation against myself, which I'd gladly undertake. The agents listened to my speech. They said, "Oh, you don't want us to get sore, now . . ." and left. To this day I remember their sad faces and the smell of their rubber jackets. On my way home a couple of days later, I spotted them. A song died on my lips. I went to a friend of mine and spit out the whole story. I asked if I could stay with him a few days, and maybe together we could think something up. He agreed, and so did his wife. He made tea, and she went out. I was sitting across from him, and I saw beads of sweat flowing down his face. At a certain moment he stood up, took me by the hand, and led me into the corridor. He told me that his wife had gone to the police, and he advised me to run. I said I was already too tired of it all and I wouldn't run; let them come, let them take me, and do whatever they want. Then he knocked on the neighbor's door, pushed me inside, and said to some young, sleepy girl: "Hide him. The police are looking for him." And he disappeared. The young girl lived alone, and she turned out to be a student.

At night her fiancé would come, and negotiations would begin. They lasted until dawn. The fiancé would pull up underneath her window and sit on his motorcycle with its engine revving nonstop, and he'd deliver these classical speeches, modeled after the speeches of Cicero. But then, from the most important issues, like love and desire, he'd turn to matters concerning all of mankind, which wasn't his strong suit, and he'd come back to love, and then at dawn he'd appeal to her sense of justice and he'd finish with the issue he'd begun with: love and desire. From time to time he'd rev the engine on full throttle. The motor was an old type, and it would burn out. The neighbors, awakened by the mighty roar of the 600cc engine, would tune in to the speeches. Some offered him good advice, a second group warned him about women, and others threatened to go to the police, and still others embellished his drama with derisive commentary and told him what they would have done in his place. The entire apartment house took part in the drama. From time to time the police showed up. They'd been summoned by one of the spectators, someone with no sense of tragedy, who'd wanted to sleep. The fiancé would be sent off, but he'd turn up again. This went on for a while.

A few years later I was reminded of the whole story. I was already in Israel at the time. When I was living in Tel Aviv, I occasionally went to the movies on Ben Yehuda Street. The movie theater didn't have a roof, and they only showed Eddie Constantine films. These films had plots that were full of noble simplicity. Eddie Constantine would just slap the other actors around for two hours. It's worth mentioning that he hit them with an open hand, not with his fists, which made for unforgettable sound effects. Since he was also the producer, he could beat the poor actors any way he wanted, so the drama gathered real speed. Half the seats were missing in that theater, whose name I can't remember anymore. The viewers would start to beat one another during the film if somebody took an unfavorable view of Constantine and made mocking comments. And just like in the apartment house in Warsaw, the viewers would put in their two cents, offering the actors advice or telling them how dumb they were, and there wasn't an ounce of derision; they wanted to participate in the drama. But if a man tried to grab a chair and beat somebody over the head with it, the manager of the theater would switch the picture off and let the viewers have their fight, and then he'd turn the projector on again. The manager was probably a fan of brave Constantine, too, and didn't want the viewers to miss anything of the drama unfolding before their eyes. When they walked into the theater, people didn't pay attention to the name of the film. They'd just ask the ticket seller, "How many dead bodies?" and if the given number satisfied their spiritual needs, they bought a ticket. Later, the theater burned down. A friend from Tel Aviv said they'd been screening an American picture. The bold story had a heroic German woman, an American prisoner of war, and some nefarious Soviet officers: one of them plays the piano and breaks out in a cloying, sentimental song. He does this in order to distract and kill a member of the dumbfounded German family with a single shot. The victim turned out to be the daughter of the heroine. And that was the end of the theater, where tickets cost only sixty piastres. The public felt that the image of the Russian soul was presented too simply. They sent the theater up in smoke, and the manager to the poorhouse.

In the end, the girl's fiancé tormented me just as much as my two sad secret agent spooks and their raincoats that smelled like rubber. The affair came to a predictable end: the guy was drunk on his trusty steel horse, flew off a bridge, and broke his arms and legs. He went from a young man in the bloom of health into a tear-jerking invalid. Which all would have been fine, except that I became next in line as an eventual candidate for marriage. Natural process of elimination, as they say. I whispered whatever holy words I had to and headed off in a direction, I didn't even know where.

I knew I wouldn't be able to fool around with my secret agents much longer. I was scared they were analyzing my denunciations and making progress. I went to one of my writer acquaintances who I knew used to work for Military Intelligence, and I told him every-thing. He laughed genially and promised to help. He said, "Don't be concerned about it, son. They say that young Adam Mickiewicz also used to dabble in denunciations. Daniel Defoe was a police agent. They say the same thing about Kraszewski, and about Brzozowski, too. Go bravely on down that road. But if you don't want to, I'll help."

And I never saw them again. I only remember their sad faces and the smell of their rubber raincoats. Connected with that, the revving of the motorcycle from nightfall to sunup. I'm not sure it's fair to write about my secret agents so briefly, and absent any warmth. After all, they did inspire me to be creative. I'd get carried away sometimes writing denunciations, and I'd quote from made-up speeches and put words into the mouths of different victims, taking care that each one spoke with a distinct style and used different constructions. In literature you don't have to do that; in literature, vision and madness decide everything. It's actually good if people speak the same way, cut each other off, rave endlessly about the same things. As a genre, the police denunciation demands classical form and style, plus a certain refinement. Maybe this is beneficial for a young writer, but for an old pro it's annoying. In terms of the composition of police denunciations, ever-present in Polish literature, you have to make sure each character says something serious enough to warrant a couple of years of jail time. You've got to be equally vigilant against being too subdued, which can arouse the suspicion of the police higher-ups. Some instances demand crude and heavy language, masculine and brutal. For instance, when you're writing about prisoners who've been locked up for a long time and don't even have the right to smoke. For derisory cases, say, up to two years on criminal charges, you can write like a columnist, using anecdotes and providing your own personal commentary. Just be careful, because too much commentary embarrasses the character you're writing about. I was wet behind the ears, and I wrote several hundred denunciations thinking I was the only à rebours informant in the world. I think about my snoops today, and I'm almost grateful. They came into my life at a time when I still hadn't given much thought to writing, and their words encouraged me: they promised a long period of unpleasant abstinence. If not for them, I'd probably have wasted my health in restaurants, telling accidental friends the story of my broken life. I think it was exactly during this time that I gained an appreciation of the short and concise form, first out of necessity, then out of affection. That's the one thing I really value from the whole business. You can replace a thousand policemen one day, and you can chase a thousand prisoners a thousand miles the next. It doesn't matter. The only thing that matters is that in your life, there may arrive one thousand days when you don't manage to write a single page. If my achievements in writing allow me to give some advice to young people, I'd say to them: Every one of you ought to work for the secret police for a little while, to learn about style and precision. Books have to be written like denunciations. You've got to know that a poorly written denunciation can destroy you more than anything else.

I finally got rid of the secret agents, but I didn't have a cent to my name, nor any place to live. I went to see Józek Lenart from *Sztandar Młodych* and asked him to send me out on an assignment. Lenart gave me an advance, and I took a trip to a place near Wrocław, where I was supposed to find a young female doctor who'd been sent to work in a village a year prior. I was supposed to write about her situation there and her sunny worldview. I found the village and started asking around for the doctor. I got the feeling the peasants I was talking to were giving me strange answers, looking at me with pale eyes, acting like Ophelia in the madness scene. Finally, the doctor appeared. I asked her why all the people looked like lunatics. At first the young woman told me they were peasants from the other side of the Bug River. They were forever mourning the loss of their homeland, and they walked around in a complete fog, consumed by longing.* But that explanation, rooted in psychological and historical motives, didn't hold much water with me. Finally, after the doctor and I had drunk quite a bit of high-proof alcohol, I was able to uncover the truth: this was a village of morphine junkies. The doctor, who was scraping by on pennies, came up with a plan so simple it was brilliant: she got the entire village hooked on morphine, the peasants became addicts, and they bribed her to dispense whatever they needed to keep their addiction up. I asked her what she would do if the prosecutor got wind of her plan. She was fed up with everything, she told me, and if he found out, if he threatened to arrest her, she had a big dose of morphine and barbiturates to transport her from the living to the dead. Nothing ever came of that assignment.

My second assignment screeched to a bizarre halt, too. I was sent to one of the government farms, where the peasants were supposed to establish an amateur theater. The wife of the director of the farm was the gem of this particular theater. I traveled there on a Saturday. Sunday was supposed to be the premiere of a play by one of our masters of socialist realism. I can't remember the details of the play anymore: I think it was something about discord between a driller and

---

* The Western Bug River flows from Ukraine into Poland. During World War II, it became the dividing line between German and Russian forces. (RU)

a machinist, with a generational conflict lurking somewhere in the background. That's about as specific as I can get.

I arrived in the evening. The director of the farm understood immediately that this was an occasion to honor a guest from Warsaw, and took me to an actor who specialized in amorous roles. The lover was busy making sausage from a pig he and the director had pinched and slaughtered beforehand. We had a cordial, sophisticated conversation, raising our cups and consuming the sausage, and then we headed off to sleep. The next day, in the evening, we all gathered in the common room. Once again, to honor the guest from Warsaw, the theater manager instructed the local tenor to sing something before the performance. A young man ran onto the stage and began to bellow: "San Remo, white city on the sea—I love ye . . ." The peasants sat gaping in their padded jackets, but I had a good time. The show was next. At the moment when the main hero, a noble character full of pathos, was delivering a long tirade in honor of machine tools, friendship with the Soviet Union, and other such things, a wild-looking man ran onto the stage. With a cry of "This'll show you to fuck Jadźka!" he plunged a knife in the hero's chest; it was a personal emotional vendetta. Nothing came of that assignment.

I went back to Warsaw, where I already had a publishing contract with Iskry Publishing House. Celina Milska, the director at Iskry, knew I was a perpetual beggar, so she sent me to Władysław Broniewski to help him select some of his own poems for a "young citizen's reader." Iskry was a publishing house geared toward that sort of thing. I'm not being ironic with my language. Of course, it would be easy just to call it a "youth reader." But by documenting everything, I'm endeavoring to keep alive the language of those times: that odd mixture of slang, official communiqués, the language used at party rallies and on the street. I'm too young and insignificant to write a memoir; I'm writing about people I knew and loved. As I've already said: I want to explain, for the benefit of these very people, why I'm not living in Warsaw. I'm writing because I'm so greatly indebted to them that I haven't stopped loving them, and I can't forget them. On the other hand, I don't know if this makes sense: as I was reading Adolf Rudnicki's book last night—one of the people who helped me and to whom I owe a lot—I came across the following sentence: "Exactly two years ago, when a certain favorite young man, 'one of ours,' abandoned us and began dragging our name through the dirt in Paris, I asked myself the question: 'They can give him more money, more freedom, more of everything, but what will they give him for a court? Where will they find a court for the court poet? And what will he do without a court?'" Was I really that young man? And how did I drag their names through the dirt? And if I really said I'd only want to live in a country where a gesture of brotherhood doesn't become a gesture of self-destruction?—well, aren't all of Rudnicki's books an identical cry for that one, that single thing? Has Rudnicki ceased thinking, too?

So I went to see Władysław Broniewski, who lived in the Mokotów neighborhood. Broniewski didn't want to discuss the selection of his poems without first taking a drink, and after a terrible inner battle I gave in. He was an odd man: an officer of the Legions, a communist who didn't belong to the party, a prisoner of our capricious brothers, the most Polish poet one could dream of . . . And he needed communism for one reason only: because he, Broniewski, more than anything, loved writing about it. No other points of view would ever be taken into account, and nothing else interested him in the least. At the same time, he was an argumentative member of the nobility. He told me how Bierut invited him once to Belvedere and, taking him by the arm, walked with him to the garden. At a certain moment he said, "Comrade Broniewski, it's high time already you wrote a new national anthem." Broniewski told him to go to hell, after which he wrote a poem in Polish that genuflected before the Soviet revolution, hat in hand.

About the only thing I remember from the time I spent with Broniewski is one tragic incident. One day Broniewski gave up drinking and began writing poetry again, and things were going well. After a few hours someone called him up and asked how he was doing. Broniewski said that he'd gotten down to things and hoped to work solidly for a month or two. Unhappily for him, he mentioned he wasn't drinking. The person on the other end congratulated him, and the conversation was over. Broniewski got back to writing. Five minutes later, the telephone rang again: somebody else, who had talked with the previous caller and learned that Broniewski had stopped drinking, was calling to congratulate and encourage him to persevere in his decision. Broniewski thanked him and got back to work. Ten minutes later, again, the telephone: more advice and again a thank you from Broniewski. The eighth telephone call was from Comrade Jakub Berman. Broniewski, pale and jittery, came up to me and said, "Go get some vodka." Afterward, he told me that on the day his beloved only sister died, he went directly from the funeral to Wonieść, a rehab center for alcoholics. On orders from the Central Committee.

If only people knew there's no better way to knock somebody off the wagon than to remind him of what might happen if he starts drinking again. Then maybe they'd stop sharing their damn wonderful advice. People still don't realize that the feeling of gratitude contains a vast amount of hate. I wouldn't write about this if not for the fact that for half my life people have been making me sick by meddling in my affairs and giving me warnings.

So Broniewski began a cycle that would last many days. He was a strange lush: he could be dead drunk and stagger from corner to corner, but if I started to declaim his poetry—say, "Miła Street"—and made a mistake, Władysław Broniewski immediately corrected me, and harshly, too. I felt bad for him: people tormented him toward the end, and I'm sure they harassed him throughout his life. And he was an odd bird: a Captain of the Legions, Knight of the Order *Virtuti Militari*, he was proud he'd received that medal battling against the Bolsheviks, whom he later kneeled before, hat in hand. Himself a former prisoner of Stalin, he asked me what I thought about him. I said it was tough for me to say anything about Stalin because I'm afraid of bandits when there's nowhere to run. He nearly had a fit, which could have ended tragically for me, or even worse. It didn't matter that dear Uncle Joe had killed however many millions of people and built the largest concentration camp in the world. That wasn't important for him, a man who himself had sat in a Soviet camp. What was important was that I had insulted a man he, Władysław Broniewski, had written poetry in honor of. He rushed upstairs, shaking with rage. In a little while the terrified housemaid ran downstairs and told me to clear out right away, because Broniewski was drunk and was calling the Security Office. I grabbed my jacket and ran out swiftly into the darkness.

After 1956, when he was already a sick old man, he had enough
courage to come and ask me, a little picayune, for forgiveness. Not
that he was apologizing, but he was asking for forgiveness. It was unpleasant for me. We went out again for vodka, and again Broniewski
corrected me until the moment we both completely passed out, falling
asleep on the same bench, with me nestling up to him like a pup to its
mother. I think about him a lot; I thought about him when I was reading Miłosz's excellent essay about Gałczyński. Was Broniewski really
the same kind of court poet? Mieroszewski wrote that Broniewski
didn't have any clue about Marxism, dialectics, economics, and politics. Communism captivated him with its images: Marshal Tukhachevsky's hordes rushing forward in 1920; the furnaces of Magni-
togorsk; a power plant on the Volga; the White Sea Canal, during the
building of which so many thousands lost their lives; the Siberian bat-
talions marching for the relief of Moscow; the war speeches of Gen-
eralissimo Stalin, with that coarse and grating voice of his, urging the
Soviet people on to civil and world war . . . That was the communism
that interested Broniewski. He didn't care about anything else. He
even forgave them his time in jail, because he was able to write poetry
about it. To my good fortune, people didn't take Broniewski's nighttime telephone calls seriously. It could have ended in a very unamus-
ing way for me.

But what if I'm the same type of Pole as he is? I try not to think of
him any way but warmly. I try not to stop reading his poems, and I try
not to stop loving them. And when I think about him, I'm reminded
of the absolutely brilliant death scene in *War and Peace*: a man has
just died, and another man asks, "And where is he now?" I ask myself,
too: And where is he now? A communist who despised the party; a
Bolshevik who was given a medal for his action in battle against other
Bolsheviks; a prisoner of Stalin who wanted to lock up another man
for offending his tormentor; a great, unfortunate poet and a good
man. Where is he now? Does there exist for people, for us, a place
where we all meet, pure, good, and without anger, like in those Negro
spirituals? And if I do meet him up there, what will he write about,
and what will he believe in?

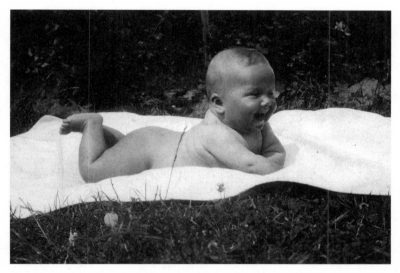

First photograph of Marek Hłasko. Summer 1934. (Archive MH)

Marek Hłasko. Wrocław, 1947.
(Andrzej Czyżewski)

Maria Hłasko, Marek's mother, with second husband Kazimierz Gryczkiewicz.
Warsaw, 1960. (Archive MH)

Marek Hłasko (middle) with friends at the High School for the Theatrical Arts.
Warsaw, 1949. (Archive MH)

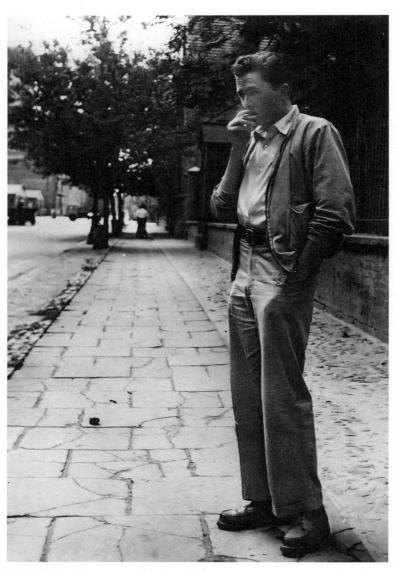
Marek Hłasko. Warsaw, 1953. (Archive MH)

Marek Hłasko with his aunt Teresa Czyżewska and her husband, Józef Czyżewski.
Wrocław, 1953. (Andrzej Czyżewski)

Marek Hłasko with writer Wilhelm Mach. Warsaw, 1954. (Archive MH)

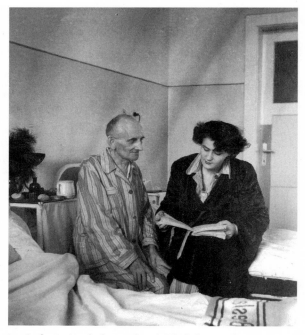

Polish writer Stefan Łoś in the hospital, with Hłasko's second cousin Zyta Kwiecińska. Wrocław, 1955. (Archive MH)

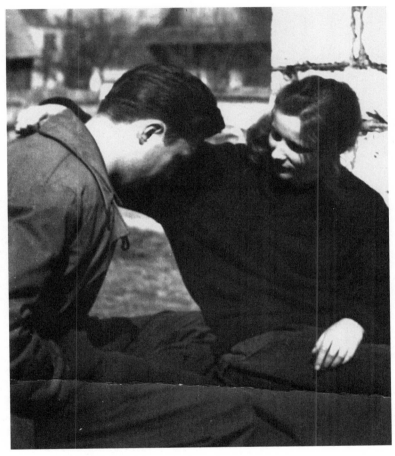

Marek Hłasko with Polish poet, writer, lyricist Agnieszka Osiecka. Kazimierz Dolny, 1957. (Archive MH)

Marek Hłasko with his wife, the German actress Sonja Ziemann. Kazimierz Dolny, 1957. (Klaus Otto Skibowski)

Marek Hłasko with Sonja Ziemann at the office of his publisher in Cologne, Germany, 1958. (Klaus Otto Skibowski)

Marek Hłasko with Sonja Ziemann at the office of his German publisher in Cologne. Germany, 1958. (Klaus Otto Skibowski)

Marek Hłasko at Maisons-Laffitte in 1958, office of his publisher in France, Jerzy
Giedroyc. (Henryk Giedroyc)

Marek Hłasko. Tel Aviv, 1959. (Henryk Stillman)

HLASKO WIEDENMAYERSTR
KLINIK DR WESTRICH MUENCHEN =

02744

Datum   Uhrzeit

Gesendet
Platz   Namenszeichen

Leitvermerk

I PRAY FOR YOUR HEALTH AND TO FIND A WAY TO HELP YOU =
LOVE LOVE SONJA +

Telegram from Sonja to Marek, in a hospital in Munich. February, 1964.
(Archive MH)

Marek Hłasko and Sonja Ziemann. Germany, 1964. (Archive MH)

Marek Hłasko. Germany,
1964. (Archive MH)

Marek Hłasko with American film and television director Ted Post (middle) and Polish composer Roman Maciejewski. Hollywood, 1966. (Archive MH)

Marek Hłasko. Hollywood, 1966. (Archive MH)

Portrait of Marek Hłasko, by Polish artist Witold Kaczanowski. Paris, 1966.
(Archive MH)

CHAPTER THREE

Reporter for the Most Courageous Magazine in Poland

I don't remember how I joined up with the gang from *Po Prostu* anymore. There's only one logical explanation to the vexing riddle of how I became an employee there, or even how I found the place. On the ground floor of the building where the most courageous magazine of its time had its offices was a bar called Jontek. Maybe one day I took a wrong turn, walked into *Po Prostu*'s offices, and asked for a double vodka and some fresh herring. But that still doesn't explain why I wasn't thrown out of there. They wouldn't have needed any justification. My belief in predetermination was upheld when a few months later I finally did get fired.

Jontek was no classy joint. Back then people went to Kameralna. Kameralna was a brilliantly conceived restaurant: it had two day halls and a night hall. The novelty of the gastro-architectural idea was that you could begin drinking in one of the day halls early in the morning, go have a meal at the other day hall, tipple until evening, and then, when the night hall would open, you could have a proper good time. Any scoundrel could get into the two Kameralna day halls. The night hall, in contrast, observed a certain etiquette: guests had to have a jacket and tie. For all they cared, the customer could have been pulled straight out of a trash dump after twenty-four hours—he just needed a jacket and tie. Since I didn't have a steady place to live in those days and I'd ruined all my clothes in frequent scuffles with other residents of the capital, I stumbled onto an idea so simple it was Spartan: I bought a tie and a velveteen jacket in the government department store and left them in the coatroom of the night hall of Kameralna. When I got to the bar, I'd immediately transform from a dirty scoundrel into a classically educated youth, auguring hope for the future. I'd skip merrily into the hall.

The hall manager and the cloakroom attendants kept watch over public morals and calm. I remember once, after a horrible fight had been broken up and the teeth had been swept off the parquet, the night manager walked in, right hand raised tragically in the air, and announced: "Gentlemen! Calm and cheer all around!" Then the Sarmatians got back to having fun.* If one of the Sarmatians was singled out for having too much fun and the police had to be called on him, he'd be banned from Kameralna for a time jointly determined by the manager and the cloakroom attendants. That was a terrible punishment. Once I walked into Kameralna and witnessed the following scene: two of my friends, Andrzej Roman and Paweł Minkiewicz, were carrying a body through the hall, making their way to the bar. They were shouting, "Heads up, cash is on the way." The body turned out to be Jurek Cukrowski, passed out cold, and Misters Roman and Minkiewicz were carrying him to the bar, because etiquette didn't allow them to take money from the pockets of their unfortunate benefactor.

My pal Wojciech Frykowski, a promising, aspiring future alcoholic, got annoyed one day at an overly insolent waiter. To let the waiter know he should get back to work, Frykowski bombed him with a cucumber. But Frykowski was so tipsy he couldn't get off a good shot, and the cucumber hit the bartender instead, a solemn old man in glasses. It bounced off his glasses and hit a lonely customer poisoning himself at the bar. The latter, without bothering to hear an

---

* Sarmatians, followers of Sarmatism, a cultural and ideological movement that dominated the life of the nobility in the Polish-Lithuanian Commonwealth in the sixteenth through nineteenth centuries. A unique blend of Eastern and Western traditions, Sarmatism called upon the Polish nobility to maintain the ancient traditions and good name of their families. Here, the term is used ironically to refer to a specific "Polish" national character. (RU)

explanation, dealt the barman a blow to the skull. This was the opening bell for an all-out fight. The operating principle was "Every man for himself."

I'd just gotten to the cloakroom when the bartender ran in. "Three cop squads with blackjacks!" he yelled to the cloakroom attendant.

The attendant ran through the hall, and a minute later he was gauging the brawlers with a professional glance. He came back to the cloakroom.

"Two squads with blackjacks will be enough," he said, and soon he was on the phone with the cops.

I was interested in the specialized terminology they were using, and I asked for an explanation. They surprised me by graciously giving me one. The level of drunkenness of the patrons was calculated into cop squads, and you can imagine what the blackjacks were for. For a small fight, one cop squad was called; for a bigger fight, two. The upper limit has never been established, and it could be an object of infinite interest for researchers.

The most affable of the cloakroom attendants was Miecio. A terrifying giant, he never hit a client in the skull or the face. He'd just gather them all up in a heap, like the eye of a radar condensing thousands of nautical miles, and throw them out the door with the strength of a tornado. The clients were flattened against the wall on the opposite side of Foksal Street, which used to be called Młodzież Jugosłowiańska Street, and before that, Pieracki Street. The other attendants would throw jackets, caps, and canes at the guests, plus other articles of masculine elegance. At the same time, they wished them good night and addressed them politely, saying, "Mister Editor, you must be exhausted."

Life had been cruel to Miecio. Once, I was coming back from the funeral of the president of the Polish People's Republic, Bolesław Bierut. It was indeed a spectacle worth remembering. Comrade Tomasz, as Bierut was sometimes known, was being escorted from the airport at Okęcie, and crowds had gathered along the entire highway. They didn't want to miss the final ride of the beloved leader and thinker. Of course, bedlam ensued, and the casket with the body got caught up somewhere along the road. Drunk people on the streets kept asking, "Has the body gone by already?" Or, "What's with the body? They should have had time to pickle it." Others answered calmly, "The body's getting cold; it's getting cold." Finally the body passed by, and the heartbroken people all went back home. Then I ran into Miecio. His face was lined with worry. I offered him my condolences; he did the same. I asked him if the worry on his face was because Comrade Tomasz was, frankly speaking, dearly departed. But it turned out Miecio had other concerns: he'd been fired from Kameralna.

"I was too nice to all of you," the poor guy added. To illustrate his point, he told me he'd gotten a little annoyed and hit a pushy customer in the head with a key. The patron had to be taken to the hospital, where they identified twelve stab wounds. To be sure, the lock on the door of the nighttime Kameralna was heavy. The key brings to mind Saint Peter. As we know from the story and from pictures, he holds a gigantic wrench in his hands, the kind that plumbers usually use. In spheres prone to religious ecstasy they like to call it "the key to the kingdom."

Poldek Tyrmand wrote about Kameralna in his day, and I don't have much to add. Those were good days and nights. I scoured the world for years for a joint like that and couldn't find one. In Jaffa, for example, there was a joint that was always completely dark, and they only let you in if you were accompanied by a woman. I told them I was a loner, my erotic life a composition of fainthearted and ill-fated attempts at masturbation. They didn't let me in. German nightclubs are boring as all hell. In Zurich there's only one joint that stays open until twelve. Finally, after years of investigation and effort, I was able to fill the painful void in my life: I discovered La Bohème in Paris, on rue de l'Odessa. I walked in there wanting to get out of my head as soon as possible. I was sober as a child for the first time in my life. Some drunken Irishman mistook me for his twin brother, whom he was having a row with, and gave me one right in the kisser. It wouldn't have been so strange except I'm skinny and dark-haired, with a faraway look in my eyes, while the brother was red-haired, fat, and short. The owner of the joint, Tony, told me it was a mistake and to let it drop. It's an incredible joint: the last time I went there, covered in blood from head to toe, I didn't arouse the slightest interest. They ushered me into the kitchen and anesthetized me with the help of a Tony Special, which is a drink made by mixing pure spirits with a dry martini. Then, to my complete shock, Jack the waiter pulled out a great big box with lancets, saws, clamps and forceps, and stitching thread. He washed his hands expertly with pure vodka, which he then poured back into the bottle. He stitched me up and spanned my wounds with clasps. In a bored voice, he told me to come back in six days to get the clasps taken out. I wanted to ask him where he'd picked up his knowledge of anatomy, but there wasn't time. A man with a knife in his thigh had just been carried into the kitchen, and Jack briskly went into action.

The patrons are mainly American soldiers, their thirst for entertainment out of proportion with their income. Tony devised a method to deal with this: everybody got a hand stamp. But there were some hitches: some wily black soldiers wouldn't wash their hands for a few days, trying to reenter on the sly. So Tony ordered a few dozen phosphorescent stamps, visible only under a glow lamp, and he would change the stamp every evening. Admission to La Bohème now works like this: a giant black man in the entryway grabs the paw of everybody trying to come in and glances at his hand, bringing it under the light I've mentioned. If the stamp matches the schedule made by Tony, the guest can come in. If not, the black man kicks the guest out on the street. If only the bard Mickiewicz had lived in today's times, he would have had what to think about on the Paris streets. He'd have run about all day wheeling and dealing, trying to borrow a few cents, so that in the evening he could live it up at La Bohème.

I don't know why I've written so much about Kameralna and La Bohème. It's like what happens to a schoolboy who sits in the last row of the classroom and everything reminds him of a rear end. It's an old joke, but for the sake of the young people who are reading *Kultura* and are about to embark on their lives, I'll retell it here in full, to illustrate why I got so off track from the story of the most courageous and most uncompromising magazine in Poland. This story's for the young reader:

A school. A teacher is investigating the intelligence of his pupils. He takes a white handkerchief from his pocket.

Teacher: "Kowalski, what does this handkerchief remind you of?"
Kowalski: "Bonfire smoke and fog."
Teacher: "Why is that?"
Kowalski: "Because in the fall I always have a cold, and we usually see fog and smoke from the shepherds' fires in the fall."
Teacher: "Excellent, Kowalski. You've got a future ahead of you. You may be seated." [To the next student.] "Rappaport, what does this handkerchief remind you of?"
Rappaport: "Summer vacation."
Teacher: "Why is that?"
Rappaport: "Because when I leave for Catholic youth camp, Mama always stands on the train platform and waves her handkerchief at me."
Teacher: "Excellent, Rappaport. You've got a future ahead of you." [To the next student.] "Sierzputowski, what does this handkerchief remind you of?"
A gloomy giant stands up in the last row. Pimpled. It's obvious that despite his most sincere efforts he can't complete a grade in less than three years. The camera zeroes in on Sierzputowski's face. Close up. You can see the gigantic straining of his thoughts painted on the face of this unfortunate giant.
Sierzputowski [mumbling to general delight]: "A rear end, sir."
Zoom in on teacher.
Teacher: "A rear end? This handkerchief? Why is that?"
Sierzputowski: "Because everything reminds me of a rear end."
That's how it is with me. As soon as I start writing, everything reminds me of drinking.
The first time I went out on a story for *Po Prostu*, I wasn't a full-time employee yet, just a freelancer. I went to Lublin. Two young students, living in a dormitory, had killed their homeroom teacher and looted his valuables, worth around three hundred zlotys. Both of them were underage. It was impossible to give them the death penalty. The boys were polite; they weren't bad students and had been the teacher's favorites. Thus, they were able to drop by in the evening, because the lonely old man loved them. Here I should add that the tutor wasn't a homosexual, he was just a lonely man, to whom the presence of those

two youths brought pleasure. I specifically asked the defense lawyer for these two if there hadn't been some sort of homosexual blackmailing going on. The lawyer said it had been attested beyond any doubt that the tutor was as normal a person as they come and there'd never been any sort of homosexual activities discovered in his past. In the court transcript both boys had stated in agreement that their tutor had never tried to come on to them in any "urogenital sense." (That's how the satirist The Great Wiech so splendidly put it.) Both of them barely even knew what homosexuality was. They couldn't say what actually happens during an erotic encounter between two men.

When the prosecutor asked what they were going to do with the loot, both testified they hadn't thought about this aspect beforehand. They simply got the idea of murder in their heads and decided to carry it out because they were convinced they'd get away with what crime novels cleverly call "the perfect crime." To the prosecutor's repeated question of what they needed the money for and how they planned to allocate it, they said they'd wanted to go to the movies and drink two bottles of domestic wine. To the prosecutor's question of whether, knowing the tutor's cheery disposition, it wouldn't have been better to just go to him and ask for money, both replied that this simply hadn't occurred to them. I couldn't get my hands on the rest of the case materials. For reasons unknown to me, I wasn't given the police report from the incident. But I did see the testimony, and it was precisely this point that struck me: They knew this man was friendly and kind. Why did they kill him? Why didn't they just ask?

The defense lawyer was a very busy man; he didn't have much time for me. I asked to talk to another lawyer, a young, intelligent guy, and we agreed to meet at a certain café on Krakowskie Przedmieście. I asked: Why did they kill him? Why hadn't they asked for the money? As a lawyer, he said, he was in a position to offer only one response: from his point of view, there exists only guilt or innocence. The position of attorney, especially of criminal defender, has been a fictional profession here for many years, he added, with the possible exception of divorce lawyers. If the two young men killed, and didn't ask, they did so because the image of public evil weighed heavily in their minds: the image of corruption, the knowledge of political assassinations, witnessing the

Soviet occupation, the proximity of drunkenness, theft, prostitution, decay . . . The goodness and kindness of that lonely man couldn't out-weigh those other matters. The cunning salesmen at the city's national-ized retail stores have hollowed out the weights on the scales of Themis. And he told me something else: we can't require them to be moral be-cause we only teach them what they're supposed to think, but we don't teach them wisdom. We promised them an increase in living standards. Instead, again and again they saw the increasing impoverishment of the country. We promised them rule of law, then condemned Bishop Kaczmarek when every Pole in the country knew he was innocent. We promised them freedom of speech and thought, yet we showed them Soviet tanks in Berlin when the enraged Germans could stay silent no longer. In the name of *what* can we demand they have faith in the love of a lonely and unselfish person? It's not easy to be just in Gomorrah.

I asked him: If he were their lawyer, would he have been roused to give a speech in their defense with all he'd just told me? "Of course," he replied, "but under one condition."

"What would that be?" I asked wisely.

"If their case was being tried at the International Court in the Hague."

Two years later Leopold Tyrmand's book *The Man with White Eyes* became a Polish best seller. Tyrmand, who knew how to translate the atmosphere of Warsaw brawls, of Warsaw streets and pubs, ruined the book by demonizing crime in Poland. Tyrmand's heroes shoot at each other, race their cars, run in sophisticated gangs, build a criminal organization, and so on. They're villains in the grand style, whereas the modus operandi of Polish crime is inferior: robbery, where the victim is killed for one hundred zlotys; a drunken fight over a place in line at the movies; stealing a pair of shoes; some small affair in a nationalized store. That's the modus operandi of Polish crime. Later, fortunately, things changed a bit: there were cases of corruption like the meat scandal, the tanners' scandal, the textile scandal. But what can you do: Tyrmand's favorite actor is Humphrey Bogart. Mine, too.

I returned to Warsaw and tried to finish my story. Two-thirds of it got tossed out. Eligiusz Lasota made the cuts. As I'm writing today,

Lasota is no longer the chief editor of *Po Prostu* or a representative in the Sejm of the People's Republic. Too bad. Lasota was the one at *Po Prostu* who was most afraid. One day he became a representative in the Sejm—the most popular person in Poland besides Dymsza. The students supported his parliamentary seat, but the man was a coward. Hanka Bratkowska made the magazine: she turned it into the most widely read and loved magazine in Poland from the rag that *Po Prostu* had been through the end of '55. When I started working at *Po Prostu*, I picked up the beautiful Mira Michałowska's translation of one of Hemingway's best stories, "A Clean, Well-Lighted Place," for my department. Lasota had it printed on the last page. When I wrote my short story "A First Step in the Clouds," Lasota threw me out on my ugly mug. I went to Wilhelm Mach, and Mach stuck it into *Nowa Kultura*. As soon as it was published, Bratkowska attacked me like a rabid dog:

"So, you rat, why'd you publish your best story in *Nowa Kultura* and not in *Po Prostu*?"

"Your immediate superior—my chief editor—is sitting right there," I said, pointing to the door of Lasota's office. "Let him explain why."

Bratkowska gave Lasota hell. And then there's this: the Bim-Bom Theater came to Warsaw with its second production, with Kobiela and Cybulski directing. Bim-Bom's first production had been charming; its second one was idiotic. Somebody walked onstage and said, "Nothing." Then he ran off. Somebody else walked on and said, "Nothing." And ran off again. The lights went out, then came on again. They "detonated" an atom bomb. Some balloons burst. It was supposed to remind you of broken dreams, but meanwhile, as any fool knows, the first thing cracked rubber brings to mind is an inflated doctor's bill, the idea we've gotten ourselves into a fix, and the prospect of our wife raising hell. An angel came out and played the balalaika. Then Satan flew onstage, tore the balalaika from the angel, and fired a shot from a toy pistol. Afterward a crazy cyclist rode across the stage. He wasn't there a half a minute, the son of a bitch, when suddenly some Jewish actress appeared and muttered something about how there wouldn't be any spring. Then everybody insisted there wouldn't be *anything*

anymore. And that was it, no ending. I wrote an article about it, and
Lasota kicked me out. Some people liked the play. Lasota enjoyed it,
even though he hadn't seen the performance: the majority of people
liked it, so Lasota liked it, too.

My career as a court reporter ended with a similar mishap. I had
gone to the trial of Władysław "Władzio" Mazurkiewicz. Mazurkiewicz had invited various people to have a drink and take a ride, the
kick being that he didn't say good-bye to them in the morning with
a kiss, but put a bullet in the back of their heads. The trial was one
of a kind: Mazurkiewicz was a sleuth and provocateur for the Security Services, and the witnesses were afraid to expose the bastard
at the trial. Everybody knew Władzio was a murderer, but they all
thought he was just carrying out orders from his bosses at the Security Service. And you can't forget: Mazurkiewicz's trial took place
before October. The trial was a sham. The witnesses were afraid
to speak up; the prosecutor deftly changed topics. Mazurkiewicz's
dim-witted lawyer defended him by proffering the argument that
Mazurkiewicz was a born killer, a pathological type with hereditary
sinister tendencies—he pickled his victims under the concrete floor
of his garage at home—but the lawyer completely overlooked the
fact that his client-lunatic was conscious enough to develop an emotional attachment to his victims' valuables. The trial was a farce. It
was obvious people were afraid to talk, that Mazurkiewicz had cun-
ningly circulated information about his partnership with the Security Services. It's impossible to imagine a similar situation occurring
in a country where the police maintain at least some semblance of
decency. But it wasn't Mazurkiewicz who was put on trial. The entire
city was on trial. Hofmokl-Ostrowski, whom I'd contacted with a
request for an interview, started to explain that Mazurkiewicz had a
squinty-eyed scowl, which is the best proof that his criminal tendencies were hereditary and he didn't bear responsibility for his guilt.
The old boy raved, and I listened. Suddenly Attorney Ostrowski became ghostly pale.

"Sir?" I uttered. "Would you like some water? What's wrong?"

"You, too, have a squinty-eyed scowl?" muttered Ostrowski, and
quickly said good-bye to me. I wrote an article about it, "The City Is

on Trial." Lasota threw me out of his office.

At the end of 1955, Warsaw's great son, Kazimierz Brandys, wrote a short story called "Before He Is Forgotten." The subject was Czesław Miłosz, who'd betrayed Poland and stayed behind in the West. Kazimierz Brandys didn't disappoint his readers, but at the same time, the story was idiotic, like all the rest of his work.

A few months later a metamorphosis took place in Brandys's heart, and he wrote a novella called *The Defense of Grenada*. It was all about how things aren't good, but they'll get better. They aren't good, because they have to be bad, but from a certain moment, there'll be peace and happiness. Brandys didn't serve any surprises to his readers this time, either. He didn't undermine their trust. Artur Sandauer, a man without illusions, dissected Brandys's epic with a professional's pen. Sandauer mockingly referred to it as "opportunism of epic proportions." One day Maruś Perelmann came to the office and suggested that Lasota print *The Defense of Grenada* as an insert and arrange a special discussion about it at the Crooked Circle Club. Lasota was at euphoria's peak and agreed immediately. *Po Prostu* sponsored the Crooked Circle Club, but I became furious and went to Lasota.

"Lilek," I said. "Throw Perelmann out of here together with his shitty *Defense of Grenada*. It's a shame if *Po Prostu* does this sort of thing. Either we publish new writers we believe in, or we publish writers who haven't whored themselves out. Let's face it. Things are bad if a writer like Miłosz left the country. And this one here suddenly went through a metamorphosis? The hell with Brandys."

Lasota didn't want to hear it. He published *Grenada* and organized the discussion. After that, the affairs of *Po Prostu* ceased to interest me. I gave it another shot and wrote an article about Dostoevsky. Lasota threw me out, so I decided to play a joke on him: I took Dostoevsky over to *Trybuna Ludu*, where they published it and even paid me. Lasota, a representative in the Sejm and the editor of a magazine that was and is an icon, was afraid to publish something that *Trybuna Ludu*, the mouthpiece of the Central Committee of the Polish United Workers' Party, published so eagerly. For Lasota, the article was too dangerous. Staszek Brodzki, the cultural editor at *Trybuna*, didn't even have to think twice.

Am I being fair, writing all this about Lasota only now, when he's neither the editor of *Po Prostu* anymore, nor a representative in the Sejm of the PRP? I don't know. I'm not writing about Lasota as he is today, but as he was back then. I remember, I was witness once to a conversation between American lawyers. They were discussing whether or not to execute Caryl Chessman, the cause célèbre. The argument against execution was that a person who has sat in prison for twelve years has changed, and even if he can't begin his life anew in society, at least he ought to be spared his life. The counterargument was simple: an execution order ought to be executed. We're not killing him for who he is today, but for who he was then. Lasota was a coward.

But did *Po Prostu* have any chance to remain an appealing, courageous, and honest magazine? I don't think that question needs an answer. Poland is an occupied country, and as long as you don't forget that for a minute, you have to think about and try to help Poland. Any other kind of thinking about Poland is the thinking of a non-Pole, the thinking of slave drivers and fools. Of course *Po Prostu* didn't have a chance, and anyone who thinks otherwise is doing wrong to the good, honest people who worked there, to the people who walked kilometers through the mud to organize a discussion club, who wrote about and tried to help folks who'd received work orders in the boondocks. The magazine had an excellent cadre of local reporters. Crawling through the mud, malnourished and thin, they were fine, fine people. As far as I can recall, we had six consumptives in the office, which means every other person had TB. The party, from its point of view, had played its cards perfectly with the magazine. *Po Prostu* had worked for the party; *Po Prostu* had agitated the masses; *Po Prostu* was the first magazine in Poland to conduct an interview with Władysław Gomułka; *Po Prostu* fought for Gomułka; and *Po Prostu*, by Gomułka's hand, was brought to ruin.

Before October 1955, *Po Prostu's readership was mainly students. Eighty percent of the magazines were returned for recycling. But aft*er the summer holiday that year—they halted publishing every year for a two-month period, probably the only magazine in the country, or anywhere, to do so—*Po Prostu* began to sell hundreds of thousands of issues. When you look at the old issues today, you see the circulation numbers on the cover steadily increasing. *Po Prostu* stopped being a magazine for students and became a magazine for the young intelligentsia. It was a magazine for the entire nation. They started a campaign to help out young artists, and my immediate superior sent me out in the city to look for some candidates. For hours I ran from attic to attic and saw how these starvelings were living. *Po Prostu* was the first in Poland to discuss the functionaries behind, and to sound the alarm on, the issue of the fate of young people who'd finished their higher education and received work orders dispatching them to the provinces, where they wasted away. *Po Prostu* was the first in Poland to raise the issue of the Home Army heroes. *Po Prostu* was the first in Poland to show the lifestyle of the princes of socialism, to describe the stores behind the "yellow curtains." This is to the eternal credit of people like Hanka Bratkowska, Misza Grzelak, Janusz Chudzyński, Jurek Urban, and others. My direct superior was Juliusz Garztecki. Rumor had it he was working for the Security Service, too. I don't know. In Poland there are three things they usually say about people from that so-called milieu: that they're agents of the Security Service, homosexuals, or drunks. I can't say either way. I know Garztecki worked like a devil for *Po Prostu* and was constantly busting my balls. And I well remember, it was he himself who brought up the issue of the rehabilitation of the heroes of the Home Army. But I'll say it again: Marxism doesn't help a person obtain wisdom. Dialectics is knowledge not of how thinking ought to be done, but of how one ought to think. When *Po Prostu* began to think for itself, it was shut down.

The mistake of Bratkowska and other members of the staff was allowing in the scum who turned up in our offices on Wiejska Street as soon as *Po Prostu* became the number one magazine to work for. Lasota can't be held responsible, since he's a coward. But Hanka should have gotten rid of them all. People say different things about Hanka. I only know good things about her. When Jerzy Andrzejewski sent me his incredible short story, "The Escape," Lasota was shaking with fear. Hanka tore into Lasota, and he just sat there and took it. We received thousands of letters from people who said it was the best story Jerzy Andrzejewski ever wrote. Andrzejewski himself considered "The Escape" to be a weak story, a failure. I begged Andrzejewski to give us "The Escape," getting on my knees and kissing his hands. In the end we both ended up in kisses. The tragedy with Jerzy is that he doesn't recognize his enormous, God-given talent, and he has a lack of self-respect. A lack of pride, in place of which there's hubris. The man tears things apart in his writing, but he's convinced himself he's got to moralize, too. The idiots from the Polish Film Studio, in their complete and quite frankly puzzling ineptitude at making films, didn't know what an incredible war movie they could have made out of "The Escape." Even Professor Aleksander Ford, the colonel, couldn't have ruined that story, though he manages to screw up everything.

There's one more thing I want to say about Hanka. When I received my summons for army service and was called to go in front of the military commission, I first went to the newspaper offices. I went up to the third floor, to the typists' room, and I started to write a letter to a film director I knew. I told him I couldn't write him a screenplay because, as the song goes, "And he was called to war, and she cried over him . . ." In the letter, I wrote, "Poland has more need for spies . . . than journalists." I was referring to the fact that those who volunteered to be informers for the secret police were exempted from military basic training. I was shaking in anger when I wrote the letter, and I ripped the page out of the typewriter, not noticing that I'd inserted a carbon, like I usually did. Like a purebred Polish conspirator, I left a copy of the letter on the table.

Two hours later Lasota called me in. He looked like Jasiński: a young lad, handsome and gloomy.

"Listen, old man," began the editor of the most courageous magazine in Poland. "I've got to ask for your resignation."

"Why?"

With a tragic gesture, Lasota pulled a copy of my letter from his drawer and showed it to me. Bratkowska patched up the whole thing, of course. But who had brought the copy of the letter to Lasota? The typists, eighteen- and twenty-year-old girls, whom we used to flirt with. What use did these people have for independence? They should remain their brothers' keepers until the end of the world, and their lives should be dull and colorless.

I am reminded of something that happened to me in Israel. A friend of mine, Jerzy Buchbinder-Press, found me a hell of a job; namely, in a foundry. Keep in mind, it was a hundred and twenty degrees outside, and the oven in the furnace room was four thousand degrees. An inferno, and on top of that I was working under the table, since I didn't have working papers. And so, while my friend Buchbinder-Press sat in a café, stroked his considerable beard, and conducted business— that is, *vent about his bizniz*, in the professional lingo of Israel—I was loading sixteen and a half tons of material into the oven and making friendly conversation with my boss, Mister Szapiro. In that factory, everybody from the manager to the last scoundrel who emptied the trash in the furnace room knew I wasn't Joram Buchbinder-Press but just "Hłaskower"—which sounded more Jewish than Hłasko. After a few months I found better work, so I went to the factory to say my teary good-bye to everybody. And suddenly one of them didn't want to shake my hand.

"Why not?"

"Because you're a *sheygets*, and you're not Joram Buchbinder-Press."

"You had half a year's time," I said. "Why didn't you go to the police?"

"Because when you came here, I saw you were hungry and needed a job. I won't give you my hand. Your people should be cursed, and so should you, and your land."

That's how it is in Israel with the Jews, who for two thousand years wandered around the world. Beaten, tortured, spat upon, and marched through every prison and camp in the world. The government of Israel was established in 1948. During the battle for Jerusalem, insubordinate soldiers were punished in one manner only: they were forced to leave the front line for a period of time. And that was the worst punishment for an Israeli soldier—for a Jew, who for hundreds of years had been an object of mockery and derision. The Jews were picked on only because they wouldn't stop saying, "Hear O Israel, One is our Lord and One is our Homeland," when they entered their home. They have their homeland, and if there really is a God and He is merciful, they'll never lose it. Every person who truly believes in God should wear a Star of David next to the cross around their neck, until the last anti-Semite is dead, and until his body turns to dust, which the patient earth will receive in shame.

My career at *Po Prostu* ended when they printed *The Defense of Grenada*. I didn't care about anything anymore. I only showed up on the first of the month for my paycheck. Still, it's a shame about the magazine. The only thing I don't feel sorry about is the person who, from the second *Po Prostu* turned into a magazine for the young intelligentsia, insisted on publishing a programmatic column known under the winged title of "On the Intelligentsia." That was an expression taken from the pen of the Russian who explained to us in a speech at the Eighteenth Congress of the Great Communist Party of Bolsheviks that the intelligentsia are also people, to some extent. The Russian thinker was a man by the name of Stalin. Who insisted on printing his columns goes without saying. To use a quick analogy: when my friend KP and I tried to join the cobblers' union in Legnica in 1949, the director asked him, "What can I help you with?" "Cash," my friend said with a smile and flashed his TT pistol, just like it was supposed to be done. And that's how my career as a reporter came to a halt.

I still didn't have a place to live, and my friend Bereza and I used to sleep at the Central Railroad Station. Frequently we were "put up" at certain police stations and drunk tanks. Finally, I found a temporary place with another friend who lived at his grandmother's. This friend hated alcohol. At the same time, he was a great fan of adultery. But what to do with the old grandmother? It was simple: we lived in the Powiśle neighborhood, so we would buy the grandmother a ticket to the movies somewhere in the Ochota district. A movie lasted two hours, the tram ride was three hours there and back, so that's five hours already. In that time you could get something going. After a while my friend's grandmother began to talk like the heroes in the movies. For example, she'd say, "You, Marek. Keep your hands down when you talk to me, or things might get unpleasant." When another friend came by to say hello to the grandmother, the grandmother said, "I never shake hands with a lefty. It's saved my life more than once." Or another one: "Don't be such a nice guy, Mark. Remember, you came to Frisco to rest up and get your health back." Everything was going well, but my nymphomaniac friend got too smart for his own good. They were showing a four-hour Soviet film called *Admiral Ushakov*. And just around the time when the girls were about to give up what the good Lord gave them, the grandmother showed up.

"A scandal!" she started shouting. "Thugs! Animals! Unacceptable! A nightmare!"

But she wasn't talking about the naked girls at all, which is what we thought at first. What happened was, somebody who looked like a real lowlife was starring in the film as Admiral Nelson. His partner, Lady Hamilton, looked like the type of girl you'd find at night on Chmielna Street. They slap themselves on the behind and yell, "What do you say we give this ass a little spanking?" Lady Hamilton was dressed in a lace nightgown that was meant to be the peak of luxury, on top of it all. Admiral Nelson, devilishly arching his brow, approached her and extended his only hand. In a resounding bass he called out:

"Kak pozhivaiete, Ledi Gemilton?" *How do you do, Lady Hamilton?*

That was too much for the grandmother to watch. And I was thrown out again. I remember how I walked sadly along Krakowskie Przedmieście on that immortal October day, and my friends stopped me in front of the university.

"Come to the Żerań district tonight," they said. "We're going to distribute the guns."

"What do I need a gun for?" I asked.

"We're going to fight."

"Friends, put off the freedom movement for a day," I said. "Tonight I'm invited to a name day party at Kropka Minkiewicz's place. I can't miss it."

And I walked on.

CHAPTER FOUR

Goofy the Dog

Not long ago, as I was reading one of the latest issues of *Kultura*, I came upon an anonymous article titled "A Voice from the Motherland." The author of the article was discussing the attitude of Poles toward America. During the Korean War, he reminisced, Poles who were walking by the American embassy would remove their hats to show respect to the starry flag. I belonged to that group as well. I was a student at a high school for the theatrical arts, and I was expelled a year before the outbreak of the Korean War. As far as I remember, the American embassy was located on Ujazdowskie Avenue, and our school was in the YMCA building on Konopnicka Street. After classes we would take Ujazdowskie Avenue and doff our caps in front of the embassy, and the soldier standing there would look at us with interested benevolence, the kind usually meant for hunchbacks and idiots.

We would go to the Information Center at the US embassy as well. None of us knew English back then, but we'd look at the pictures in magazines like *Life* or *Time* and other American books and periodicals. Sometimes the Information Center would organize film screenings. We would go, and after the show, undercover agents from the nearby police station—on Piusa Street, I think it was—would detain us. They'd check our ID cards and rough us up. It took about two hours to regain our freedom. But there was an upside: we could discuss the movie we'd just seen with others who'd been in the audience and were now awaiting their turn, sans belts, shoelaces, or ties. This happened time and time again.

At the film showings at the embassy I got to know a character by the name of Goofy the Dog. Goofy always had pure intentions and good thoughts, but instead of being able to realize any of his ideas—for example, cheering up his owner or a bulldog acquaintance from across the street, or his son—he'd cause a short circuit or a tanker accident, or he'd slam his paw in the door and let out a howl. This would wake up the very bulldog Goofy had been trying to pleasantly surprise, and the dog would give Goofy a shot to the snout. From then on, Goofy became a favorite character of mine, right alongside Nikolai Stavrogin. And there's probably no pride or exaggeration if I say about myself, "Goofy, that's me," just like Flaubert said, "*Madame Bovary, c'est moi.*"

It was about that time Stefan Martyka, a third-rate actor with a show on Radio Poland called *Wave 49*, was getting his start. This bastard would interrupt programming primarily during dance music hours and say, "This is Wave 49, Wave 49. We're signing on." Then he'd get his digs in at the imperialist countries; mostly he sank his teeth into America's backside. He'd spew all sorts of crude, vulgar, idiotic things and finish up his vitriol with the words, "We're signing off." One day a certain student did away with Martyka. At first they suspected it was an act of revenge by Jan Cajmer, who was the director of the dance orchestra at Polskie Radio. It was usually during Cajmer's program that Martyka would come on. But soon it was discovered that Martyka's murderer was a steady guest of the Information Center at the US embassy, and the place was shut down. My friendship with Goofy the Dog came to a halt for many years, but Martyka signed off forever.

The unrequited love of Polish people for Americans was the subject of a host of publications, articles, and discussions. Essentially, it wasn't a flattering picture. In American films, Poles overwhelmingly are drug addicts, spies, or petty thieves. Jerzy Putrament, the eminent Polish thinker, has something to say on the subject in his book *On the Literary Front.*

Here's Putrament the Thinker: "There's a certain American crime novel set in Chicago. It's a hot afternoon, a private eye sits in his office and in a half sleep overhears the cleaning people arguing next door . . . in Polish."

And then:

"In general, Poles (or rather, Americans of Polish descent, as they're officially called today) quite frequently make it onto the pages of modern American literature. In the classic degenerate psychoanalytical play *A Streetcar Named Desire*, the hero is a Pole who turns out to be the lowest type of swine. He abuses a poor American girl, in spite of the fact that she's mentally ill. When another character in the work wants to offend him, she calls him a 'Polack.'"

That's the Thinker for you. However, purely out of respect for the vastness of his thoughts, I'll allow myself to note that things aren't exactly as Putrament summed them up. Undoubtedly, Stanley Kowalski isn't the sort of person you want to make fast friends with or lend money to. However, it escaped Putrament's attention that the poor American girl was once a Corinthian call girl, as they were called, either by profession or predilection. And that's exactly what got under Kowalski's skin. The whole time, the miserable American girl is provoking our unfortunate countryman. In the end, to get her out of his head, he rapes her. At the same time, the sick thing clearly enjoys it, goes completely crazy, and ends up in a madhouse.

To aid Putrament in further lamenting the fate of our compatriots in the US, I'll allow myself to quote a few examples at length. In *The Naked and the Dead*, one of our countrymen has a part, too: Mister Kaczynski, a professional pimp from Chicago. In the film *Stalag 17*, another one of ours appears. He doesn't say a word, just takes out his dagger from time to time to do away with the next German or Arab or whomever. Our Pole opens his trap only once, to unmask a German spy who's passing himself off as an English prisoner of war. He simply asks him in German, "What time is it, friend?" and the spy automatically answers in his mother tongue, "Six o'clock." The Pole pulls out his dagger, slits the guy's throat, and the German falls down dead. The Pole glances at his watch, leans over the suffering villain, and tells him politely in German, "Your watch, sir, is fast by five minutes." Then he hides his dagger, and the action continues.

In Otto Preminger's film *The Man with the Golden Arm*, another countryman makes an appearance. For a change, this one's a morphine addict fresh out of a drug clinic. His lifestyle isn't very complicated. He cheats at cards and shoots up morphine. The other gamblers rough him up. His wife eventually throws herself out the tenth-floor window. Despite fluttering her hands, she can't reduce her landing speed. Frankie Machine is left a charming widower. He's the only Pole since Tadeusz Kościuszko to actually have any luck in the States. All that's left of the wife is a mess of guts. Kim Novak falls in love with him, and though Frankie Machine is momentarily saddened at the sight of the puddle of his wife's remains, he recovers his humor and his health as Kim Novak puts her head on his shoulder, and they walk off together into the distance.

It would be hard to accuse Fyodor Mikhailovich Dostoevsky of being overly generous in his treatment of Poles, but the Americans decided to revise this. In the film version of *The Brothers Karamazov*, Grushenka is seduced by a Polak—a man named Gronowski. Grushenka goes to see him, but Gronowski doesn't give her a minute's attention. He's engrossed in a dodgy game of cards. The unhappy woman sits with a glazed look in her eyes and watches her seducer, played by a pimply extra.

In walks Yul Brynner, as Dmitry Karamazov. He sweeps everybody up in his burning gaze. Puts a small case on the table. Grushenka, played by Maria Schell, runs up to the table and opens the case. We see two high-caliber pistols (a darling present for your worst enemy):

Maria Schell: "Dmitry. What are the pistols for?"

Yul Brynner: "Usually for killing."

Maria Schell: "But, Dmitry! It's a terrible thing, what you want to do."

Yul Brynner [after a moment's thought]: "I know. But I am a Karamazov!"

Dmitry sits in the corner and watches the Polack. We see that Maria Schell doesn't love the Pole any longer, but Dmitry. The owner of the tavern enters, carrying a samovar. The Pole slaps the unfortunate Russian man as a token of thanks for the hot tea. The Russian looks with eyes of a beaten dog toward Dmitry, who slowly rises and pulls at the Polack's hair, standing him at attention. Then he begins to beat him, first with the back of his left hand, as he slaps him across the face, then he flips him around as his hand comes back the other way. The Pole drops out cold, hitting his head on the floor.

Yul Brynner [cheerily explaining]: "It's not nice to hit people, sir."

And we see that Maria Schell will never stop loving Dmitry. In *The Brothers Karamazov* Dmitry doesn't want to beat up the Polack. He's just bought caramels for the gypsies, and champagne and cigars, and he's resolved to end his own life at dawn, when the revelry will be at its peak. But the Americans transformed the grim Russian. The Pole lies on the floor until the end of the action. Such is our representation in Hollywood.

Putrament the Thinker was unhappy with how Poles were portrayed in American novels and plays and tried to correct the situation in *Noah's Ark*, his epic. But it didn't turn out well. The Polack is a spy, working reconnaissance for some undefined Asian government, and his superior is a terrible little Chinaman named Li. The Polack sucks up to him, but a contemptuous smile wanders across the face of this terrible Asian. In order to garner his readers' sympathy for the hero (the lack of which, among other authors, annoys the Thinker), and in order not to wound national pride, Putrament has our countryman smoke marijuana, drink whiskey, and so on. A Polish woman decides to sacrifice to the hero the holiest thing she possesses. Our hero not being up to the job, however, there arises what Stendhal calls a "love fiasco." Nature has endowed our countryman with no great intelligence, either. The Chinaman Li orders him to plant a bomb on an airplane. The Polack sneaks it on, but being an idiot he boards the same plane himself. They take off, and the stewardess informs him politely that he's gotten on the wrong plane—which he's just placed the time bomb on. He's frightened out of his mind. Everybody is crawling around on all fours, searching for the bomb. The plane is flying over the ocean. Time is passing. The Pole is whimpering; the bomb is ticking; the situation is grave. The other passengers are panic-stricken. The bomb has been placed on the airplane for the sole purpose of killing a Russian journalist. That's what the Chinaman Li ordered.

There was a story once about an American writer who was serializing a novel. One day his boss approached him.

Writer: "Boss, from this morning on I want a ten dollar raise per chapter."

Boss: "Get lost."

The writer leaves, whistling carefree. The boss buzzes his secretary and orders her to send in a fellow named Rappaport.

Enter Rappaport.

Boss: "Rappaport, from now on you're going to take over writing this damn nonsense."

Rappaport: "Yes, boss."

He nonchalantly grabs the manuscript and leaves. The boss plunges back into his work. After an hour Rappaport returns. He's completely drunk and pale as a ghost. He places the manuscript in front of the boss.

Rappaport [mumbling]: "It's a lost cause. I shake off the dust of my feet, and I curse . . ."

He totters out the door. The boss asks for Treppengelander to be sent in.

Enter Treppengelander.

Boss: "Patrick, from this morning on you've got to continue writing this lark."

Treppengelander: "Sure thing."

He leaves. Returns after an hour. Pale as a ghost. Drunk. Throws the manuscript on the table, and without saying a word, he walks out. The situation is getting serious. The printer's office is calling. The boss summons a fellow named Najlepszy.

Enter Najlepszy.

Boss: "You . . ." and so on.

Najlepszy: "OK."

He returns after an hour, drunk and pale as a ghost.

Boss: "What's going on?"

Najlepszy: "There's nothing to be done. The hero's just jumped out of an airplane at sixty-five thousand feet without a parachute. There's a squadron of fighter jets nearby, and they're firing missiles at him. Down below, three sharks are circling, jaws opened wide. And now

I'm leaving. I shake off the dust of my feet, and I curse . . ."

Najlepszy leaves. The boss calls the first fellow back in and promises him a raise. A day later the next installment of the novel appears, beginning with the words, "By a superhuman effort of will, having escaped from these irritating disturbances, Mike Gilderstern returned to New York."

I only remembered this anecdote as I was trying to understand Putrament's novel. The bomb is ticking, and the airplane is soaring through the endless sky. I used to know a little something about plane crashes, and I even have a sport pilot's license. I read up on emergency water landings. A passenger airplane is usually equipped with life jackets, and it can actually land on water. Besides, it doesn't have a fixed chassis, which means it won't flip over. When a plane does have a fixed chassis, flipping is inevitable. Those types are unfit for water landings, unlike the hydroplane. None of this is accounted for in *Noah's Ark*: the plane stays in the air, despite the fact that the pilot knows there's a time bomb about to explode any minute.

It goes off and everybody dies. There are only two people left, the Russian journalist and an American journalist. The Russian pulls the American onto a rock ledge and mumbles something brotherly to him. The Polack has been turned to dust. Retribution was terrible. However, a new character had arrived in the pantheon of Polish literary heroes.

William Faulkner, a writer no less talented than Putrament, had a completely different view of Poles. In his novel *Wild Palms*, the hero, Harry, arrives with his girlfriend at a mine in Utah. The Poles who are working there know absolutely no English. These Poles have a unique way of settling personal grudges; namely, if somebody falls from their graces, they stick a piece of dynamite in his pocket and he gets blown to bits. The Poles, as Charlotte and Harry observe, are bleary-eyed from lack of sleep and working overtime. Harry says to the director of the mine, "Why do these people work themselves senseless, if the mine is going to be bankrupt soon anyway?" The director tells him the Poles don't know English, and he can't manage to get through to them that the mine has gone to hell. "These are strange people," the director of the mine says after a minute. "They don't understand dishonesty."

In all three of these stories—in *Noah's Ark*, in the story about the American editor, and in *Wild Palms*—the same elements are present: danger, explosions, terrible Poles. It would be interesting for a literary scholar to explore these interweaving mutual elements of plot and content. Faulkner's novel has an unfortunate plot. *Wild Palms* is a story about a love that a man is afraid of losing. As a result, fate gives him a choice between nothing and sadness.

Without overdoing the commentary, we'll let the Thinker have the floor. Here's what he has to say on the Korean War: "We are grateful to Truman and Adenauer, mortal enemies of the Polish nation, for their sincerity, at least. For the sincerity whose reasons we need not look for in our enemies' feeling of power, nor exclusively in the foolishness and mess of the American political propaganda machine. The reason the imperialist Americans don't hide their invasion plans from us, the destruction and dismantling of Poland, is first of all a deep contempt, which they harbor toward everybody who is not American, and especially toward the nations of Eastern Europe, the Slavic peoples. For them we are an undifferentiated ethnic mass, unable to think, unable to react."

The story of the battle raging in America today, simply put, doesn't stem from a feeling of power. On the contrary, it was exactly the defeat in Korea that pushed Mister Truman into a new series of irresponsible threats, because it's only in the course of the past half year that it became possible to conceive of the peace camp as a powerful force. The defeat of the imperialists in Korea and Vietnam, which expanded the peace movement in the Western European countries, in Latin America, and in the Near East, coupled with the conflict and friction among the countries of NATO, alongside the economic and political successes of the USSR, the People's Republic of China, various other people's republics, and the DDR, obviously hints at something: the tide of history is turning to our side.

But what guarantee do we have it's really this way, and not otherwise? We oughtn't worry, in general. The Thinker explains everything: "Over the threats of war, over the hysterical shouting, carries the voice of Stalin, the voice of His party. He will show us the way to a better humanity. On this path there is a place for our nation."

Reading the above, let's think for a moment about the losses America suffered in Korea. Colonel Paweł Monat, who defected to the West and published some recollections in *Life*, argues that there were days when the commies lost thousands of soldiers. Colonel Monat might come across here as a person who's not quite objective. Considering that, let's talk about the economic successes mentioned above. The East Germans were so happy with the improvement in living standards, they organized a demonstration in 1953. Maybe it was all due to some misunderstanding that Soviet tanks were used against them. Overjoyed Hungarians stormed the streets of Budapest in 1956, but it must have just been a case of wires getting crossed here, too. Władysław Gomułka spoke about the economic successes of the Polish People's Republic in his report; the economic success of the Soviet Union came to an end with the purchase of capitalist grain. I'm not a journalist or commentator, that's for sure, but there's one more thing I want to say: the Americans should have given Putrament the highest military and civilian honors, because he did more for their side in Poland than they ever managed to do for themselves.

In 1952 an exhibition, dramatically named "This Is America," was organized at the Warsaw Arsenal. Who the hell knows how many items they collected: spy pistols, napalm bombs, comic books based on *The Brothers Karamazov*, and the corpses of several black people. The exhibition produced dreadful results: people waited in line at the entrance for hours, because they thirsted for anything at all that was American. People wanted to collect information on the country with forty-eight stars. They wanted to have a brief look at things produced by the people on the other side of the ocean, people who would never lend a helping hand. It was an unhappy love, a perfectly unrequited love, perhaps also a final love.

Our image in the United States is represented by a man who has the nickname "Killer Kowalski." He's the most brutal wrestler in the world. He always loses by disqualification. A cruel Pole endowed by nature with murderous tendencies, he can't control his villainous instincts in the ring and always gets sent to the corner by the referee.

As a fan of that kind of fighting, the last time I was in Paris I saw a fight between the *champion soviétique* and the *champion américain*. The Russian stepped into the ring: a straw-haired fellow in a gold jersey, with the face of a degenerate syphilitic. The public greeted him with joy and howls of delight. Nobody even thought about the minor details that in the USSR there are no professional sports, and American freestyle wrestling is regarded as "brutal." Thus, the *champion soviétique* must have been born not on the steppes of the Don but, rather, in the neighborhood of Pigalle Square, maybe even on Saint Denis. The American champ walked into the ring: a giant so terrifying that if this match hadn't been so carefully orchestrated, the champion of the USSR would probably have hailed a cab from the ring straight to a small green cemetery.

The public is booing and threatening the American. They're throwing orange peels and matchbooks at him, shaking their fists. The match begins. The poor American is trying as hard as he can to lose, but something here has been poorly planned out. No matter how much the referee kicks the American when he forgets himself and begins to get ahead, and despite help from the judge and the public, too, the blond-haired Slav conks out. The audience is made up mostly of workers, petty artisans, and a few bored leftist intellectuals. They begin shouting at the American: "Dirty pig, go fight in Vietnam!"

And that's the tragedy of America. They waste millions of dollars on a local war that Italian and French workers can't understand. Americans have to support people like Moise Tshombe or Syngman Rhee; Americans have to reconstruct West Germany; Americans have to stand by General Franco. The American worker pays for all this, yet it's not the Statue of Liberty who garners applause, but the blond-haired cretin, fighting against an opponent three times stronger than he is. And he wins, because this is what the poor people want—the poor people who can't rid themselves of the illusion that freedom comes from the place where the best of the best have perished.

Poles are aware that, in the case of a conflict with Russia, the Americans won't send a single soldier; nevertheless, the love continues. For many years they didn't show American films in Poland. Finally, in '57, they got ahold of a film called *Apache*. The Apache was played by a blond-haired, blue-eyed Burt Lancaster. The film premiere oddly co-incided with another event. The air balloon Gwiazda Polski II, the Star of Poland, was released into the skies, twenty years late. The thousands of people waiting at the theater weren't paying attention to the balloon that had finally been launched. Everybody just wanted to see Lancaster, who has all sorts of escapades in the film. He slaughters, shoots, blows up wagons with dynamite. He strangles a guard with his shackles and says to him, "And now return, you white dog, to your people, and tell them who they are dealing with." He mops the floor with them, but that's nothing compared to what happened before the film. Fights were breaking out every minute. The police were constantly intervening. Finally, two guys took out a knife, and the wife of one of them began to search for somebody named Zenek. He was the only person, apparently, who could control the situation. Everybody burst out shouting: "Where's Zenek? Where's Zenek?" Finally, this Zenek ran up: with a veteran's eye he sized up the situation, threw off his jacket, and began to fight like a ram, butting his head into people's chests. And nobody was paying attention anymore to the lonely Gwiazda Polski II taking off. Lancaster and Zenek upstaged the efforts of the Polish engineers.

It's not easy to talk about the relationship of Poles to Americans and everything American: the chatter about Count Kazimierz Pułaski and General Tadeusz Kościuszko doesn't amount to much here. It's best to leave statistics out of it. A comparison between American and Polish literature isn't worth the time. At least in my case, for the simple reason that I haven't the foggiest idea about my native literature. I suppose I can thank my Polish literature teachers for that, because they were always tormenting me with the classic question, "What did the poet *mean*?" My repulsion at reading Mickiewicz's national epic *Pan Tadeusz* is something I can't overcome even today. Teaching literature in school ought to be a criminal offense. It's a wonder the commies haven't figured this out. So many masterpieces of socialist realism are compulsory in school. This largely proscribes young people's interest in that type of literature.

During the Korean War there were murmurings going around that Poland would have to send volunteers to Korea. It's unclear how the rumor spread. Maybe because they extended military service by a year for people who were twenty-seven years old (and some who were twenty-six). The people who were affected were called the "Korean class." Maybe it really was true: in expectation of a war, they decided not to give soldiers their release. They were following the advice of Uncle Joe: the more sweat in training, the less blood in battle. Many people who'd previously managed to get out of military service by arguing they were unfit for service due to angina pectoris, bilateral hernia, or deafness suddenly began reporting to volunteer. The goal of these schemes was clear. People wanted to walk up to General MacArthur with arms raised high in the air. Of course, most people didn't realize you could lose your life at the hands of the very Americans everybody was looking to for escape. Anyhow, those were ugly years, and the possibility of losing one's life or becoming permanently disabled didn't discourage potential volunteers. The rumors turned out to be wrong, though, and the "Korean class" wasted away in the army.

Mass meetings were organized where they condemned American aggression in Korea, and people cheered in honor of Kir Im Sen, or whatever his name is.* They called him the great son and liberator of the Korean Nation. His enemy was Syngman Rhee: a "low-down dog"; at other times, "a dog on the leash of American imperialism." Both of their pictures were in the paper every day, but the problem was, the men looked as similar as two drops of vodka. I remember once, during a mass protest meeting, the party secretary held up a newspaper with a photo of the Great Son and Liberator of the Korean Nation. He shouted, "We won't allow this scum to drown the 38th parallel in blood!"

They didn't have a hard time organizing the mass protest meetings at work: the exits were blocked off, or the director personally kept an attendance sheet that you could only sign after the meeting was over. Every worker had to sign the attendance sheet twice: when he arrived at work and when he left. So there were a lot of protesters. People signed protest sheets against the American aggressors, but these damn lists could only be signed after the speakers had finished their orations. Then you could finally go home. When General MacArthur

---

* Kim Il-sung (RU)

announced his nuclear arms project, there was a well-known song: "Truman, Truman, drop the bomb, we just can't take it very long . . ." and so on. On the other hand, people in the borderlands and in Lwów had their own song of hope. It began the same way, and the last couplet sounded like this: "One hydrogen bomb and we'll return to Lwów. Though all ashes and sand, we'll be back in our land."

But Truman didn't drop any H-bombs. Even the hope of being turned to ash and returning to our land was for naught. And the Poles were right in assuming everything would be ashes after the war. I remember a fragment of a speech. It was probably James Forrestal, Secretary of the Navy under Truman, who delivered it: "We'll turn sky and land into a fiery oven. We'll drop the atom bomb and the hydrogen bomb on them. We'll kill their children in their cribs, old people in prayer, and workers in the field. Where today there is a city, tomorrow there will be only smoke and flames, and our blind enemies will wander through them." That speech, oft-recalled by Polish radio and newsreel announcers, became, paradoxically, a hymn of hope. It's like in insane asylums when people who suffer from chronic insomnia are given a cup of very strong coffee before sleep, since sometimes it can induce the opposite reaction. Since the American statesman's promises were considered a hostile text, obviously the speech found favor in the eyes of the Polish people.

The author of the speech knew his Bible, people said, and judging from the imagery, the Revelation of Saint John the Divine was his inspiration: "And the fifth angel sounded, and I saw a star fall from heaven unto the earth: and to him was given the key of the bottomless pit. And he opened the bottomless pit; and there arose a smoke out of the pit, as the smoke of a great furnace; and the sun and the air were darkened by reason of the smoke of the pit . . ." On the other hand, the people comparing the American statesman's text with Saint John's completely missed the latter's prophesying angel and the end of days. Dropping the dreamed-of bomb might have accomplished too many things at once.

The H-bomb wasn't dropped and we didn't return to Lwów, but the Poles' love for Americans didn't lose its fervor. When I worked as a driver, there were basically four automobile manufacturers: General Motors Corporation, Diamond, Studebaker, and the Stalin Car Factory, aka ZIS. The aristocracy rode around in Diamonds, but the drivers' favorite was GMC, which we called "Jamesie." The Jamesie was an incredible machine: we'd roll down the window and peel back the canvas roof when we drove. We felt like Gary Cooper. The GMC really roared. It had an overhead valve engine, and the drivers used to nonchalantly hang their left leg out the side. That was the essence of cool. When one of the drivers slipped up at work, or was late, or didn't fulfill his quota, the party secretary would call him into his office. He'd say:

"How'd you like the GMC to be taken from you? You're stepping out of line, eh? You want me to take you out of the GMC and put you in a shitty ZIS, eh? You want to ride around in that shitty ZIS so your friends can laugh at you, eh? Is this why Comrade Stalin tamed nature and built dams on the Volga, so that you'd have to ride around in that damn truck, where there's no starter and the gearshift sticks? Mend your ways."

And the man would mend his ways, as much as he could.

But the height of chic was a lined American army jacket. In those days, a jacket like that in your wardrobe could set you back three and a half thousand zlotys. You had to be satisfied with an army jacket with epaulets for a grand and a half. I bought one like that. The previous owner's pleasant-sounding name was printed on the left breast: ANDERSON. The ink was so permanent I couldn't wash it off. With the party secretary and the director of the work council watching, I rubbed that ANDERSON with benzine and denaturant, but nothing helped. Which is how I became the coolest guy on all of Sokołowska Street.

Who can forget General MacArthur's face: the hard face of an old vulture. And MacArthur wore shades. The cartoonists from *Szpilki* always used to draw him like that: sunglasses resting on a criminal's face, an atom bomb in one hand, and in the other, General Douglas MacArthur was strangling a Korean patriot. After that, some hustlers in private enterprise began manufacturing shades like his. And people bought them, even if it cost them an arm and a leg. After a while people stopped calling them shades and started calling them macarthurs. And if the party secretary said, "These macarthurs shall not be worn," he'd start receiving medical notes from people claiming they had chronic pink eye. After a while, all the young drivers seemed to contract it. Eventually, the factories making the macarthurs were shut down, and that was that.

But not for long. It was pretty easy for Warsaw hooligans to figure out the prevailing trends in men's fashion in America, and only a few weeks later we saw young people in roomy homemade jackets, colorful hand-painted ties, narrow trousers, and shoes with a so-called "bacon-fat" heel—hard white rubber soles. But the most important attribute of that style was the *plereza*, or ducktail—a special haircut. It consisted of hair shaped like waves above the forehead, and in the back of the head it came together somehow like a duck's tail. According to Wiech, the *plereza* came in three types: the sugar *plereza*, the egg white *plereza*, and the linseed decoction *plereza*. Hair isn't meant to hold on its own, he explained. But, if you used sugar, the *plereza* would hold for a day; with egg white, it would last three days. The *plereza* held together by the linseed decoction was the longest lasting and would hold for a week. The moment a brawl breaks out, one man tries to mess up the other's hairdo, and the second guy can't tell which way is up. That's the negative side of the *plereza*. There's a character in one of Wiech's stories who stands before a judge and explains why he mauled six men and turned a nicely appointed apartment into smoking rubble. The young man tells it like this: "I heard somebody screaming, 'Bigosińczak, mess up his hairdo.' When my hairdo got messed up, all I knew was I couldn't see nothing." People who wore *plerezas* and painted ties were called bikini boys. This was supposed to be offensive, but it didn't bother young people.

To get back to the attitude of Poles to Americans: I could easily find quotations from our Marxists talking about degenerate, gloomy American literature, and contrast that with what was written a few years later, when they actually became familiar with the literature. They discovered that Faulkner wasn't a pervert or a sadist, but a great Christian and a commentator on the Bible; Hemingway ceased to be an instigator of war and instead became the last great romantic; Steinbeck got out of pornography and turned into a moralist; and so on. But why bother? What interests me is the young workers who most likely won't ever read the Sartoris family saga, and yet they know it wasn't General Rommel or Marshal Zhukov who was the greatest commander of the Second World War, but probably the officer fighting the war in the Pacific. The only thing they know about him is that he's an American general battling communism. Their gesture of brotherhood is so ridiculous it's embarrassing: dark glasses, ugly haircuts, hideous ties. But it all stems from the conviction that that's how the people of the starry flag dress, so we'll dress the same, even if the authorities brutally shave our heads in the police station and hang our names on a board next to the names of shirkers and hooligans. And along with that, we stick with our old American cars, the cars that carried the Americans to victory. We dress in old American clothes. We look at the comic strips, even though we can't understand them. Our gesture of brotherhood toward Americans is ridiculous and pitiful, and the Americans will never notice, nor understand, it. But it's the only gesture we can manage. None of these young people will ever travel to America. None of them will ever receive a grant from the Ford Foundation. And none of them will ever write and say American culture is a culture of plebes. For that, you can only count on the correspondents for *Nowe Drogi* or *Trybuna Ludu*. No, for these poor young souls, America isn't even what Israel was for the people of Moses. It's not a promised land. But maybe that's how things work: the lack of a promise offers more hope. The commies promised everything: bread, work, freedom, brotherhood. He who promises everything, really promises nothing.

I heard there was an attempt to organize a demonstration in front of the American embassy during the blockade of Cuba. I don't need to explain the character of the demonstration. The cops gathered with their helmets on and took along some tear gas and blackjacks, but found themselves with nothing to do. Of course, a few foreign correspondents showed up to photograph the sad cops and the overjoyed people. In the nearby pub, plainclothes undercover agents negotiated with hooligans, begging them to smash a few windowpanes and yell some sinister lines regarding America. The cops promised them impunity if they'd knock down blind old women and throw cripples from trains. But the Warsaw hooligans were tough, and they refused all the propositions that, under normal circumstances, would have been very enticing. This anecdote obviously can't be true, because it's not too difficult to dress a few cops from the police academy in civilian clothes and have them pretend to be angry Poles. But the anecdotes are born out of real conditions and sympathies, so, while it's not the truth, the idea behind it is true.

I didn't know much about American literature back then. Piotr Guzy told me about Faulkner; Edward Bernstein told me about Hemingway. I found out about other books the only way possible. I'd get the people I wanted to talk drunk and pay their tabs at the bar. It really ended up costing me. Some of them got drunk fast and mixed up different authors and situations. After the war, only one book of Hemingway's, *To Have and Have Not*, and Caldwell's *Tobacco Road* were published. The first one to break the wall of silence was the editor Marian Eile, who published two stories of Hemingway's in *Przekrój*, in Mira Michałowska's translation. Later they published him just about everywhere, and Zygmunt Kałużyński was right when he proclaimed, "The triumph of Hemingway united the Polish nation." Then all the young prose writers who were just starting out began to write like Papa Hemingway. They called me the Hemingway of the Polish boondocks. That I'd started writing during a period in Poland when Hemingway was still considered a degenerate and an atom bomb enthusiast, and that I couldn't read him because I didn't know English back then, and that I stopped writing at the point when Hemingway was beginning to be published in Poland—all of this escaped the attention of our critics.

Papa Hemingway says something like this about critics: "When a man needs help, he receives only bile from them. I am sure the majority of them wish there were no books at all. Then they'd be able to write about themselves and their opinions. Perhaps God or Nature will afflict them all one day with a terrible incurable illness, one only they will contract. Then there will finally be an end to them." The quotation is inexact. I read the statement many years ago, and I can't remember where anymore, or in what language, but the idea from the author of *The Snows of Kilimanjaro* is probably conveyed accurately. The clever old American's dirty words don't apply to the Marxist critics, though. The sliding scale they use is limitless. *For Whom the Bell Tolls* was accused of defaming the Spanish Civil War. After '56 it became known as a great work of romantic literature, Robert Jordan was an excellent soldier, and in general everything was how it should be. What was actually Hemingway's weakest book came to be known as his greatest. Simply, a young man appears on the scene in order to blow up bridges, kill other people, and die like a man. Without too much reflection, he dives headfirst into the greatest misfortune that can befall a nation: a civil war. He's neither a communist nor a fascist, despite everything. He wants to die like a man.

And what if I don't want to die like a man? What if I want to die as the owner of a small plot of land in the Grochów neighborhood in Warsaw, surrounded by a gang of children and grandchildren? And what if I don't want to run across a field with a rifle and stand bareheaded before a firing squad?

Nevertheless, they say it's Hemingway's best book. And that's how they did him in. But what else could you have expected? Hemingway is the last romantic, Faulkner was a commentator on the Bible and something like a modern-day Dostoevsky, and maybe one day we'll discover that Henry Miller's just another Lysenko, Orson Welles is a student of Nikolai Cherkasov, and James Dean stole his rage and shame from Pavlik Morozov.

It was about that time Poles began to flirt with America. First Putrament went to visit, carrying back the fruit of his ideas in his book *Two Gulps of America.* The following are some of his reflections. Here is Putrament looking at slot machines:

"I stare at these shrines, and I'm inclined to admire them. Although they arise out of some crook's mean desire to earn a few bucks off a poor lost simple soul, they're preying on a certain preexisting objective human desire, no matter how tastelessly they meet that need.

"And what about in our country? With all of our gabbing about the rising cultural needs of the masses, how many opportunities for entertainment are available to the ordinary, average laborer or worker, if he goes out at night in the city? Movie houses, theaters? If only! That's not even to speak of other cultural programs. What people wouldn't give for a chance at admission on the spur of the moment, without having planned it out and reserved tickets beforehand from the ticket office!"

In the final analysis, Putrament concludes, the only available entertainment is the consumption of alcohol. It's a worthy conclusion. Still, if they want to, Polish workers can try reading: they have Ostrovsky's *How the Steel Was Tempered* or books by Putrament himself, even if it's *Crossroads*, a book about American spies and Gomułka's secret service. It was only two years later, in *On the Literary Front*, that Putrament, taking a cue from the Soviet champions of socialist realism, recommended going to the movies and the theater. At the same time, he cautioned against destructive American writers like Williams and his play *A Streetcar Named Desire*, which Putrament described as psychoanalytical. If that's psychoanalytical, I'm the Prince of Poland.

Putrament walks along Wall Street, surprised by how narrow and short it is, like Chmielna Street in Warsaw. The modesty and unexceptional nature of the street at the "Heart of America" is worthy of imitation, he remarks.

Putrament was quite taken with the exterior and interior of the UN building. Of the prevailing boredom there, he offers the following reflection: "In our day, it takes a famous polemicist like the late Vyshinsky to risk a joke and polemical sarcasm. He had an additional audience thanks to the role his homeland played on the world stage." Indeed. The UN, an organization whose aim is peace and happiness across the whole world, is an ideal place for the late Andrei Vyshinsky, the prosecutor of the Moscow trials and the man who frequently requested the death penalty based on evidence that was either falsified or extracted via suffering and torture. We'll probably never know the whole truth, and if we find out, it'll be too hard to believe. Yet this is what goes through Putrament's mind as he stands in front of the organization that's supposed to provide hope for the downtrodden?

Putrament's book is interesting in its own way, but I'm already too tired to keep quoting from it. The most interesting chapter is the one on Czesław Miłosz. Putrament looked to Vyshinsky for how to construct a denunciation. He takes a page straight from Cicero, from the classical school of rhetoric. Putrament begins high and noble: he was dazzled by Miłosz's poetic talent and depressed by his own verse.

Miłosz was, for Putrament, a star. If he'd gone on any longer, I was expecting he'd ape what Piotr Verkhovensky says to Nikolai Stavrogin: "You are the leader, you are the sun, and I am your worm."

Putrament felt insignificant beside Miłosz: he adored Miłosz, but Miłosz didn't pay him much attention. Miłosz was nonchalant, arrogant, haughty. Finally, they came to blows. And at that moment Putrament's voice breaks through: following the classical recipe, this is the moment when he should arrive at an argument that appeals to universal feelings of justice. Instead of that, he initiates a lampoon.

Putrament admits he was against Miłosz's escape to the West, if only out of fear Miłosz would squander the great poetic talent Putrament values so much. What the connection is between going to the West and squandering one's poetic talent, I can't say. Why one writer has the right to decide the fate of another by administrative methods, I can't figure out, either. Why a person must beg to be let out of a country's borders, which is a normal freedom even in Latin American countries—on that, too, I can't muster an answer. Miłosz fled.

Putrament explains why: having been removed from his diplomatic position, Miłosz didn't want to accept the fact that he would no longer be paid in foreign currency, but in Polish currency instead. Putrament explains in his sketches in *On the Literary Front* that the economic success of the people's republics guarantees high and progressive growth in Poland's standard of living, as well as the inevitable decline of the dollar and the pauperization of the West. Considering that, how does his argument hold water, since the zloty is supposed to be first-rate? If Miłosz wanted to be better paid, he should have stayed in Poland, according to *On the Literary Front*. But by claiming that material opportunism is the key to Czesław Miłosz's character, and using what Putrament said in *Two Gulps of America*, Miłosz went to the West precisely because it's not the zloty that's good, but the US dollar. And maybe the whole thing just comes down to Putrament being so goddamn full of it.

Putrament prophesies that nothing will come of Miłosz's career in the West. Why? Poor timing. "Nineteen forty-eight wasn't a bad year. One could invoke Gomułka's defeat, which had just recently opened the deserter's eyes." Putrament means here that *Miłosz* could have deduced Gomułka's fall from power in 1948. The fact that Gomułka went to prison could have become a stepping-stone in Miłosz's life and career. Maybe Miłosz chose a bad year, but Putrament chose an even worse moment to write about Gomułka's defeat. The book *Two Gulps of America* was sent to the presses on May 14, 1956, and it was released that month. Two months later the once-defeated, newly resurrected Gomułka had occasion to shake hands with his comrade and fellow member of the Central Committee, Jerzy Putrament.

In the end, Putrament reaches some final conclusions about Miłosz. Miłosz fled because war was close at hand. Putrament: "To remain in Poland at that time? To wait here for the arrival of terrifying mushroom clouds? Yet again to experience this poor, flat country being leveled by the most awesome instrument of war?" But what war and what danger is he talking about here? After all, we were safe the whole time (according to *On the Literary Front*): Stalin's voice, ringing like a great bell, promised us there would be no war, and Putrament himself wrote about the Americans' defeat in Korea and assured us of their weakness and impotence. So what the hell is the story with Miłosz?

And now, a few blows below the belt. Miłosz used a Lithuanian passport during the war, which guaranteed his personal safety. In those days everybody had some sort of phony papers. Nobody could ever tell me what the difference is between having a phony ID card and holding a Lithuanian passport. And doesn't a person with such immense literary talent, as even Putrament says, have the right to do everything possible to become a chronicler of the terrible times? And if he doesn't have a right to do that, will keeping him in Poland by force really protect his enormous talent? If they wanted to save him *after* the war by confiscating his passport, then why couldn't he save himself *during* the war with the use of that passport? Putrament didn't learn too much from Vyshinsky. As a former police informer myself, I can't believe Putrament was an NKVD agent, something he talks about fondly and with humor. The man writes a poor denunciation.

And there was one more cheap shot: after Miłosz chose freedom, Putrament writes, the Americans wouldn't give him an entrance visa. It's not hard to imagine how this happened, and Putrament should understand it best, but I'll explain it myself, based on personal experience. When an informer gets planted somewhere, a wave of disinformation follows soon after him: rumors that he's a reactionary, that he's unfavorable in his attitudes toward the regime, that he dreams about the return of capitalism, and so on. This way, he's provided with safe and reliable cover. People take him for one of their own and tell him everything they think. He knows what to do next. If a person of Miłosz's stature flees to the West, they spread disinformation in his wake, too: they say he worked as a secret police agent, that he's anti-American, that he informed on colleagues for money and the good life, and so on. They forge copies of documents, take oral testimony from "witnesses" who make up all sorts of stories. It can take years to set the record straight, and it's not always possible to fully rectify it. Putrament disappointed me as an informer. I've never read his fiction, but I think personal confession is the same for him as it is for me: a genre he cares deeply about.

I've written a lot about Putrament and Miłosz that apparently doesn't have much to do with the title *Goofy the Dog*. But what I want to say is this: If Putrament should ever decide to stay in the West, he won't face the difficulties Miłosz and I were up against. Even though he's not a very capable informer, he won't have to worry about money for a few years. But on the day he decides to write a single page of prose, he'll be doomed to die of hunger. In any case, I owe him a lot. Once, when I was sitting in the Berlin Journalists Club, I read a scathing article in *Izvestia* about myself, and about how people like me shouldn't be tolerated, and more in that vein. *Izvestia*, of course, is a Russian newspaper, but the author of the denunciation was the Polish author Jerzy Putrament. This was in July of 1958. Putting down the newspaper, I realized for the first time it was a real possibility I'd never return to Poland. And I never have.

When the turmoil began in Vietnam, I, Goofy the Dog, went to the American consulate in Palermo and asked to join the American Army and be sent to war. They told me I could go under one condition. I had to get an immigration visa and join the army on American soil. This, even though President Kennedy had said in his inaugural address, "My fellow citizens of the world: ask not what America will do for you, but what together we can do for the freedom of man."

I, Goofy the Dog, can't do anything, but Putrament and his ilk can do a lot. After I chose freedom, American journalists asked me what I thought Americans could do to show their sympathy for the Polish people in some way. I couldn't give them an answer. But today I can: they should award people like our Thinker with all sorts of grants and perks. Let them go to America, and let them spit on that great and beautiful country. The people in Poland will see through every one of their lies. Let them call America's incredible literature rubbish. Let them call America's outstanding soldiers criminals. Let them call General Patton a coward, and let them claim that the factories providing American people with bread are ovens that deprive man of his dignity and intelligence. Just let them write that; meanwhile, all I had to offer was my own blood, but it wasn't good enough for the Star-Spangled Banner. So don't ask me, for God's sake, what together we can do for the freedom of man. I can't do anything.

CHAPTER FIVE

Felix Dzerzhinsky and Bogart

Young man, contemplating life,

Deciding how yours should be led,

I say, don't break your head,

Live as Comrade Dzerzhinsky did.

—Vladimir Mayakovsky

Sure, it *would* be best to live like Felix Dzerzhinsky. But you can only live like Dzerzhinsky on the backs of the working class, and that's not always possible. A person understands this sad truth only after he has requested political asylum, and when his sole personal property is an oilcloth suitcase containing gifts from the American people to refugees from behind the Iron Curtain: a toothbrush, a towel, and soap. You can sell the stuff for fifty cents, but you've got to get lucky finding an idiot who's willing to buy it.

But what to do when you want to keep on writing? You'll be fine, so long as you were once a communist, a member of the Central Committee, a high functionary in the Department of Security, a spy, or a diplomat. A man who was a spy for the Kremlin behind the Iron Curtain, who tore out his compatriots' fingernails or put a bullet in the back of their heads, will always find a good career. He'll be used as a propaganda trump card and a pawn in the battle against communism.

An honest man who has never been a communist or a spy just becomes an unnecessary burden for the people of the West. As everybody knows, the people of Eastern Europe hate the commies, and it's impossible to exploit them for propaganda purposes, since to say that evening is dark and morning is bright isn't a revelation in the West. A person who hates commies is greeted by years of misery, humiliation, waiting on a visa: years of emptiness and despair.

It's no good to pretend to be a disillusioned communist writer, either. It had been a decent trick until 1956, but then Khrushchev fixed everything from the top down. Today a red intellectual can't rend his garments and cry that he didn't know about the millions of people tortured in concentration camps and prisons. He can't express public surprise about the increasing impoverishment of his country and the growing despair of his brothers and loved ones. He can't claim he didn't know and didn't hear the same things on the street that everybody heard, every worker and every passerby. Not much could ever be expected from these red intellectuals, and even less today. On the other hand, spies and high dignitaries will be welcomed warmly and safely. For a while. *I Was Stalin's Agent*, the memoir of Walter Kryvitsky, a Soviet spy who defected to the West, ends with the words, "I was lucky one more time." He was talking about surviving an assassination attempt. A half year later his body was found in a hotel in Washington. The commies don't excel at much, but this is one area where they always succeed.

But what can a writer do, especially one who's never been a member of the party, never written hymns in honor of the political police, and whose work was never published in his own country because he was labeled a counterrevolutionary? That's a tough question. Let's consider what he can do in moments of hunger, when not a single publisher will give him an advance, and creditors lurk on the street corner, whip in hand.

1. Insanity

Feigning insanity isn't easy, but it can be done, provided one has the necessary courage and character. The easiest thing is to fake a persecution complex, but that takes time. When you see you've just got enough money to live for two months, you get started. You turn up one day at the police station to request a gun license. When the officials ask what you need a fifteen-round FN pistol for, you tell them that for the past week you've been followed by some man in a leather coat and black glasses, carrying a cane. Furthermore, you suggest, inside the cane is a sword (from the movie *Gilda*, starring Rita Hayworth and Glenn Ford). Of course, the police officials will throw you out unceremoniously. A few days later you show up again and repeat. The only difference is this time you say you're being followed by somebody else entirely, a man with a briefcase. Suggest that inside the briefcase this man's got a time bomb, which he wants to put in the trunk of your car (*Touch of Evil*, directed by Orson Welles). When the police official asks if you own an automobile, tell him no, but you've been known to take a taxi once in a while. The person who's been tailing you could slip a bomb in there. You'll get another kick in the ass, but they'll know, at the police station, that this is your second time there. You can even go three or four times, but no more.

Under no circumstances should you go see a doctor in the beginning. After all, you're insane, you don't know anything about the illness affecting you, and you believe you're being followed for political reasons. When your friends advise you to see a psychiatrist, respond negatively or even with a slight touch of anger. In the end, break off contact with the outside world. Buy some sleeping pills and head to a hotel. Call your best friend in another city and tell him you've got a surefire opportunity for him to make some serious easy dough; he's just got to call you the next morning at twelve. The friend promises he'll call. You take the sleeping pills, write a farewell letter to your family, and explain that on account of your being followed, and the fact that nobody is willing to help you, you've decided to commit suicide. You pray for the children, for your little brother, etc. Then you go to sleep.

The friend calls the next day, but the hotel reception can't get through to you. In a little while, a concerned porter comes knocking on your door. Eventually he busts it open, and you wake up in a mental hospital surrounded by psychiatrists and loonies.

That's one way to do it. The best place to attempt suicide is in Munich, because they take you to the hospital in Haar, where you're not alone: the hospital has more than 4,200 beds. By law in Germany, every attempted suicide is required to stay in the hospital under medical supervision for three months. Three months isn't long, but you can eat your fill and think up a new story, which you can write down later and make a few bucks off of. A countless number of Julius Caesars, Jesus Christs, and illegitimate sons of the Duke of Windsor help the time pass pleasantly. When I was there last, I lived in a room with the emperor of Abyssinia. In the next room was a priest the Nazis had tortured so badly he lost his marbles, and when they finally let him out of jail at the end of the war, he couldn't understand the war was over and he was free. He kept on waiting for his execution order. My face reminded him of an SS man he knew, and he would ask me every morning, "Am I going to be executed today?"

I'd answer him soothingly, "No need to hurry, Father. We're busier than hell."

Another one of my neighbors was a certain Mister R. Mister R had been in Auschwitz for three years and was faking a persecution mania. He pretended that he couldn't sleep because he saw ghosts. We became friends. Since I was a so-called "free" psychotic, or a psychotic with the right to leave the hospital grounds, I took a car and drove to Munich, where I bought amphetamines and bennies to help him stay awake. All this because Mister R wanted to get compensation from the German government, and they sent him to a psychiatric hospital to get a doctor's attestation of his sickness. Mister R received permission to go for walks under my care. He'd get in the car, and I'd drop him off in the forest, where he'd fall fast asleep. I'd go to the tavern for a beer. All the alcoholics being treated by German psychiatrists would meet in that tavern. Since I was an alcoholic, if I wanted permission to walk around outside the hospital grounds, I had to swallow an Antabuse or Antikol pill in front of a doctor. No problem—you swallow the pill, the doctor has a look inside your mouth, and you can laugh about it on your way to the bar.

You order a beer and take a small sip. After twenty minutes the first reaction comes: a bit of a commotion in your head, and you turn as crimson as the poppies at Monte Cassino. You've got to wait for that first reaction. Then you take a little sip again, but the second reaction's already weaker. You take your third sip an hour later, singing Bavarian tunes with the other damned alcoholics. They're not the greatest songs, but you get used to them. I'd spend two hours in the tavern, pick up Mister R, then load him up with amphetamines so he could howl through the night again.

When you're faking insanity, don't forget how helpful it is to refuse nourishment. Claim to be afraid of poisoning, and don't pay attention to the doctors' gentle persuasion or to the fact that the orderly will taste every spoonful before putting it into your beak. You should yell, resist, and spit. After a few days they'll start giving you infusions, a huge heap of vitamins, intravenously. You have to resist, until the doctors are forced to tie you to the bed. When you feel the needle in your vein, scream without letting the bottle with the life-giving nutrients out of your sight for a minute. Then, fall into a depression. After a few days, you're no longer terrified when you look at the bottle, just dejected. After fourteen days you start to eat, and you eat so much, and for so long, until the doctors and the judge decide to let you out.

I don't recommend using drugs like morphine, mescaline, or coke. For drug use, you've got to spend two years in the hospital. That's the law in Germany. It's an exit, but you really have to think about it. Keep in mind, too, that manic-depressives are rarely drug users. Or so the psychiatrists in Berlin told me. You should consult a doctor on this one. Faking alcoholism is expensive and takes a lot of time. The best option is suicide. If you don't have money for sleeping pills or a hotel, all you need is a bridge where you can take flight.

It's a little boring in the hospital, which is why I said the best hospital is in Haar. It's a nicely laid-out complex of buildings in the forest. Beyond it there's a nunnery you can visit if you have permission to take solitary walks. You have to do it discreetly, because if a sister is caught having a romance, she'll be disciplined and possibly expelled. There's also a cemetery there. You can nap in the shade of maple trees when you get back from the tavern and want to sober up. After three months, you're cured, but there's a chance they'll hold you longer if your depression sets in again.

Now you have to consider how to make a few bucks. There are lots of ways. You can buy pills in Munich for the sleeping pill addicts in detox, and cognac for the alcoholics, just so long as you do it carefully. Patients in treatment are constantly subjected to urine tests to make sure they're not using barbiturates or alcohol. The best thing is to sell bennies, which are used by people who were in the concentration camps and who now pretend to have nightmares so they can get compensation from the FSG. These folks don't sleep at night because they see the ghosts of the crematorium ovens, SS men, and barbed wire. If you can't get ahold of amphetamines or bennies, try to get your hands on some Nesco instant coffee. The psychotic will drink the entire contents and wander around the whole night. When he tells the orderly about his nightmares, the orderly will answer with a sweet smile.

"Everything will be all right yet. Why don't you try to get some sleep? Tomorrow you can chat with the doctor."

Talking to the doctors isn't difficult. Doctors have yet to cure a single psychotic, and meanwhile they go crazy themselves or become morphine addicts. It's not worth exaggerating your horrible life in your stories. A so-called "difficult childhood," on the other hand, is always reliable. You can drone on about it. There's not a single person who *didn't* have a terrible childhood. Just don't tell the doctors the reason you're depressed is your pathological family. Don't say your father was an alcoholic, your mother was a nymphomaniac, your grandmother committed suicide, your grandfather was a sadist . . . There's no theory yet that explains childhood, and you'll get bogged down in the mud if you take this approach. But you *can* rave to your heart's content about what you went through in the People's Republic. Blackmail by the political police is a good one. They wanted you to collaborate; you resisted. Footsteps on the stairs send you shivering. You fall apart at the sight of a uniform, even if it's just the uniform of a fireman or a member of the Papal Guard. You tremble when somebody sings "*Oczi czernye*."* But you weep when you catch sight of the red standard, because you feel like a renegade since you left the country of Uncle Joe's constitution. Your feelings about morals and honor

---

* "Dark Eyes" ("Очи черные"), a popular Russian folk song (RU)

tell you the land where a man was born is more important than any events that might occur there. And that's your problem. Nostalgia for a nightmare. You'll glide through the explanation, and this way, it's the doctors who'll soil themselves.

Doctor: "Try to remember back to when you received a toy you really wanted."

You: "A toy?"

Doctor: "Yes, a toy you wanted as a child."

You [Composing your thoughts. Plaster an angry expression on your face, as if you can't remember. Finally]: "For my wedding, my wife gave me a car."

Doctor: "But please, try to remember back to when you were a child and you received a toy you really wanted. Did that ever happen? Can you tell me when?"

You: "When?"

Doctor: "Yes, when was that?"

You: "December 1943. Christmas. I was walking home, and the Germans stopped us on Twarda Street . . ." [Break off speech here.]

Doctor: "Please, go on. Remember, I'm a professional. I know this is difficult for you."

You: "Obviously, Doctor, it's very difficult for me to talk about this with you. I have a lot of friends in Germany. I know that hunger and terror can do anything to a nation. As a Catholic (Protestant, Jew, Greek Catholic, Baptist, etc.), I don't have the right to think any one nation is better or worse than another. There are conditions under which any nation is liable to do anything to another."

Doctor: "Please, try to relax. This is very important. So, what happened?"

You: "I was on my way home, and the Germans stopped us. It was on Grzybowska Square. People were standing around, waiting. Then two trucks of hostages arrived. Their mouths were stuffed with gypsum. No, I'm sorry, their mouths were shut with sticking plasters. With plaster like . . ." [Look around.]

Doctor: "You mean wide plasters?"

You: "Right. Their mouths were taped up with these plasters. The Germans lined them up against the wall and shot them with a machine gun. And when they were lying on the ground, an NCO went up to them, and he shot the ones who were still alive right between the eyes. But he didn't shoot standing up. He crouched down and shot from the side so there wouldn't be a ricochet. You know, the NCO didn't have a Luger pistol, he had a revolver. You know the difference between a revolver and a pistol?"

Doctor: "Yes."

You: "Well, that surprised me, because the German Army didn't have revolvers, only pistols, like the P-38, the Mauser, the Luger. But I remember exactly. It was a revolver, because when he emptied his chamber, he had to load it another time. Bullet by bullet . . ."

Doctor: "But what did you get for Christmas? It was on Christmas, correct?"

Now, a moment of consternation and a terrifying silence. You're thinking about something you can't remember. Finally, you say you remembered, but forgot again when you were telling the story. It was on Christmas that you got the present, but what it was exactly, only God knows anymore.

The bit with the revolver is extremely important. Witnessing the public execution eclipsed everything else. You only remember that the German NCO had a revolver, not a pistol. Twenty years have gone by, and you can't forget it. You don't need too many details; one is enough, ostensibly without meaning. After all, what's the difference if somebody's killed by an automatic or a P-38, in the end? But that's what remains, and that's what you can't forget. Not whether people had their mouths plastered shut or stuffed with gypsum; in the six years since then you've witnessed a lot of nightmares, and that detail won't leave a trace in your memory. Death, the most certain thing of all, is taken for granted in these times. In our memories, the only detail that sticks is the one with no special meaning. That's what's important for the idiot psychiatrist sitting across from you. Executions, crematorium ovens, atom bombs: they all count for nothing. What really matters is the one small detail fixed in your memory through the years. It grows to symbolic proportions, and in the end, it becomes the most terrifying thing of all. Your sense of good and evil is beyond the range of your intelligence. Evil ceases to torment you. The only thing that surprises you anymore is certain minor details. Thus, the matter of the unusual revolver. And the memory of the NCO preventing a ricochet as he shot the dying prisoners. It's not important that five minutes prior, you said he shot them between the eyes—which is absurd, because how can an officer shoot his victims between the eyes when he's squatting? But your story can't be too consistent. You're a psychotic, and you can't piece together your desperate thoughts. You have to avoid consistency in your stories.

If the doctor asks you later if you want to go back to your wife, tell him no. When he asks for the rationale behind your decision, tell him you've come to the conclusion it's impossible to love a sick man. You've decided to leave so as not to ruin your beloved wife's life. You've even written her a letter admitting to infidelities you never committed. This proves you love your wife more than anything, but it also proves that your depression remains, though in a somewhat gentler form, and now you have it under control. It only makes sense to say this if you actually have a wife you want to get away from for a while. If you don't have a wife, tell the doctor you've got a girlfriend who's just as poor as you are, and you don't want to ruin her life. You know a certain butcher from the neighborhood, or an athlete who's got a car, and he's in love with her. You know your baby loves a fast ride, and you can't even give her that. So you've got to split.

Poverty is an extremely important factor. It's the reason for your suicide. Pitiful: you're already thirty-some years old, and the only thing you own is an electric razor given to you by the American people after you sought asylum. You are what's politely called in English a "loser." If you're a writer, you can invent scenarios where you're the loser, with no trouble at all. Say you worked for a year for a famous Hollywood director. Your future was in the balance. The director became your closest friend. However, the wife of the millionaire director fell in love with you, and you were tossed out with the trash. A few of these situations, and finally, the tormenting poverty and the shame are reason enough for desperate measures. A lack of luck, poverty, awareness that your wife is supporting you—if that's how it is. Then the conversation between the idiot doctor and the idiot patient looks like this:

Doctor: "What was it that made you decide to take your own life?"

You: "I can tell you. But it'll take thirty-two years. As long as I've lived. Do you have that much time for me?"

Doctor [gently]: "Just tell me, if you can, what was the final straw? It's very important."

You: "With the likes of me, the only thing that's important is that others steer clear of us. But I'll try to tell you. When a man dies free, a life full of danger, of battles fought, of happiness, is gone. But when a pauper dies, the only thing that's lost is shame."

You've got tears in your eyes. You stole that last line from *Spartacus*. Kirk Douglas chooses to die along with his people, since Crassus has paid off the ships Spartacus was planning to escape on. There's only one ship left, and the pirate captain tries to convince Spartacus to take Jean Simmons and his treasure and start a new life. Douglas, indignant, rejects the proposal.

Captain of the Pirates: "Why do you choose to die, Spartacus?"

Kirk Douglas [after a moment's thought; laughing bitterly at first, and then the laughter turns into an expression of arrogance]: "When a free man dies, a life ends, etc. But when a slave dies—only pain dies with him."

Generally speaking, Germany's not a bad country to fake insanity in, but it's even better to fake being a psychotic in Israel. First of all, you have friends who are doctors—lunatics themselves—and they'll do everything in their power for you. Second of all, as a result of the suffering they went through at the hands of various beacons of humanity, like Hitler, Stalin, and our Comrade Bierut, the number of psychological illnesses among immigrants from Europe is high. You can stick with the difficult childhood and the horrors of the occupation, but you've got to say you were persecuted by the political police. A large number of agents in the security apparatus were recruited among the Jews. What people don't know is the NKVD, who in many cases forced Jews to join the ranks of the security apparatus, blackmailed them. Brilliant Stalin was able to encourage that most shameful Polish trait: anti-Semitism. His schemes were smarter than Hitler's. He knew what the average Pole feels when he sees a person of the Semitic race sitting across from him in the uniform of the security apparatus. The Jews, who suffered such terrible persecution during the war, were now persecuting the Poles. Brilliant Uncle Joe understood that suffering ennobles, but only in stories like *Anne of Green Gables*. It's strange that none of the Polish journalists ever rose to the defense of the people who were sent from the NKVD prison to the Security Bureau to act as their brothers' keepers.

In Israel, the life of a lunatic is a bed of roses. A beautiful country, with sun and orange groves where you can dance and get your fill of vitamins. In some insane asylums they administer work therapy. The patients work in construction or on the roads system. They receive free room and board, and the money they make is set aside for a better future. After they're released from the hospital, this allows them to begin a new life, or to return to their precious addiction. The latter seems to me a more typical phenomenon; as an empiricist, I'm basing this on my personal experience.

All that's left is the matter of persecution by the political police. You remember your difficult childhood—the public executions, the detail with the revolver and the squatting NCO—but you take a new tack when you talk about blackmail by the political police. You present it like this: You were offered work in the security apparatus as an informer. You refused, but now you're terrified of everything. Footsteps on the stairs, midnight phone calls, the uniforms of the Papal Guard, etc.

Doctor: "Please, tell me how it happened."

Silence.

Doctor: "Please, tell me. And remember, above all else, I'm a doctor."

Silence.

Doctor: "And did this officer—"

You interrupt.

You: "Yes, Doctor, obviously it's hard for me to talk about these things. I have many friends in Israel. I know terror and hunger can do anything to people. There are conditions under which every person is liable to do anything toward other people. As a Catholic (Protestant, Baptist, Greek Catholic, and so on) I know that all nations . . ."

And you gain some time to stuff yourself with food and think of a new novel or story. After a while you can ask to be sent to work construction, and a few months later you've saved a pile of dough and you can write to your heart's content. Only, it's extremely important to choose the right kind of disorder. The easiest kind to feign is a persecution complex. But let me stress again, you need to refuse food for a few days in the hospital, under the guise of you're doing it because you suspect the doctors are in cahoots with the Gestapo, the Security Bureau, or Cosa Nostra, who are trying to finish you off. The infusions will protect you from feeling hunger. It's also not a bad idea to pretend you're hearing voices ordering you to do different things, like kill your mother-in-law, commit suicide, etc. But if you find yourself in temporary financial straits, an attempted suicide is the thing to do. In three months, you can write a lot of interesting things.

2. Disillusionment with Communism

This is a dead horse, and it won't pay you any dividends. The commies created a fantasy world, and the average person has neither the desire nor the ability to think about things like the gulag camp in Kolyma, Lubyanka prison, or nighttime interrogations. I heard that in the camps of the Far North, when prisoners were planning an escape, they would sometimes bring along a new arrival so they'd have something to eat along the way. I know it's the truth, but even so it's hard for me to believe it. When I was reading Tolstoy's *Resurrection* not long ago, I came upon a similar story about a prisoner who tried to run from Siberia. He convinced his friend to come along, then killed him and dragged him for hundreds of kilometers, munching on his flesh. But these things don't interest anybody, and besides that, it's impossible to make people believe it.

When I would tell people what life is like in Poland, they'd listen to me with polite boredom. Then I stopped telling people about it, and my anger passed. Who was I to demand from people a belief in such things: that a gesture of brotherhood turned into a gesture of self-destruction; that I earned more money here, in the prison in Jaffa, than I did over there? I don't know much about morality. I think it's an elastic idea, but I don't know how you can demand people believe you when you tell them such things.

We, the Poles, don't stand much of a chance. Any Russian book, even the worst one, will always be a thousand times more successful than a good Polish one. *The Wall* by John Hersey doesn't hold a candle to Adolf Rudnicki's writing. Just making such a comparison is offensive to Rudnicki. Leon Uris's *Mila 18* is so dull, it's in a class by itself. *One Day in the Life of Ivan Denisovich* is a weak story, but it enjoyed incredible commercial success. Grudziński's *A World Apart* is shocking, but its sales were dwarfed by *Ivan Denisovich*. *Darkness at Noon*, a modern-day classic, is a weak piece of literature and completely idiotic, proving that the author didn't have any idea what a jail looks like. The hero sees his friend being led to his death from his cell. The only way you can see through a peephole in prison is if you're standing in the hallway. The other character in the story has paper and pencil and draws a map of the USSR for Rubashov during his walks in the courtyard. In prison you're not allowed to have paper or pencil, or even nicknames. Another guy wears a watch chain. All three characters—Rubashov, Ivanov, and Gletkin—are paper-thin, which Koestler himself even admits in his autobiography. He says his heroes aren't living people, but puppets spouting ideas. When you read his book today, you can't help but feel it's all just a sentimental lecture on totalitarianism. Neither quotes from the Bible, nor quotes from Machiavelli, can save it. All these are books written by Russians, or people from over there, which is easy to explain. If I wanted to learn about the United States, I'd rather spend an hour talking with a regular American than spend four hours learning about the States with somebody from Puerto Rico, no matter how smart he was. Anyhow, it's not worth spending any more time on this topic. It won't earn you a dime.

3. Pimping

Pimping is an incredibly hard profession. It requires an exemplary combination of cool, composed acting, strong nerves, and quick decisions. On top of that, you've got to be able to dispatch a wide range of feelings: from extreme cruelty to the gentleness of a lamb. In order to become a pimp, even the schools of Reinhardt, Kazan, or

Stanislavsky offer little help unless you've mastered the craft of acting yourself, through a strong work ethic and character. I heard once that Burt Lancaster, the American actor, used to order his butler to lock him in a room with only a mirror and a chair for hours at a time. He told the butler to open up only at the agreed-upon time and not to listen until then to his pounding on the door, when the desperate Lancaster could no longer endure loneliness. I don't know if this story is invented or true. But you've got to act similarly.

Contrary to what most people think and what we're taught from movies and books, it's more difficult to steal a career prostitute from her pimp than to make a prostitute out of a decent young girl. Every woman can be made into a prostitute if you convince her it'll help her finish her music or medical studies, buy a little house outside the city and start a new life and have a moral reawakening. On the other hand, it's hard to filch another pimp's prostitute for two essential reasons. The first is, a prostitute loves her shepherd and finds moral and physical purification through her everyday relationship with him. The second is, a friend of the shepherd-pimp can very easily stab you in the back, and the police won't do a thing. Every policeman in the world has his paws greased by pimps and their wards.

Let's say you see a pretty prostitute. She's sitting in a pub. You walk in and look at her with a hungry look. The first evening you don't say anything. You drink your beer and leave. At the door, you stop for a minute and look at her again. You look at her with hatred; you're already opening your mouth to say something, but you turn away violently and leave. You go home to your fiancée and have a long discussion about how Schiller was a better writer than Goethe. Or the other way around, it doesn't matter.

The next day, you go see a Humphrey Bogart film. *Casablanca* would be ideal. It's total rubbish, but Bogart's brilliant in it. You learn how to act from watching him. Pay attention to the following scene: Ingrid Bergman, Bogart's former lover, comes to ask for help. Her husband is about to be arrested by the Gestapo, and only Bogart can save him. It's unclear why, in all of Casablanca, only Bogart can save this pain in the ass, but that's beside the point.

Bogart is sitting and holding a big glass of whiskey in his hands.

It's midnight. In front of him sits an ashtray with a hundred cigarette butts. A black man is playing the piano—Bogart and Bergman's favorite song. Footsteps, and in walks Ingrid Bergman. She stands in front of Bogart. Not a muscle twitches on his face.

Bergman: "You must help me. This man is fighting for the most important thing in the world."

Bogart: "I'm sorry. The only thing that interests me is myself."

Bergman: "If you don't help, this man will die."

Bogart: "What of it? I'm gonna die in Casablanca." [He's silent for a moment, then he adds calmly]: "It's a good spot for it."

Bergman: "Listen. When I met him, I was a young girl. This man showed me that there are beautiful things in the world—"

Bogart [interrupting]: "'When I was young, I met a man who . . .' Yeah, yeah. Pretty story. I've heard plenty of 'em in my life."

Bergman takes out a pistol. Bogart breaks out into satanic laughter, but he never puts down the whiskey glass.

Bogart: "Go ahead and shoot. You'll be doing me a favor."

The scene's brilliant. Bogart says his lines freely, taking his time. Meanwhile, his face is tired and tormented.

When some journalists asked him what he was thinking about when his face took on that expression of resignation and fatigue, Bogart said he wasn't really thinking about anything at all. He'd arrived at the strange facial expression thanks to a simple trick: he put his right shoe on his left foot, and the same thing with the left shoe. Obviously, in a situation like that you can't have an expression as sunny as Uncle Joe's in Shurpin's painting *Morning of Our Fatherland*. There, our leader stands against a background of the setting sun, and we also get a glimpse of power lines, oil rigs, airplanes, and combines. But that's off topic.

The most important thing is to learn the dialogue. Bogart was the film actor who turned everything on its head. Up until Bogart, all the actors tried to recite their lines smoothly and flawlessly. In *The Petrified Forest*, Bogart, for the first time, showed how dialogue should be spoken. Bogart spoke poorly, haltingly, looking off to the side. Long sentences he spit out quickly, and short ones he stretched to the absolute limit. He looked as if he were searching for the words, like speaking came to him with difficulty, tortured him. Before that he used to speak very flat. Brando, an actor from Kazan's school, talks the same way. He speaks haltingly, like he's tormented. But Brando doesn't have Bogart's sense of truth. Maybe it's because he lacks the resignation and the calm that Bogart had. Newman, Cliff, Dean— they're all Bogart's children. It's no coincidence Bogart has achieved his reputation ten years after his death, when millions of viewers have seen his prodigious offspring, none of whom have the desperation and cold determination of the father.

With Bogart in mind, the next day you go to the pub where your girl is sitting. You're poorly dressed; you look like a mess. It's because you can't think about anything but her. You need a shave. You've got on a poorly tied tie and have dark circles under your eyes from lack of sleep. The furrows on your brow have deepened, and your hand trembles lightly as you smoke a cigarette, standing with legs spread wide on the threshold of the pub. Remember, there's nothing more charming than a man who knows he's gauche and doesn't try to do anything about it.

You walk up to her.

You: "How much?"

Prostitute: "One hundred."

You look at her in shock. You're broke; that kind of money could support you for a week. Shock slowly gives way to despair. You don't have that kind of cash. And then you look at her with hatred, because anybody who does have the money can have her. Anybody who's got the money . . . but not you. You turn the hatred inward then. You're already past thirty. Other people your age have homes, cars, and bank accounts, and you've got nothing. You're a failure. Your future is lost, and now this night is, too. You crush out your cigarette and leave.

Prostitute [calling after you]: "Eighty."

You turn around violently. There's no more hatred and despair on your face, just a cold awareness of trouble, but only for a fraction of a second. Then you're back to thinking about all those young people driving Jaguars and seducing minors and acting bored in Portofino. You look at your shabby coat sleeves, and your face lights up with rage.

You: "I don't need your pity."

You walk out, return to your fiancée, and tell her that Schiller is better than the author of *Faust* or vice versa; it doesn't make a difference, whatever you talk about. Walk into the same pub the next day and silently show the girl the requested sum. Take her upstairs. Pull out a letter from your pocket addressed to a foreign name.

You: "If I don't come back tomorrow, send this letter."

Prostitute: "Why?"

You: "I bumped off some guy today. I wanted to have you."

You tell her you smashed a man's head in with a crowbar in the hopes of acquiring the necessary capital. You obeyed your heart and gave in to the storm of emotions brewing inside. You committed a crime so you could have her. Then, give her the holy medallion you bought two hours ago off some Jewish merchant, but tell her it's a keepsake from childhood—your only one. If you're not back tomorrow, she should send the medallion to your mother. A murderer doesn't deserve to wear a medallion or a cross.

When a journalist asked William Faulkner what's the best profession for a writer, Faulkner said it has to be a "bawd," that is, a brothel keeper. Faulkner's reasoning was simple: good food, a cordial relationship with the police, the local riffraff call you "sir," you don't have to work mornings, and in the evenings there's always a good party. But in Europe such a setup isn't even a dream.

Pimping isn't bad work if you approach it logically, as a temporary vocation in order to make a few bucks so that later you and your beloved can open up a little hotel, have a moral reawakening . . . In that case, it's not a bad job. Pimps with more than one girl don't sleep with them. Everybody knows, a pimp loses control over his prostitute once he sleeps with her. It's not up for debate. As soon as you've got even one girl, you've got to make her promise not to perform certain favors for her clients. For example, she can never take her bra off. These are delicate issues; each person has to decide for himself. At the end of the day, I'm a writer and a moralist, not Doctor Kinsey. But it's imperative to insist she keep something holy, reserved for you only. Slap her around every time you get the chance, like a jealous bastard. She'll be happy and so will you. The first time she brings you money, tear it up and throw it out the window, where your friend will be waiting to catch it. He can tape the money back together, bring it to the bank, and claim a kid pickpocketed his wallet and ripped up everything inside.

Then you've got to attempt suicide. Take a razor and try to cut yourself below the elbow (never below the wrist), where the veins are surrounded by a big chunk of fat and muscle, which fact you pretend to be ignorant of. You're acting in a fit of passion. You'll spend your days floating on a river of wine and roses.

4. Quiet Harbor

As for somebody helping you out of a tight spot, forget about it. Twice in my life I turned to Polish organizations for help: the first time, when I was in Israel and didn't have a work permit and was dying of hunger; the second, in an analogous situation. Both times they turned me out, although I must say they were polite about it. If the insane asylum fails you (in the sense of a quiet harbor), and pimping, too (in the sense of making money), and you're looking for a moral reawakening and a way to write a story about the budding feelings of a young woman, there are always a number of shelters available. They're called prisons.

The prison in Munich isn't bad, especially if you want contact with the mother tongue, which is vital for a writer. Every third prisoner is a Pole. The folks there lead an uncomplicated way of life. They sleep in the train station, and in the daytime they gather in the big department store in the city center and pool their money together for a bottle of Pushkin vodka. (The vodka for real men: the advertisements show two guys with glasses in their hands. Nearby sits a bear, watching kindly.) After our countrymen head back to the train station to catch some sleep, they're picked up and sentenced to eight days in prison for vagrancy. In prison they perform the necessary ablutions they can't do on the outside, since they have no place to live and no working papers. A few years ago there was a hotel in Munich called Bunker, where you could spend the night for one mark, but that's impossible today. Italians sleep in the train station, too—failed pimps and matrimonial frauds. In the prison in Munich you hear three languages: German, Polish, and Italian.

The food is terrible. The scenes in movies where you see people frantically pacing their cells are unrealistic. In prison you spend a lot of time on your back, because every unnecessary movement brings on hunger. It's terrible, and you can't even write. You work everything out beforehand—scene by scene, dialogue by dialogue—but you can't write anything down. Prison rules forbid activity for financial gain.

Contrary to what pedagogues and film directors like to think, the guards aren't nice to the polite and helpful prisoners. They're fond of the "toughs," as they call them: the crooks and the brazen bastards. If your sentence is served and you don't have a penny, and you want to sit in jail for a little while longer to collect your thoughts, there's an easy way to go about it. Smash a cross against the wall and summon the guard. They'll give you an extra six days for profaning religion. Bavaria, the site of Adolf Hitler's first triumph, is a Catholic land.

God forbid you get the stupid idea into your head to visit the prison hospital. Smoking's not allowed, and it's boring as hell. But if you really feel terrible and need to get some rest, collect some bread and tell them early on Sunday you want to go to Mass. During the service there's a chance to trade grub with the guy from the cell next to yours. You can get cigarettes in exchange for sausage or bread from the brownnosers who don't smoke, but who still have the right to buy tobacco twice a month. The best time to swap merchandise is during the Elevation. In prison you're not allowed to read Jerry Cotton books, but in the sick ward they have stacks of the goddamn things. During the homily you can trade.

When the priest says, "For this cause therefore have I called for you, to see you, and to speak with you: because that for the hope of Israel I am bound with this chain . . ."—that's when you've got to bark above the head of the *Wachtmeister*: "I got a Jerry Cotton book. The one where he traps Jack the Bulldog and murders him with a Colt Cobra."

Then they bark back: "Kiss my ass with that Jerry Cotton. We want the one where he hacks up that Malay woman."

Then you say: "The one who spread her legs for Jack Diamond?"

They answer: "No, the one who spread 'em for the Ryan brothers in San Francisco . . ."

The priest says: "And when they agreed not among themselves, they departed, after that Paul had spoken one word, Well spake the Holy Ghost by Esaias the prophet unto our fathers . . ."

You've got to synchronize with the voice of the spiritual shepherd. Anyway, the church service is broadcast over the sound system, but the prisoners from the sick ward sit by themselves, and the *Wachtmeister* keeps you separated. After a few Sundays you'll have the skills to tell them the whole story of Mike Hammer right in the middle of Holy Mass, and nobody will be able to catch you. It's expedient to be familiar with the Holy Scriptures, or at least the New Testament, so you can know when the priest is about to strike a pathetic note, and then you can barter how you like.

You should always have a place to fall back on when you're short of cash. A place where the prison sentences aren't long, but they're reliable. You cross the threshold, and it feels like home. One place you don't have to worry about this is in Paris, because that's the only city where you can still make a pile of money when you're short. It's easy to crash and burn there, though. And remember, whoever hasn't taken one in the face from a French policeman doesn't know what it is to be beaten. If you wind up in prison in Jaffa, don't make a scene. You'll get such a thumping, in the end you'll be convinced nothing will ever happen to the Israelis; they can damn well take care of themselves. In Palermo, when they work you over and tear the medallion from your neck, kneel down on the floor and kiss their feet. The guards will give you cigarettes, and if you're a good boy, they'll even let you drink beer during the interrogations. And in general act nice, but tough.

If you're sitting in a cell with other "innocent" prisoners, don't fall into despair and whine when the others don't appreciate your acting abilities, although acting skills in this type of refuge can be extremely useful. Take part in their conversations but don't be too bold, and never complain about being unjustly convicted. Remember, in the entire world penal history, there has never been a guilty prisoner. Don't barge in on others' conversations, even if someone's spouting nonsense that makes your head spin. When I was locked up in Stadelheim, two prisoners—both innocent, of course—carried on an endless debate between themselves for months. They were deciding where to go when they got out. Naturally, they wanted to go to a restaurant where they could get drunk quick and cheap. The problem wasn't easy: the lockup in Stadelheim released prisoners at five in the morning. At that hour, all the bars are closed.

One of them suggested going straight from jail to Schwabing, where they could get down to business. The other insisted on going to the Central Train Station: the road's a little longer, but it's cheaper at the station and you can drink more. Besides that, you don't have to worry about what happens next. You'll be rearrested for sure: the police in Munich start their "razzia" right at the Central Train Station. The second prisoner, who clearly was the more serious alcoholic, firmly insisted on heading to Schwabing. Finally both fellows found a compromise: they would go to the market and begin their mission in a huge beer hall, whose name I can't recall. They agreed on the finest details: they'd be let out at five; they'd grab the first tramcar at five fifteen; it was a half-hour ride, and they'd have fifteen minutes left (the beer halls open at six), so they'd make a little conversation. The next Sunday I asked the fellows why they hadn't been released. It turned out they both had six years left on their terms.

There's a certain hierarchy of conversation in prison. Topic number one, obviously, is each prisoner's innocence and the painful error committed by the justice system. Topic number two is women and their wickedness and deceit. Further, there's sports, important life decisions, remembrances from the war; the stupidity of the current chancellor or president; the existence of God; and laments over the terrible food. This last problem jumps ahead of female deceit to become topic number two on Fridays, when they give the prisoners a piece of fish in a revolting slime sauce. On Saturday there are the usual troubles, and the regular hierarchy is restored.

Another ripe topic for conversation is the warped memories of time spent in other prisons. German prisoners are generally of one voice that the most pleasant prison in the FRG is the prison in Stuttgart. It's modern; it's got a radio and running water. The Stuttgart prison is equipped with a radar alarm system, and there's not one chance in a hundred you'll get out of there by your own hands. The Italians are of several opinions on the subject, as the Sicilians have no great love for the Italians from the north. I don't think the prison in Palermo is so bad. In American prisons they feed you better than anywhere else, but experienced prisoners warn they run an extremely tight ship.

Be friendly in prison, but don't try to become the lead dog and don't become the life of the party no matter what, because you'll arouse the resentment of other taciturn and tight-lipped prisoners. Don't gab about yourself too much. Remember, all the crooks and pimps are there because of some mix-up, and they want to talk about it, too. It's a plus if you've seen a lot of films and can reenact scenes. If you have a good memory, try *Gone with the Wind*, *Waterloo Bridge*, and *Casablanca*. Stay away from gangster films and cop films, though. As a rule, they're pretty dumb, except for *The Asphalt Jungle*; God forbid you get it in your head to act out *Rififi*. It's impossible to make a decent, accurate spy or police film because, in order to be a good stool pigeon, you've got to be able to blend in among the crowds, and a man like Gary Cooper or Sean Connery just can't do that. Stick to moral dramas and adventure films. Prisoners love Eddie Constantine. His films are easiest to act out because they're all so similar to one another.

If you want to really shine with erudition and learning, first of all you've got to tell them some Mickey Spillane stories. He's not well known among the German prisoners, and you'll have a lot of success with him. But beware of mixing things up: if they catch you, you'll lose their trust forever and they'll never give you their cigarette butts.

In the Stadelheim prison there's a cell block the prisoners call the "Porsche Abteilung," or the Porsche Corps. General directors and presidents of different banks and factories are held there. They have to atone for their sins. The police catch them with their whores, drunk behind the wheel. Porsche is a popular sports car, hence the name. The people from the Porsche Corps are very distant and haughty. They're objects of derision and hatred of the other prisoner-paupers. You've got to remember in prison that God is always on the side of the stronger army. Remember that a rich man will never help you, because he's of the mind that alms corrupt. And don't think it was poor people who thought up the above sentiment. And don't believe what Frederick the Great said. If you get the itch to punch somebody from the Porsche Corps, and you want to gain sympathy from other prisoners and three days in the lockup, then you should repeat what a certain Swedish king said to God: "Lord, if you don't want to help us, at least admire how we, the Swedish nation, can do battle."

When they put you in the hole, you have to give up your regular jacket for a red one. This marks you off from the general population so other prisoners don't approach you when you're exercising in the courtyard. But don't sweat it. If you've proven yourself in the cell, the prisoners will pick a fight among themselves, the guards will jump to separate them, and one of the prisoners will throw you a packet of shag. If they find it on you when you're returning to the cell, just say you found it on the ground. Three days isn't a long time, but nonetheless you can't pass the time masturbating. You'll only unnerve yourself. Think about your book: calmly, scene by scene, tell it to yourself from beginning to end, and then start over. That's the best advice, from Igor Newerly. Don't think about your wife, and don't think about women at all when you're in the hole. Try to think about scenes from your childhood. About frogs you cut open with a razor, about the time you snatched your old grandma's gold wedding ring as she lay in her cata-falque, about how you told your family you just wanted some time to be alone with the beloved corpse and then traded the eighteen-carat gold for pinchbeck. Don't sing. It'll only make you feel tired, and when you're too tired, you can't fall asleep. Try to imagine living somewhere beyond space and time; try not to pay attention to the ticking of the clock. Remember what Shatov said to Stavrogin: "We're two people who have met in infinity, outside of space and time."

Don't think about today, and don't think about tomorrow. Instead, think about the past and what's dead and gone, about happy things that lead you to gentle laughter and light ruminations. For example, I thought about the invasion of Soviet Falcons in '45. I was in Cze-stochowa, and I was living on Sobieskiego Street, 84. The Russians arrived: they'd smashed a vat of moonshine, and afterward people fell to the ground, drinking the high-proof alcohol together with the crushed-up snow. This is well known. That's how it is in every war and in every place. For two weeks I watched the Russians pass by beneath my window, on the road leading to Warsaw. But they didn't ask about Warsaw. From time to time, one of them would enter the house and ask for a little hot tea. He'd say, "Where's the road to Berlin?" He wouldn't ask how many kilometers, just the direction. Behind him was the Ukraine, the Urals, and the Caucasus, Moscow of gold and Leningrad of stone, and now he was going to Berlin, not even asking about the distance, just the direction.

They walked for days and nights, singing the same song about the hero Chapaev, who blew through the Urals. At night they raped our women; the soldier who was holding back the struggling husband of one of these women would whisper to him, "Ty chevo bespokoish'sia? Razoczek zhonku pere'ebem i dostatochno." *What are you getting all worked up about? We'll give your wife one quick fuck and that's it.* And they'd walk down the street and sing about Chapaev and the letters they received from their mothers on the First of May. Their mothers wanted to know if they were still alive. They had a lot of good songs: about their holy anger, foaming like a wave; about their mothers taking heart and wishing them a fine road ahead while marching under victorious skies; and about drinking for the Fatherland and for Stalin. Then they'd pour themselves another drink. Only now do I realize that Russia can't be understood except through song. Their boring books lie and their stupid newspapers lie, but their melodies are true and lead them to victory. That's where the strength of the people is. And it's true every soldier can be defeated, but not a Russian soldier.

They went to sleep on the snow near the gates of our home. They didn't want to come inside and fell asleep right away, woke up early and shook themselves off like a wet dog. They cooked their kasha with a piece of bacon and walked to Berlin. They took our watches and our wedding rings and they took our women, but they didn't want our hospitality or our roof over their heads. I remember how they were raping one woman in a courtyard, and another woman, trying to save herself from a similar fate, went up to the sergeant and gave him a glass of vodka. She said, "Vashe zdorovie, Komandir." *To your health, Commander.* He had his fly unbuttoned. The sergeant tore the bottle from her hand and threw her against the wall. That's when I realized there's nothing as terrifying as the contempt of a Russian soldier. They trampled the glass and joined the others on their way to Berlin. They were singing about Chapaev.

The NKVD war unit arrived after the combat troops passed, and we all went outside to see how they were going to dispose of a family with ties to Vlasov's Army, who were living just a few houses away. The men from the NKVD pulled up in a Willys Jeep. Without switching off the motor or getting out of the car, they started shouting: "Come out, brothers!" The people came out, they set them against the wall, and the sergeant sprayed them with a machine gun. The NKVD men pulled away without even checking to see if anybody had hidden. We were all trying to steal whatever we could, and we saw that nobody had even tried to hide. The dead lay there, brushed with snow. So when you're in the hole, think about that and remember: if they ever make it to where you are, don't bother running. A real man never runs away, but with the Russians, nobody escapes anyhow.

Don't take comfort in the fact that you've got a refugee passport and can live in Switzerland, France, or Italy. One way or another you'll end up alone. But before you end up alone, it's a long lonely road getting there. Nobody will believe what you could tell them, or what you'd like to tell them. On the other hand, maybe it's better not to think about that when you're in the hole. You can think about it when you're back in the general population cell again, together with people who still have faith that six years from now, they'll return to their old pub and drink their usual beer. Don't laugh at their faith. It may just be holy.

5. Honest Work

You'll never find decent, honest work. Forget about espionage. Poles are no good at it. After I chose freedom, I was asked if I knew where the military airfields in Poland were. I knew of a few. My interviewer perked up.

"Where are they?"

"In Warsaw, in the Boernerowo district," I said.

"And where else?"

"Near Legnica."

"Do you know of any others?"

"I think there's one near Gdynia," I said. "Between Gdynia and Gdańsk. I'm not sure, but there should be one in that area."

"Have you seen this airfield?" asked my interviewer.

"No," I said. "I've never seen it."

"Then how do you know about it?"

"From Radio Free Europe," I said. That was the end of my spy career.

To my great sorrow, it's not even worth fantasizing about becoming a spy. I personally object to Jerzy Putrament, who, in his masterpiece, *Noah's Ark*, portrayed a congenial Polish spy working for some intelligence agency. My protestations also extend to Tadeusz Konwicki and Jarosław Iwaszkiewicz. As we recall from reading their books, Poles who choose to live in freedom in Western Europe are lured by CIA officers who tempt them with invisible ink, pistols with silencers, poison, and dynamite. But the thoughtful Poles reject the offers of the American officers and repentantly return to the bosom of their fatherland. In the film Tadeusz Konwicki wrote the screenplay for, *The Career*, we meet Jan Świderski, who's become an American spy. In *The Chase* we meet an American spy who's been sent to Poland by the CIA in order to poison or castrate a number of stallions. In the film by Wanda Jakubowska, whose title I can't remember, there's also a spy; in another one by Jakubowska, *Victory's Soldier*, there are two English spies. One of the spies is called Władysław Gomułka; the second spy, Marian Spychalski. Based on this, you might assume you'll immediately be engaged by the Americans to poison horses, castrate chickens, and cut telephone wires. But disappointment's waiting for you: instead of dynamite and a pistol with a silencer, you'll simply get a kick in the ass. All the books you've read and the films you've watched, the desire you were full of, your hopes of starting a career—it'll all be for nothing. Your argument won't convince the officers who grant asylum.

Writers who want to write spy novels should be warned about that type of composition. It's quite difficult to send a spy behind the Iron Curtain. The person who gets sent is either an American officer who's had God knows how many years of training, which cost God knows how much money, or else he's a scoundrel who can't be trusted and who's in it for the money, so there's always the risk he'll go work for whoever offers him more cash. It's pretty clear-cut. Technically speaking, to send a spy across the border in the modern system is difficult. You can send him on a business trip or as a cultural attaché, but it's not easy.

On the other hand, Russians and Poles can send thousands of spies a year to the West, and there's no risk involved. They simply arrive here and ask for political asylum. Their appeal sounds like a song that used to be popular in Poland: "Truman, Truman, drop the bomb, we just can't take it very long." For a number of years they remain here, quietly working in their professions. Only after some time has passed do they begin their true mission. They're not just any scoundrels unworthy of trust. They're party members and fanatics who know their road is in fact short, and ends with twenty-four thousand volts. This doesn't deter them, and they get to work. We know from Leon Kruczkowski melodramas how the Rosenberg couple had their heads shaved so the electrodes would fit more snugly. Impatient Eisenhower was waiting by a telephone that had a line straight to their cell, in case the Rosenbergs decided to inform on other spies. But they only kissed each other and spoke about Stalin until the moment the executioner connected them to Western Electric and released the currents into their bodies. Eisenhower at that moment understood the failure of his nation and its politics, and the stupidity of American intelligence officers.

But if you've already asked for asylum, you should avoid any delusions. Your friends from childhood, from your school days and your youth, who've managed to escape, will have already spilled their guts and revealed all the skeletons in your closet. The CIA officer hearing you out will know things even you can't recall. It's foolish to lie to the Americans in the hopes of finding a quiet harbor for a little while. You'll fall under the horse cart and get trampled. But before that, you'll get a punch in the face you'll still remember when you're dead and buried.

You won't find any honest work if you're a writer and you never belonged to the party, and aren't a disciple of Światło, Monat, or Fejgin. I'd gladly become an American spy in order to hook a few commies, but I know I'd get caught right quick. And anyway, like I already said, there's no chance of becoming a spy because they have no need for people like us. The fact of the matter is, people like me don't know anything about the country we're living in. Knowledge of misfortune is good for nothing. And what more can you say about Poland besides the fact that it ceased to exist on the day the Radio Moscow announcer read the following words:

TODAY, THE SEVENTEENTH OF JANUARY, NINETEEN HUNDRED AND FORTY-FIVE, OUR WORTHY SOLDIERS LIBERATED THE CITY OF WARSAW. ETERNAL GLORY TO THE HEROES OF THE RED ARMY WHO FELL IN ACTION WHILE LIBERATING THE FATHERLAND. DEATH TO THE GERMAN INVADERS.

—STALIN

CHAPTER SIX

Two Wardrobe Doors for Sale

Despite what you might have read, the brief period of free speech in Poland didn't begin with Władysław Gomułka's ascent to power. In fact, that's when it came to an end, under the guise of *"raison d'état."* That was the reason given by Gomułka, the man we had pinned our hopes on. Gomułka didn't have to use metaphors and figures of speech to underpin his argument: Soviet tanks in the streets of Budapest and fifteen thousand dead Hungarians (if you believe the official figures) served as a serious enough warning.

Hungarian flags were flying on the streets of Warsaw, and thousands of people volunteered to donate blood, which was then airlifted to the embattled city. The Hungarian national anthem could be heard; *Po Prostu* printed a Hungarian poem on page one called "Air"; people mourned and drank. And thus the national feeling of tragedy was placated.

Today, it's not easy to write and talk about October. All of a sudden, it seems like nobody back then really believed in it. It's not worth dwelling on the topic. I can't think of a better-known example in world history of when a tyrant tears his robes and declares that, starting tomorrow, he'll reform. There's an article by the chief editor in an old issue of *Po Prostu*, which claims the "Polish October" came about as a result of the revolutionary boiling over of the masses of workers and peasants, and of their healthy instincts and political experience. This led them to demand rule of law and democracy from the leaders of the party and the nation. But it's doubtful how seriously one can take the proud declaration by the workers of the Żeranie automobile factory: "We won't let them in!" If you want to know to what extent three thousand people armed with handguns and bayonets were in any condition to stop the Soviet Army, ask the soldiers. In any case, the party pulled off its tactical maneuver faultlessly, in terms of spectacle and coordination. People were made to feel they'd achieved something that would be an important turning point in the nation's history.

On the other hand, it's hard to assess the whole thing from a humorist's point of view. I don't know how eleven years of experience and proximity to the Soviet border let people harbor different expectations after October. Maybe it can all be chalked up to faith in one man: Władysław Gomułka. Maybe they believed that the man who'd been a prisoner of and had suffered at the hands of his fellow believers (the commies) would lead us without forgetting what he'd gone through and suffered himself. These are the ethical premises of *Anne of Green Gables*. But from an empirical standpoint, and taking into account what police and prison wardens with years of experience have to say about the subject, suffering has never been known to ennoble.

A second entertaining element in this whole canard is the feeling of disappointment in Gomułka, as if the guy ever had a real shot at changing anything for the better in the near future. Shortly after coming to power, Władysław Gomułka stated in one of his speeches that a quick increase in the standard of living was impossible because there was no money to pay for anything. He also discussed the colossal Polish debt and the catastrophic state of the national economy, without failing to mention how the Soviet Union had generously relinquished parts of its claims against the People's Republic of Poland. But people didn't listen to his words carefully enough. When he traveled to Moscow, the crowds who had gathered at the train stations cheered joyously at his appearance. At the same time, they told him not to expect a free lunch. They gave him good advice: "Wiesiek, hold your ground." It became a slogan of sorts for the people. Everybody completely forgot the fellow was a communist, probably the most stubborn and hardest of them all. The whole story is perfect for moralizing writers:

the people were oppressed, a boot up their ass for eleven years. After painful experiences and a lot of suffering, they believed things would suddenly be different, all thanks to a single person. From the point of view of police literature, though, at whose feet I was baptized and which I still am interested in, a plot like this never turns out.

After a certain period of time, writers and intellectuals trumpeted the myth that Gomułka despised them. I'm sorry to say, it wasn't all so simple. I'm afraid the writers and intellectuals invented the myth themselves. Gomułka was labeled a spy and a villain; they spit on him; they organized mass meetings where they condemned him publicly, accusing him beyond a shadow of a doubt of working for the French, English, and American intelligence agencies. They didn't grant him that privilege afforded to even the most vile of criminals: to stand before a court of law and tell the truth to the people and the judges. Writers who wrote about Gomułka's spies and about the damage caused by what they called "Gomułka's tendencies" received national awards. After many years of work and reflection, and the squandering of immense financial resources, the film *Victory's Soldier* was shot: Gomułka was mocked and derided, and there was not a single Simon of Cyrene to be found. After that, according to Putrament, the defeated Gomułka returned. And nothing happened: the same people who spit on him back then are still making films and writing books. No heads rolled; nobody shared the fate of Boris Pilniak, Isaac Babel, or Gorky. Gustaw Herling-Grudziński wrote his essay "Seven Deaths" about the latter. When you're dealing with a real human being, hatred is something that must be earned, and it doesn't matter whether the person is a communist or not. But it's a nice myth: the leader of the government hates us. I wish it were true, but I'm too old to convince myself that scorn is the same thing as hatred. As they say, anybody can kill, but only a king can spare a life. So they received a kingly gift, and it was the gift of one who scorned them, not who hated them. I'm sorry to say it.

By 1957, there was nothing left for me. In '56 my debut short story collection was published. It was called *A First Step in the Clouds*. It was also the last step. The only thing that interested me in literature besides police denunciations was the story of a woman's love for a man, and their bad luck together. I don't know how it came to be that way. I've only loved once in my life, eleven years ago, and since then I haven't loved anybody even for a minute, despite constantly building illusions for myself. Everyone who knows and remembers me, knows that literature ceased to interest me the moment Hania and I separated. But she didn't leave me all alone. I had the right to an apartment, in either the Old City or the Ochota neighborhood. I chose Ochota, if only because the building I was living in, the site of my former domestic bliss, had a children's nursery, and Hania had children. So Hania left, and I stayed behind with the nursery school. I'd return home at 5:00 a.m. from the pub, awash in tears, and at seven there would already be a chorus of children's voices waking me up with a song. It sounded three hundred strong. I only remember a few lines:

> Welcome to the labor of our days,
> To the joyful tumult of our steelworks,
> To a country of joyous people.
> By deed of nations we erect a building on a dream,
> Among the steppes, forests, and lush meadows.
> From the south to the Polar Circle,
> Fatherland of a hundred peoples . . .

It continued in that vein. I'd wake up and start shedding tears again. At eight my first guests would show up: colleagues coming back from a bar called Zieleniak. They'd head over there at five in the morning, after Kameralna closed. At Zieleniak you could drink till all hours. Some of my childhood friends would come by and spill their guts out. Others stopped by to scrounge some cash to continue their drunk. I'd sit on the bed and cry. Some of my guests drank and discussed politics. Once Tadeusz Kubiak brought over an elf he'd bought as a present for his son. He asked if I'd keep it at my place until next Christmas. This was in February, I think. It was supposed to be a surprise for his kids on Christmas Eve. Luckily, Kubiak's friend Janicki bought the elf from him and did who knows what with it. Down below the children sang, I cried, and my friends went to the Esplanada restaurant, which was two streets down, and came back with vodka.

Every so often Adam Pawlikowski would come by with a girl who was willing to show him a good time, and he'd kick me out of my own home for the duration of the romantic interlude. A children's choir and a round of curses from the neighbors bid me farewell. One day my friend Pawlikowski told me he was setting out on a stable marriage. The story of my family nest on Częstochowska Street came to end. I had a heart-to-heart with Poldek Tyrmand and swore I couldn't live without Hania. Tyrmand heard me out and then said with a sinister laugh:

"The only thing left for you is cold steel. But try getting out of Warsaw. Go somewhere she's not and try writing."

"All the same, I won't be able to write anything," I said.

Tyrmand gave out with another sinister laugh:

"That's precisely the problem. You need to learn to work even when you think nothing will turn out. That's the only way something will work out."

And really, nothing came of it. I went to Kazimierz and started writing a novella called *The Graveyard*. I finished it two years later.

I sat in Kazimierz and thought about my home on Częstochowska Street. I hadn't yet read "Wronia Street and Sienna Street," that great essay by Paweł Hostowiec, but our building wasn't much different from the building where Hostowiec lived. Terrifying moments of jealousy played out there, which the entire street took part in. There were scenes of wild bingeing, and like every self-respecting Warsaw street, we had our own bad guy. He was a fellow called "Lolek the Partisan." Lolek the Partisan had the strength of a bear. During the war, his extraordinary adventures led him to Yugoslavia, where he fought with Tito's Partisans. He came back to Poland with the rank of a Yugoslav officer, adorned with medals. Later, when the Russians soured on Yugoslavia, Lolek the Partisan was ordered to the nearest police station and forced not only to give up the medals he'd won for bravery, but he also had to write a letter to his former commander, vowing not to maintain any further contact with him, and letting him know he considered the officer a traitor to the workers' movement.

From then on Lolek began to drink. He'd get money for these drunks in a very straightforward manner: He'd take a crowbar, go to the corner where a well-known hunchback had a kiosk that sold newspapers, and ask him for money to buy a fourth of vodka. The hunchback would refuse. Lolek would flip over the kiosk with the hunchback inside of it, and then he'd offer to set it back right-side up, except now he didn't want money for a fourth, but for a half liter. Since it would have taken three strong men to put the kiosk back, the hunchback would agree, and Lolek the Partisan, putting down his crowbar, would set the kiosk upright together with the hunchback, pocket the cash, and go get his vodka.

I could never understand why the hunchback didn't say yes from the start. Lolek would ask for a fourth, but the hunchback stood his ground and wouldn't give him anything. It ended up costing him twice as much. He was definitely a figure from a classical tragedy, and there was an element of suffering about him—*catharsis*—that would have saved him from becoming a joke. A second figure—another character straight out of a classical tragedy—was Bill, the barman at La Bohème. Bill was an American soldier and a fixture at La Bohème who used to make all kinds of scenes, but always came out on top. The owner of La Bohème, the brilliant Tony, hit upon a truly diabolical scheme. When Bill got out of the army, Tony offered him a job as a barman, and Bill, who in the meantime had gotten married to a beautiful woman from Paris, agreed. As a barman, he couldn't hit the customers. To the contrary, he had to calm them down and break up fights, and he couldn't even kick a customer in the shin. Often, when I'm sitting in La Bohème and I see a fight, and then Bill getting in the middle of it all, I look at his face and try to imagine what must be going on inside that man's heart. I think about him and his burning desire to join the fight. He's the most tragic figure I've ever known.

On Częstochowska Street, my banker, moral guardian, and adviser was a building caretaker who had three sons. They were nice boys, calm. The scary one was their mother, who was constantly quarreling and bickering with her neighbors. The sons had to settle her problems, so you could never find all three of them at the table together. One of them was always enjoying a free cot, courtesy of the penal system. The kids loved their mother. If the mother, her hair messed up and her eyes flinging lightning, sprang upon one of them and began yelling, "Tadek, go make the Kwiatkowszczaks' mother pay!"—well, Tadek would get up from the table, take a souvenir switchblade from his brother, and run out onto the street. Tadek was the youngest son in the family, and he was the one who had to handle the family feuds on Częstochowska Street most often. I accompanied the caretaker and his family to court for one of Tadek's trials. The prosecutor threw thunderbolts, but Tadek kept making these calming gestures in his mother's direction, calling out from time to time in a piercing voice, "Mama, don't you cry. I'm gonna lay him out."

All of these are situations from Wiech. It's a great misunderstanding to take Wiech merely as a columnist. In reality, he's one of our greatest novelists and moralizing writers. His few stories are genius. There's the one about the two thieves who quarrel over dividing their profits; one about the "Angel of Goodness," or the calmest subletter on Rybaka Street; there's one with the American equestrian Tatersal on Dzika Street, coached by Mister Henek Szpagat; and one about Mister Monek Alfabeta—the greatest Don Juan of Twarda Street. This isn't news.

There's one thing I still can't figure out, despite being a son of Warsaw, of the Powiśle neighborhood: did Warsaw talk the way Wiech wrote, or did Wiech write the way Warsaw talked? I remember how the drivers at Metrobuild, the Warsaw Consumers Cooperative, the City Trade Bureau, and a few of the Warsaw boys at Paged would all buy *Express Wieczorny* just to find out about recent developments in the lives of Wiech's characters. Wiech ceased to be a great moralizing writer and became a columnist, but that was after the war, when Wiech himself said, "It wasn't I who changed Piekutowszczak. It was history." Piekutowszczak was a recurring character in Wiech's writing. And it was true: after the war Piekutowszczak's brother-in-law stopped frequenting the liquor stores and started frequenting the kefir shops. He turned from a rationalist into a positivist. From a dodger into a dialectician. He stopped using logic; in its place he learned what he was supposed to think on certain matters. And that's how the funniest man in all of Warsaw died.

For many years I searched for a writer who could replace Wiech as he was when Nalewki, Smocza, and Dzika Streets were still around, before the war. Finally, I found him: Damon Runyon. He created a cast of characters similar to Wiech's, with their special New York jargon. He's got Harry the Horse, a man who bets on the horses so long he begins to look like one; Spanish John, the criminal; and Big Butcher, the ticket ripper. I lived in a hotel in Tel Aviv where a few of its residents were called Spanish John, Big Butcher, and Harry the Horse. There was only one vacancy left—for me. As an ironic rib on my very un-Semitic looks, they called me Little Isadore. We were all in on the act. Runyon's characters, like Wiech's, have similar problems, similar joys and sorrows. When Harry the Horse, Spanish John, and Little Isadore try to convince Big Butcher to crack a safe for them, he refuses. He's the happy father of a six-month-old child, and his wife has gone to her mother's and will be gone for the night. After long deliberations, they decide to take the child with them. So, while Big Butcher is drilling through the armored cash register, his buddies are entertaining the kid, handing him a saw and a drill bit to play with. Little Isadore, instead of giving him a pacifier, gives him a bottle of nitroglycerine by accident. And here too, as in Wiech, we find people in the same situation: people in the suburbs sitting in front of their houses on chairs and staring at one another. "That's how we do it in Targówek," says one of Wiech's characters. Damon Runyon's got a line: "In fact, everybody in the neighborhood is sitting out on the front stoops over there, including women and children, because sitting out on the front stoops is quite a custom in this section."

A weapon is an extremely delicate item, of course. The Polish call it a bone, a spitter, a hoof, a splitter, and so on. The Americans in Runyon's stories take it another step further, and with more precision: "the great equalizer." Sicilian gangsters who were deported from America, old men already, whom the barmen and pub owners call *commandatore* today, told me that the name "great equalizer" dates back to the days of Baby Face Nelson. He went crazy on account of his short stature and childish face and came to the conclusion that only a Cobra .38 stuck in his grip would make him equal to his partner in crime, or to his victim.

All three of the caretaker's sons knew how to crack a whip, and since I'd been a highwayman, we had something in common. In his essay about Wronia and Sienna Streets, Paweł Hostowiec also writes about the underground world in those circles. That section of Warsaw was still completely crooked after the war, more corrupt than the neighborhoods of Marymont and Wola, which were no pictures of respectability. The reason was simple: the Warsaw Main Cargo Station, the cargo unloading station, occupied a section of Towarowa Street. The neighborhood around Towarowa Street, up until 1950, was full of private stalls whose owners worked on the sixteenth and seventeenth peripherals or the first and second coal lines, taking care of transport and unloading for firms like the State Construction Company or Metrobuild. To use a banal and threadbare epithet: it was a nest of corruption.

But now I have to explain what it was really like. Everybody from the transport firm had his own forwarding agent on the sixteenth and seventeenth peripherals or on the coal line. This agent made sure that the wagon with the goods intended for his firm was discharged within six hours, which was the limit for idling set by the Polish State Railways. If the wagon idled longer than that, the given firm had to pay a whole array of fines. We didn't have a sufficient transport system yet in those days. You had to hire private drivers, who provided their own horse and cart. But how could you manage to unload a wagon containing thirty tons within the time limit if you couldn't load more than four or five tons onto the horse platform, and the unloading point was located far away, say, in the Bielany neighborhood? Easy. A privateer would approach the agent of a given firm and offer him a pack of Giewont cigarettes. Without a word, the agent, a trusted employee of the firm, takes a cigarette. He pulls a hundred-zloty banknote out of the pack. Both men go their separate ways in silence. The agent, in turn, goes to the boss of the sixteenth or seventeenth peripheral and offers him a pack of Giewonts. The representative of the Polish State Railways takes a cigarette from the pack and pulls out a fifty-zloty banknote. On the edge of the bill someone's scribbled the number of the wagon. Instead of idling for six hours, this wagon should be allowed fifteen. Next, the state railways representative puts a stamp on the transport document and signs it, attesting to the fact that the wagon belonging to railway junction X, number Y, has been unloaded on time. In the evenings, there would be drinking bouts in one of the private stalls around Wronia and Sienna. The privateer, the trusted employee of the firm or the agent, the representative of the Polish railways, and plainclothes policemen and regular cops would all come together. Afterward they'd walk down Złota Street to Number 28, where three prostitutes were living, and they'd continue their binge there while availing themselves of carnal delights.

I know the situation well because I was an agent at Metrobuild for a little while; back then I earned a thousand or fifteen hundred zlotys in a day. My official salary never exceeded seven hundred zlotys for twelve or fourteen hours of work. There's nobody around today who can calculate the losses incurred by the Polish State Railways. I'd say they've got to be in the billions, thanks to those idling wagons. That's what you get with top-to-bottom planning. Unfortunately, I was fired from my job as an agent, and shortly thereafter they demolished the last private bordello on Złota Street. Today, that land forms part of the property of the Palace of Culture and Art.

This was on my mind as I sat in Kazimierz writing my novella *The Graveyard*. Until Hania, everything had been simple. I was only interested in relations between men and women, which seemed important and tragic. But then suddenly everything started to seem grotesque. I understood, you can't write a realistic story about totalitarianism and have it be tragic, too, and I still don't believe that kind of literature is possible. A person entering the gates of a German concentration camp knew there were only two possible ways out. The first way was through the chimney of the crematorium; the second was the eventual arrival of Allied soldiers or Soviet Falcons. From beginning to end the dramatis personae remain the same: the executioner remains an executioner; the victim, a victim; a slave driver doesn't let the whip out of his hand until he retires. A person entering the gates of a Soviet prison doesn't know anything. Maybe tomorrow he'll be shot; maybe after he sits out his ten years they'll hit him with another sentence, this time for fifteen; but it also might happen that, in the meantime, the party has changed tactics, and now the victim wears the executioner's clothes, and the erstwhile torturer crawls up on his knees, begging for a loaf of black bread before getting sent to the goners' barracks. The element of tragedy gets shaken up. The death sentence can be changed into a mandate of power, the victim into an executioner. The locus of torture becomes the locus of revenge. And the element of catharsis is gone. A scrap of paper from the NKVD stating that someone who was shot in the back of the head twenty years ago was killed based on false accusations and confessions won't make anything better.

In Herling-Grudziński's book, we read about an actor who once portrayed a boyar in a historical film, playing him with exaggerated nobility. They give him ten years for distorting the ideological thrust of the film. After some time, the film makes its way to the camp where the unfortunate actor is serving his time, and he's got an opportunity to watch himself in a very different setting than his present one. In the movie, he's sitting at the tsar's table, lifting goblets heavy with wine, gorging himself on pheasant. Even if this story isn't true, the idea is right. Writers who write about totalitarianism are absolutely helpless, because nobody's willing to accept the truths they portray.

In Orson Welles's film *The Trial*, we see the hero, Josef K, wandering around the Palace of Justice. The palace is a conglomeration of different architectural styles: part Baroque, part modern construction, and part Gothic. Josef K is walking through the dusty corridors, and all of a sudden he finds himself in the waiting room of the Gare Saint-Lazare train station. The Palace of Justice is ridiculous. Surprisingly, not one film critic paid attention to that element of the film, which is basically the key to the way Orson Welles wanted to show Kafka. It's utter nonsense that people are supposed to take it for the Palace of Justice. There's no meaning, no style or coherence. The law book Josef K looks at is a collection of pornographic photos.

Back then, in Kazimierz, the thought occurred to me, "What would happen if I wrote a story consisting of fragments of speeches, based only and exclusively on authentic facts and experiences, and simply walked the character through it all like in a story with a single plot line? Would that type of story work? And would people who've been seeing this for years with their own eyes—would they simply believe the facts that, once put on the page, inevitably become fiction? Would people believe it?" I prepared in various ways. First of all, I traveled to Warsaw and started reading *Nowe Drogi*, the monthly journal of the Polish United Workers' Party.

I wanted to search out Edward Bernstein for the occasion. I went to the dormitory where he used to live, and as I walked through the hallway I heard the sounds of a guitar and the following song:

> You sent me a letter in early morning,
> With a bouquet of white roses,
> And in the letter you wrote,
> You said you didn't give a damn for me . . .

The simple, dramatic song caught my attention. I knocked on the door, walked in, and saw two of my friends, actors from the drama school. One of them was sitting on the bed, holding a guitar. The second one was frozen in the middle of the room, posing like a dying swan, his face full of gloomy reverie.

"We're having a rehearsal," said the fellow with the guitar. "We can choose what we want to do for our exams, but we have to perform it like actors. Our lines are the lyrics to the song. Take a look."

I sit down next to the guitarist on the bed. He stands up and goes into the hallway and starts knocking on the door. Meanwhile, the dying swan fellow is lying on the bed and doesn't pay attention to the knocking. Only when the other guy begins pounding his fists on the door does the swan perk up. He absentmindedly gazes out in front of him. He starts looking for his night slippers. He looks for a minute, then finally, without forgetting how sleepy he is, goes to the door barefoot and opens up. The guitarist hands him something: a letter and a bunch of roses. The sleepy fellow's face comes to life. He takes the flowers from his sweetheart, and the situation becomes clear. She loves him, she wants him, and this morning she sent him roses. Now he has to give a tip to the postman. The enchanted lover rifles through the pockets of his wallet but with no luck, since he spent his last penny the night before, drunk and depressed. He sits the postman in the seat of honor at the table and goes to his neighbors to borrow money.

He hasn't talked to his neighbors in years on account of some feud, but everything seems trivial next to the symbol of her feelings his sweetheart has sent him. Finally he borrows ten zlotys and gives it to the postman, who leaves. Now he's got to do something with the roses, of course: he grabs a vase, but being sleepy, he stumbles over the couch and the vase breaks into a heap of shards. Once more he goes to his neighbors, this time with roses in his hand, says something in a happy mumble, then picks up a hideous crystal bowl. The bowl is a memento belonging to the master of the house, who received it when he was a marksman serving in the Polish paramilitary organization *Strzelec*, or something like that. The negotiations last a long time, but this former follower of Piłsudski is a romantic, and he finally hands over the vase. The happy lover places the roses in it. He's excited. He sits in his chair and smokes a cigarette, staring at the unopened letter before him. He's sure the letter is full of sweet and intoxicating words. He's deep in thought, thinking about those nights he crawled beneath his sweetheart's window; about her husband who didn't want to give her a divorce; about all the times he fell ill with what those in military circles call "complications from the flu," but which is cured by antibiotics and sulfonamide. He contracted these diseases when he would go on binges, and his despair brought him into the arms of a Corinthian lady of the night. And he sits there, staring at the letter and putting off opening it. Finally, the cigarette burns down to his finger, and he's brought back to consciousness. He puts out the butt and opens the letter swiftly. Its contents are fatal. He turns his face to the wall. His hand tightens around the thorns of a rose. The end.

"That's the Stanislavsky version," they explained. "The scene has it all: love, hope, despair. In the exam we'll change the words 'You said you didn't give a damn for me' to 'You're leaving me already.' Of course, it's not the same thing, but what can you do? And now we'll act out the same scene according to Strasberg and Kazan. Mietek, let's begin."

This time the guitarist lies down on the bed, and the other one starts to knock. The guitarist doesn't react to the knocking. He's smoking a cigarette, staring at the ceiling and keeping time with his bare feet against the bed frame. After a while the other one starts pounding on the door.

Guitarist: "Are you bringing me cash?"

Postman: "No, roses."

Guitarist: "For my funeral? Leave the roses with the building manager."

Postman [breaking character]: "Mietek, for God's sake, they don't have building managers like that in the States."

Guitarist: "Leave them at the door."

Postman: "You've got to sign."

The guitarist gets up and signs for them. He throws the roses on the table and starts making himself breakfast, not looking at the roses lying there, not looking at the letter. We can see from his face he's a lost soul. As he drinks his coffee he begins tearing the petals off the roses, and then, when the roses look like corpses from Bergen-Belsen, he opens the letter. He's got the blues written all over his face; he starts laughing. He picks up the skeleton remains of the roses and looks at them ponderously.

Guitarist: "It was my mistake. I should have sent flowers to Hela. She knows a watchmaker in Paris where I could spend the night."

He muses for a second, then realizes he's made a mistake in the dialogue he's been performing. "I completely forgot: I'm supposed to be married to Hela for two years. She's away on holiday now, and the roses are from some woman I started a fling with last week."

He asked me which version I liked better. I told him I didn't see any difference whatsoever in the whole affair, and anyway it didn't seem accurate to me. Women who are about to break up with you don't spend money so easily on a bouquet of roses. In the best-case scenario, if the woman is marrying some rich gardener from the Warsaw suburbs, you can count on her sending you a letter saying she's leaving because she didn't want to ruin your life. Although that seems unlikely, too. Adolf Rudnicki wrote that the easiness of women has become our inferno. I don't see that as grounds for getting all excited, but I told the guys to read Rudnicki. When I finally got around to asking about Edward, it turned out he'd been expelled two years ago and nobody had any idea where he was living now.

I went back to Kazimierz again. I remember walking at dawn down Krakowskie Przedmieście toward Jerusalem Alley, and I saw a guy standing in front of the statue there. He was throwing his key ring at the pigeons who were sitting on the statue dedicated to He Who Stopped the Sun and Moved the Earth. I'd never seen anybody hunt like that before. I walked up closer, and I saw that the lonely hunter was Paweł Minkiewicz. I watched him in action for a minute.

"Paweł, what do you want from these unlucky birds?" I asked.

Paweł said he was in a really bad way with money, and if he couldn't snag a bird, he wouldn't have anything for lunch that day. Moved by the fate of this lonely hunter, I proposed getting breakfast at the buffet at the Warsaw Main Railway Station. The hunter agreed. I remember them all: Mietek, Zdzisiek Maklakiewicz, Miszka Stanielewicz, Poldek Tyrmand, and that actor who walked into a store on Chmielna Street once, went right up to the owner of the place, put his right hand tragically over his heart, and said, "Give me a hundred-note. The *artiste* is dying."

It's hard for me to think about them now. I don't know if I'd be able to talk with them today like we used to talk back then. The most terrifying thing is I don't miss Poland at all. If I ask myself what Poland means for me, I don't have an answer, except to say that it's ten or fifteen people who were friendly toward me. I wouldn't be able say much about my colleagues who fancied themselves writers. They took me for a fool my whole life. In turn, I didn't really know what I was supposed to talk about with them, because we were interested in different things and separated by different experiences. But throughout all those years I used to think it was this half dozen or dozen people who would become Poland for me. That turned out to be an illusion, too. When I published the first part of my denunciation in *Kultura*, I ran into a close friend, one of the most intelligent people out there. After reading it, he told me, "It's really amusing, except it's Poland *à la* James Bond. Such a Poland doesn't exist." This man had never been a communist, never a communist sympathizer. He was never an opportunist, and his whole life he'd struggled against obstacles that came in no small doses: once he'd been accused of having petit-bourgeois inclinations. Another time they accused him of pornography. Once they accused him of surrealism, yet another time of disparaging the achievements of the working class.

What could I answer him? The only thing to tell him was I'd dreamed up the poverty in Poland. I dreamed up the matter of the political police. I dreamed up the treachery and the shameless murder. I dreamed up the fact that for two years I'd been blackmailed by the police. I dreamed up the liquidation of *Po Prostu* and all those other things I'd recalled, only so that Jerzy Giedroyc, my editor, would have a nice way to spend his evenings. But to think that Poland was for me those half dozen or dozen people: that was to think like an idiot. I hadn't taken atrophy into account. And I, such a diligent reader of Dostoevsky, hadn't taken into account that boredom is a shameful thing. Maybe even the most shameful.

All the fellows I started out with, they knew it was fatal, but they waited all those years just to be able to write one poem, one story, just to be able to paint one surrealist painting or make a sculpture that didn't *resemble* anything. These were people—despite the facts and despite everything going on around them—these were people who kept faith that the moment would come when it would be possible to say: "No."

We—losing our hair, no longer beautiful, twentysomethings no more—we had our moment of glory. Some of us turned out better for it, some worse. There weren't any masterpieces made in those days, but maybe the works will be useful as a chronicle of the past, as proof of misery and lack of talent, as evidence of the powerlessness of a person living in a nightmare who doesn't have the inner strength to recognize it as such. But like I said, these were people who believed they'd one day be free to say the single most important word in every individual's life: "No."

When I meet beautiful twentysomethings today and I talk with them, one thing scares me: they all know things are bad in Poland. Nobody has any illusions about the occupation of Poland. On the other hand, nobody's really concerned about it. One of the most beautiful girls I've met recently wants to become a computer engineer. Another handsome twentysomething is studying the archaeology of the Mediterranean Sea. There's one who's a metals engineer. Not a single one of them wants to be a writer, painter, or sculptor. None of them are holding their breath for the day when they'll be free to say, "No." If a painter, writer, or director defects to the West, years of anguish and sporadic work are waiting for him. Nights spent in flea-bag hotels, women who pay the bills, and personally I don't know of a case besides Miłosz where the artists who fled from behind the Iron Curtain didn't get bumped down a social class. These new beautiful twentysomethings won't have those problems. After seeking asylum, they'll work as doctors, engineers, God knows what else. They won't be tormented by boredom or hunger or by a longing for the home-land they've left behind and which never caused them any suffering. And these are the new beautiful twentysomethings.

But back then, in Kazimierz, I didn't realize there'd come a time of atrophy. As I said, Hania wasn't there, I took to doing strange things. I wrote the novel *The Graveyard*. The book was childish, unsuccess-ful. I decided to build it on authentic facts, since I didn't know yet it's not the facts that matter in prose, but apt invention. Facts turn out to be impossible to use. The story with Samba the dog is authen-tic; the speech the hero of the novel hears is from something Roman Werfel wrote in *Nowe Drogi*; the story told by the tall political po-lice officer, about the major and the sabotage, is a story I heard from Colonel Jacek Różański; the story of the sculptor who carves statues of the Great Teacher intended for a private shooting range is a true story, known all over Warsaw; the story of the child who lives in the dilapidated house and whose mother ties him to the bed every day with a rope when she goes to work, so he doesn't fall down the ru-ined staircase—that's shown in a documentary film made, I believe, by the director Jerzy Bossak; the story of the girl who intentionally got herself pregnant by a tubercular communist, in order to give him the strength to live, but he, the communist, left her when he found out that the girl's father was politically questionable—this happened to the family of some friends of mine. And the policemen who insinu-ate to the drunken hero that he made antigovernment statements is a story known best to me, because that was the way the police recruited new informers. But all of these facts didn't add up to anything. And I bet, even if a better writer than I were to build a story on these very facts, even then, nobody would believe the things seen, heard, and talked about in whispers every day.

Darkness at Noon, Koestler's feeble novel I'm tempted to call a sentimental lecture on totalitarianism, is full of nonsense. I've already discussed that. Nevertheless, it's an example of apt invention: Rubashov speaks with his first interrogator, Ivanov, who's been his friend since the October Revolution. Ivanov doesn't strain too hard trying to convince Rubashov that his execution is for the good of the party. Ivanov says, "Every year, millions of people die from hunger, sickness, flooding, and natural disasters. Why shouldn't we be able to kill a few thousand people here and there if we accept that we are conducting an experiment whose goal is the happiness of humanity?" Since Ivanov's tactics don't amount to much, Gletkin takes over for him. He's a young communist, the ideological child of Rubashov, but understanding between father and son proves impossible. If the novel has any value, it rests on the conflict between Rubashov and Gletkin, but only because it takes up an old literary thread: unnecessary people must make way for the young. Hostowiec writes that if *Wild Palms* were to be regarded as a document of the life of the American man, the reader would come to the conclusion that money is the rarest and most difficult thing to come by in the United States of America, the richest country on earth. At least it's apt invention. In another of Faulkner's books, a man stands with his back to the setting sun, speaking to another fellow. The second man is having a conversation with the first one's shadow, falling in the opposite direction. In another novel, the hero single-handedly battles crocodiles in order to save the life of a woman who's just given birth before his very eyes. He doesn't have any feelings for her. After he's saved two people's lives, he gets ten years tacked on to his jail sentence, because prison regulations don't allow prisoners to absent themselves for any reason from the locus of their torture. Another character in the novel is sentenced to ninety years in jail because he was afraid of a confrontation with a hysterical woman. And that's all we can say about apt invention.

People were saying there was only one man who could write the nightmare of our times. I don't buy that. Fyodor Mikhailovich Dostoevsky was a visionary, and he already captured everything in the eighth chapter of *Demons,* called "Ivan the Tsarevich." I can't resist the temptation to quote what Piotr Stepanovich Verkhovensky says to Nikolai Stavrogin, as he's explaining Shigalyov's plan to him. Shigalyov is the ideologue behind the group of revolutionaries organized by Verkhovensky.

Verkhovensky says, "Over there in his notebook is the truth itself. There—is espionage. Through him, every member of society keeps watch over his friend and has an obligation to denounce him. Everybody depends on the group, and the group depends on everybody. All are slaves, equal in slavery. In special cases—slander and murder. For there is always equality. It begins with lowering the standards of education, of knowledge, of talent. A high level of knowledge and talent is only good for the gifted. We don't need gifted people. The most gifted ones have always gained power and acted as tyrants. They were unable to stop themselves from being tyrants. The more they defiled, the more benefits they reaped. There, in Shigalyov's plan, he drives them out and sentences them to death. Cicero has his tongue cut out; Copernicus loses his eyes; Shakespeare gets pelted with stones. And that's Shigalyovism. All slaves must be equal. There was never freedom, and there was never equality without despotism, but the masses must have equality. And that's Shigalyovism. Ha, ha, ha. You are surprised. I am a supporter of Shigalyovism."

He continues: "From today, the slogan of the entire world will be 'We require only that which is essential.' What is also required is trembling. We, the power wielders, have thought of that. Complete obedience, complete annihilation of the individual. Once in a thousand years Shigalyov will cause people to tremble, and then some will begin devouring others: anything to avoid boredom. Boredom is an aristocratic feeling. Under Shigalyovism, there will be no desire. Desire and suffering are for us. For the slaves—there is Shigalyovism."

After '56, authors like Ionesco and Beckett became favorites in Poland, not to mention Kafka and Gombrowicz. Nobody wanted tragic literature anymore, which could have been devastating for writers. A writer chooses one of the most immoral professions for himself, and he has to be aware, even to a very minimal degree, of whether he lives in hell or a country of smiles. Accordingly, everybody tried to get their hands on Gombrowicz. *Ferdydurke* became what the Bible was to Dostoevsky when he was doing hard labor: the only book that political prisoners were permitted to read. As it was said, they dumbed us down. Even prior to Khrushchev, it was known that millions of people had perished in the camps. Formerly, everything had been OK. The engineers of the hearts of the people didn't know what every person on the street already knew, what every worker and everyone who didn't belong to the new privileged class knew. The escape to the ridiculous and the grotesque became the only possibility of escape from the merely ridiculous. It's better to be a jester playing before a full hall than Hamlet speaking to an empty chair.

In one of the stories published during that period, we encounter the following situation: the end of the world, only two men remain, and they torment each other endlessly. Finally one of them hangs himself out of fear that the other is about to denounce him. It doesn't matter that there is neither civilization, nor jail, nor political police.

Similarly, Russian literature smuggled into the West redeems itself with laughter. In a book by Abram Tertz, a Soviet writer dogged by unpleasant circumstances, we encounter a scene where a young man is under interrogation. "Speak to me with respect. I am only accused, not convicted," he says. The interrogator leads him to the window, beyond which extends a view of a giant square and passersby. "Those people down there are accused," says the interrogator, who is also, for all intents and purposes, the judge. "But you—you're already convicted."

In a story by a different Soviet writer, writing under the pseudonym Nikolai Arzhak, we find a young man who claims he can impregnate a woman so that she'll give birth only to sons. He is examined and treated by Soviet scientists. They take him seriously. But the people from that part of the world, how do they laugh? Let's say the explanation is simple. Nobody is ready to believe in the truth, in the cannibalism, in the inhuman suffering they had to go through. Maybe it stems from contempt for one's own self. We witnessed all this many years ago, but we weren't able to do anything about it. We looked upon the Golgotha of our brothers, and in spite of it all, we were able to sleep at night. We carried on as usual. We knew about the frostbit-

ten limbs of the people who were working in the North, and in spite
of it all, we stood in line for hours to buy ourselves warm boots or an
overcoat. We can't rend our garments in mourning, but we can laugh
at our own impotence. We will never create tragic literature, because
nobody will ever believe what we went through. The experience is
nontransferable. The residents of Paris or Milan who dream of communism will only be convinced of the abject misery of the idea when
Soviet tanks start rolling down their Paris or Milan streets. But until
that happens, we laugh. Our lives are in the hands of idiots who have
the power to murder us; at the same time, they aren't sure what their
own fate holds.

Professor Jan Kott once told his students it's futile to search contemporary literature for the types of discussions about literature and
literary heroes that we constantly find in Dostoevsky, Tolstoy, Chekhov, and Gorky. Indeed, in all of the novels published and written
after the war, we won't find a single scene in which the heroes start
arguing over a book or about the cost of a set of clothes. People who
read these books in however many years will never understand the
real value of money in our time. The escape into the world of the grotesque and the ridiculous has another, equal reason besides the first
one: a disbelief in what we ourselves have seen, and a lack of faith in
the ability of people to believe how we lived our lives. It's for a simple
reason: the absolute ignorance of other people's conditions. Ignorance of the conditions people are living under, and incompetence
in utilizing the facts even when they understand the moral aspect of
the problem. In one of these books, if the hero says, "Life is difficult,"
that's the end of it. We don't ever find out how much he needs to live,
how much he earns, or how much he'd like to earn. We don't find out
what a movie ticket costs because the writers have their own showings and screenings and don't have to stand in line for hours to get
their hands on a ticket. We don't find out how much a set of clothes
costs and how much a peasant gets when he sells a cow or a pig. This
small concern is characteristic in a sense. When we read Faulkner,
Steinbeck, or other contemporary Americans, we can more or less
imagine how people dressed, what they ate, and what they wanted
for. When you read contemporary Polish or Russian literature, you

don't get that kind of picture. Everything was better before; things are terrible now. But that's all they tell us. Whether it's in socialist realist novels or novels that get smuggled out, money has become taboo.

In our contemporary literature, money doesn't exist. In all the "outstanding" books, we won't find a single scene where the conversation is about money or what money can buy. We won't even find it in the most primitive form, like haggling over the price of a suit or a bill at a restaurant. We don't learn how much a prostitute costs, what's the cost of a used car versus a new one, or how much one pays for his apartment. In Balzac and Dostoevsky, in Chekhov, and in contemporary American writing, the heroes take out their rubles, francs, and dollars. In Polish literature today the heroes walk into a place and pay; they buy their clothes and pay. But they never ask about the price, or about whether another character is right or wrong. Literature, an important propaganda tool, is unmasked in an unexpectedly simple and transparent way. The heroes of one production novel don't give a damn about the heroes of another production novel, and that might be their only human trait. In modern works we don't even encounter what we find in Dostoevsky, who had a polemic with Turgenev and, in his own way, parodied his style. Today's writers, who write in the style suggested and lauded by the infallible party, don't even have the ambition to mask their debasement and make a lasting impression with their work.

I realize now I bit off more than I could chew when I wrote *The Graveyard*. I wanted to know what it would be like to write stories based entirely on authentic facts. As I write this, I am thirty-two years old. I've made up my mind that if I don't write a decent book by the time I'm forty, I'll do something else. I know seventeen trades. At any given moment I can work as a chauffeur, a welder, or a concrete layer. I have eight more years to keep trying. Up to now, I've written several dozen stories. Out of these several dozen, I can bear to read four of them. There's not one I really love. I like thinking about what I'm going to write; then everything seems all right. When I start writing, that's when things go downhill. The worst is when you read what you've already written and published. Then you see only the wasted idea, and you realize how you really should have written it.

Artur Sandauer tried to dissuade me more than once from publishing some stories of mine he read in manuscript, but I don't think he was right. You can't judge your own mistakes so long as the stories are lying in a desk drawer. You have to publish them, and be embarrassed by them. That's the only way to learn for the future, if such a thing is even possible.

I remember my first visit to Sandauer's place. I'd come to borrow money. Sandauer started reading me some of Białoszewski's poems. I sat there and didn't understand a thing. Finally Sandauer broke off reading.

"Do you understand?"

"No," I answered.

"Listen, please," said Sandauer, and started reading further. I sat there, and I still couldn't understand a thing.

"Do you understand?"

"No," I answered.

"Nothing?"

"Absolutely nothing."

"Listen a little longer, please," said Sandauer, and started reading again.

I looked at him, but despite my superhuman efforts, I had no idea what he was talking about.

"Do you understand?"

"No," I answered.

"Nothing?"

"Absolutely nothing."

"How is that possible?"

"I don't know," I answered.

After a few such showings, Sandauer took me for a moron and threw me out. This was when his project was to completely dissect Polish literature. He refused to give it a free pass. As far as I recall, Adolf Rudnicki was the first one he put under the gun. Sandauer read to me from his manuscript and pointed out sentences from Adolf's prose, where Adolf didn't express himself clearly enough in Polish. It surprised me that a man of Sandauer's intelligence took such pleasure from these slipups. A critic has the right to despair, but he doesn't have the right to schadenfreude. All this was happening during a terrible period, when a wave of anti-Semitism was rolling through Poland. Rudnicki never hid the fact that he was a member of the Jewish faith. I use that term consciously, because I can't simply call a person who was born in Poland a "Polish Jew." If I thought along those lines, I'd have to conclude that there is no such thing on earth as the United States of America, and that people born there aren't Americans, rather they're Jews, Portuguese, and Poles. Maybe that's primitive reasoning, but simple thinking is the only kind I'm interested in.

"What are you driving at?" Sandauer interrupted me.

"I don't know," I answered. "But I'm hoping you'll be kind enough to explain."

So he explained. This was when I'd received the Publishers' Prize, and Sandauer began to browbeat me. Naturally, he didn't give me a free pass. I had already stopped being published. My two most recent books had been rejected by publishers, and all the Marxist critics were calling me a pervert and a degenerate.

I finished *The Graveyard* and sent it to a publisher. They turned me down. I asked why.

They answered me: "Such a Poland doesn't exist."

I asked: "Shall I take the publisher's rejection as final?"

They answered me: "Yes."

Sometime later, I was talking with one of the most intelligent critics of the younger generation who used to work at that very publishing house.

"It just wasn't your thing," he told me. "Politics isn't for you. You need to grab on to what you know how to write about: a guy and a girl . . . And meanwhile, try not to think too much. In your case, it's truly unnecessary."

I approached another publisher, where I'd published my first short novel, or rather a long story, called *Next Stop—Paradise*. They refused me: "Such a Poland doesn't exist." But they offered to publish the book if I'd change just one sentence. "You've turned Poland into one big concentration camp, and there's no need for barbed wire and dogs because there's nowhere to run." I said I wouldn't cross out a single sentence. They told me the book was terrible.

I went to Wrocław, where they were making a movie out of the book. I'd given the script to Czesław Petelski, the director, who promised me he'd shoot the film exactly according to the story. I saw a few of the scenes and realized what Petelski had done. I demanded he change the title and remove my name from the credits. The changes had been made at the behest of Aleksander Ford, colonel and professor, who at that time was the artistic director of the film production company that was working on *Next Stop—Paradise*.

I've met a lot of double-dealers in my life. I've known people who sold sugar and called it morphine. I've known purveyors of "Persian" rugs woven two hours prior on Ben Yehudah Street in Tel Aviv. During the occupation I knew a type who made a heap selling flour to the Jews, telling them it was poison that would save them from suffering when there was no way out. I knew people who lived off blackmail, and I knew a firm that used to spray potassium fertilizer over crop fields, and they used such old and crappy airplanes not a single insurance company wanted to cover their pilots or their engines. However, in my entire wild ride, I've never met a man as perfectly cunning as Ford.

I can talk about him so blatantly because I know how many people, how many ideas and films the man sent to ruin. He was a sly and cunning opportunist, but he passed himself off as embittered and angered by the stupidity of the authorities. *Eighth Day* was a terrible story, but you could have made a decent film out of it. That is, if you knew how to make a film. Ford, whose knowledge of Warsaw is whatever he's glimpsed from a car window, set the action of the film in the Old City. Agnieszka hangs around the saccharine streets. Extras in tank tops stand in line and pretend to be the lumpenproletariat, ready to attack the girl. In the story, which wasn't very good, but I loved the conception behind it, there was one idea I wanted to get across: the girl, who sees the filth and horror of it all, wants just one thing for her and her beloved young man—a beautiful beginning to their love. Ford placed the focus of the film on people not having anyplace to screw. Which is obviously untrue. You can screw anywhere.

And so Ford made a film with the simple message being there's nowhere to have sex, but the truth is, it was a theme he had little knowledge of. He diligently removed all the risqué scenes. The film was supposed to bring him a prize at Cannes, acclaim from the Marxists, and light criticism from the party bosses. The film turned out shit. Unfortunately for Ford, fortunately for me. Although, that's not true, either: I ended up marrying a naive young actress from the film.

A well-known film critic asked me what I thought about the film. I hadn't seen the whole thing yet, but I knew Ford's screenplay, so I told him it was trash. Two days later, this guy quoted my exact words in the newspaper. A few days after that, a fellow from Ford's crew, the set manager, Straszewski, showed up at my place.

"I've got some unpleasant business to discuss with you," he said.

"I've never had any other kind of business in my life," I said. "Shoot."

"It's about what Bohdan Węsierski wrote in *Express Wieczorny*. About *Eighth Day* being trash."

"That's easy to fix. Just reshoot the movie, from start to finish."

"Ford will inform the press that you've never seen the film, and that you showed up drunk on the set and tried to fuck the ingenue."

"That'll be the first time Ford told the truth," I said. "But wait a minute."

I went to the cloakroom and asked a lawyer friend of mine over the telephone what to do and if this was a case of blackmail. He asked me if I had witnesses, so I told him I did. He offered me his services. My colleague, who was standing right there, warned me against it if I ever wanted to work in film again, or to travel to the West or do anything else in that vein. I got cold feet: I wrote an open letter to *Express Wieczorny* saying Węsierski had misunderstood my words and greatly apologizing to our foremost director, the master of Polish romantic film, for unintentionally causing him harm.

Eighth Day and *Next Stop—Paradise* are novellas I wrote ten years ago. I can't read them today or even hear about them. But they honestly could have made a good film out of *Next Stop*. Automobile crashes, black eyes, explosions, a heroine who gets screwed so often she's got a callous on her ass: a good film for a young viewer. But Ford carefully destroyed everything that was amusing and childish about it. I've never seen the film, I only read Zygmunt Kałużyński's and Krzysztof

Teodor Toeplitz's reviews of it. Toeplitz called it Poland through the eyes of a little boy named Marek.

During the production of *Eighth Day*, some elusive threads of sympathy began to form between me and the actress on the set. On the second day of Holy Week before Easter, we drove from Warsaw to Kazimierz in her car. It's the drunkest day in Poland because, as the saying goes, "the village is getting married." It should have taken us two hours to get from Warsaw to Kazimierz in a BMW that could have easily gone one hundred and sixty k/h. The road was full of drunken young men, drunken carters, drunken cyclists, and people chasing after one another with whips, knives, pitchforks, and other types of peasant implements Maria Dąbrowska fails to mention in her story "A Village Wedding." For a period of time, her story was considered the epitome of realism and positivism, or even romanticism. In any case, it was the epitome of something. When I arrived in Kazimierz, the sweat was pouring off me. It's not easy to drive a car through a drunken landscape. Trucks back then had a special system of relocating drunken peasants and their carts. The trucks were equipped with a special whip made from old tubing, with intertwining rubber and wire, and if the drunken peasant didn't move aside when the trucks honked the horn, the driver's assistant would jump down, crack the peasant with the whip, and take the horse by the bridle over to the side of the road. Meanwhile, the driver would somehow squeeze his truck through. Anyway, I didn't have a whip, only the innocent girl. Right before Kazimierz we had to stop the car. Before my very eyes, two drunken men had chased down a third. He fell onto the hood of the car I was driving, and they slashed him a few times with their knives. I kept driving.

"They'll fight again in three days," I said to the girl. "At the funeral."

"At the what?"

"At the funeral. Of the guy they just killed a minute ago."

"Of what guy?"

"They killed a man right on the hood of your car," I said.

She laughed. She didn't believe me. She'd seen it, yet she didn't believe it. And that's my problem with the commies: they ruined such a sweet deal for me. Every day I could glimpse despair, cruelty, and savagery, and I believed I could write about it, believed it was the truth. These days, if I want to see something that'll freeze the blood in my veins, I have to go either to the movies or to pick up girls, or to a meeting at a veterans' organization. In *The Third Man*, Orson Welles justifies his evil deeds by saying, "The House of Borgia and their government lasted thirty years in Italy. During that time there were more masterpieces of art created than can even be counted. Meanwhile, the Swiss had five hundred years of peace, democracy, and freedom. And what did they manage to produce? The cuckoo clock. Good-bye." Maybe in twenty years or so somebody will be positively touched when thinking about Stalin's actions. Today, nobody has the desire or the strength. And moreover, we shouldn't require people to believe in horror, crime, and vice.

Strange things do happen sometimes. In Roman Polański's *Knife in the Water*, an amazing film, we see a man who's going away for the weekend in his car. He has his private yacht, his beautiful wife. We can see he's loaded. On top of it all, he's young, handsome, and intelligent. In Poland, we already know all there is to know about a guy like that. Who has the privilege of a yacht, an automobile, traveling? Plus, there are the usual problems that accompany having a beautiful wife. Let's say, a fellow's having a shave in the shower, squinting his eyes to keep the soap out. In the next room his friend from the army is putting the moves on his wife, precisely when he's in a compromised position. In any case, he's a type, this guy holding all the aces. The yacht and the automobile weren't sent to him by some cousins in the States. He got them through various machinations, and that's what the Polish viewer is thinking about, feeling pangs of jealousy and self-loathing. The same film, seen by Germans, is received completely differently. A young, good-looking journalist who owns a yacht and a car isn't an object of hatred. Rather, it's obvious he's achieved everything through brains and elbow grease, thanks to his own intelligence and imagination. Meanwhile, the guy who flags down the car evokes antipathy. He only destroys: he's a rebel without a cause, and he's got no right to look down on the man who gives him a lift, feeds him, and offers him a good time on his yacht. The beauty of the film is that it offers a perfect picture of a mating ritual: two bucks do battle with each other while the doe nibbles peacefully at the grass. I'm not sure of the quote since I saw it in German, but at a certain moment the wife of the main character says to the young rebel, about her husband, "He was once like you are, and you'll be just like him." And it's true: that handsome twentysomething will one day have his own car, his own motorboat, his own refrigerator and television, and maybe a video camera, too. This is the rebel's pathetic last stand: because we aren't able to live like free men, we try to mimic the outline of their lives.

Another good movie, though not on the level of Polański's, is the Soviet film *The Cranes Are Flying*. At a certain moment, one of the main characters is playing the piano at a party in somebody's home, when he slams the lid closed and says, "If not for this damn war, I'd be sitting in the hall of the Conservatory and playing Tchaikovsky." Of course, any normal person would rather play Tchaikovsky than run through a field carrying a rifle and dodging bullets. But it's something else entirely when the war is being fought under the order of the Father of the Nation. That scene, in which the mediocre director tries to compromise one of the characters, arouses sympathy and fondness in the West. Both of the films, and the public's reaction to them, could easily have been the subject of one of Hostowiec's essays. But then, the only person Hostowiec cares about is Anna Magnani. Her films are the only ones he sees, and when she's not in a scene he sits there with his eyes closed, like me at an Orson Welles picture.

And so, in '57, everything was finished: two of my books were being held up, and I'd had two films ruined. My relationship with *Po Prostu* ended, too. I was an object of ridicule and frequent and poorly written denunciations. All the same, it's too bad what happened to *Po Prostu*. When I flip through the faded issues today, one thing catches my eye: the style of reporting, the articles, and the discourse have gone steadily downhill since '57. In its time, *Po Prostu* had a decent department for local reporting. Reading it today, I get the impression that their writers are just waiting for the end, from hour to hour. *Po Prostu* in its current form is a sign of the times. Witold Jedlicki wrote about the magazine in his book. He also wrote about the tragedy resulting from the closing of the Crooked Circle Club. I was there a few times, but only when there were topics I wanted to discuss with people face to face, and only when I could be sure I'd be able to reach the police station first and recount our conversation. The first version is usually the one that people believe: now that's a thing worth knowing. But *Po Prostu* and the Crooked Circle Club are already legends.

My last few months in Poland, I began working at a magazine called *Europa*. It never saw the light of day. It was really promising: Jerzy Andrzejewski was the chief editor, and Jerzy was at the top of his game then. Other editorial colleagues included Julek Żuławski, Zygmunt Mycielski, Janusz Minkiewicz, and Henryk Krzeczkowski. I covered film. We put the first issue together. It was good, but the Central Committee explained that the party saw no need to publish a magazine like *Europa*. We were all sitting and drinking coffee. We were in a terrible mood, and at last our trustworthy colleague Krzeczkowski got up on his feet.

"Fellows," he said, "we won't let them drive us mad."

That sentence from Henryk became the motto of my life, and it stuck. Toward the end of '57, all the scoundrels reappeared. They started writing about socialist realism again; they expelled students who demanded the next issue of *Po Prostu*. The censors latched onto Gomułka's words about the preservation of the state. My career as an employee at *Europa* was over. The year of high hopes was over, too. It coincided with the fortieth anniversary of the Great October Revolution. I remember how Janek Rojewski said, "Well, forty years gone by like the crack of a whip."

I was moonlighting a bit in film. My memories from back then aren't the warmest. It started in '54, when I went to Lodz, where the students at the Higher School of Film were making a movie called *The End of the Night*. There were a few screenwriters, and I was one of them. I met a devil of a guy there. His profile, viewed from the left, looked like a man making nasty eyes at a girl; from the right, he was the girl. They said he could play a door handle if he had to. In *The End of the Night* he had a minor role. He was a student in the directing department, not an actor himself, yet all the same no other student actors from the film school could match him. He didn't act; he simply *was*. When he entered the frame, it was obvious something was about to happen. He was a thin, nervous young man. Once, in the middle of a conversation, he grabbed a bottle from the table and threw it at me. When I asked him why he'd done it, he said he'd just wanted to check my reflexes. To this day I don't know what compelled him to do it. He never explained it, and the next moment he "plunged the ravenous glance of his pupils," to use Żeromski's brilliant formulation, into the soul of a new victim. I ran into him years later in Munich. Just for laughs, he pretended to be a Chinese detective hoping to catch a certain couple in flagrante. Climbing up a tree and peering through his binoculars at a steamy scene, he gave into the temptation that God so severely punished Onan for; he fell off the tree and broke his leg. The Chinese detective was Roman Polański.

I can't say I thought *Two Men and a Wardrobe* was particularly revelatory. Me, I still believed that only tragedy was able to teach us anything. Polański began making films that seemed grotesque back then, but which today I'd call apt invention. The two characters traipsing through the city, dragging the wardrobe behind them, didn't seem like believable characters to me at the time. Now I know each one of us drags his wardrobe through the city, and we're the only ones who know the value of what's inside. I went to see Polański's first feature film, *Knife in the Water*, with preconceived bias. However, if you were to ask me which Polish film I like most, that's the one I'd name. After seeing it, I believed for the first time that Poland had her own actors.

The school Polański studied at was the most interesting and amusing place in Poland. All the men there had their own personal style. They knew how to think; they had good taste and were well read. When I think about their German or French counterparts, I want to laugh. I don't really know what the title "New Wave" means. To this day I don't have a clue what "neorealism" is. But when I think about all those guys I knew in Lodz, with their tired faces and their velveteen pants, it makes me furious that a pipsqueak like Goddard can make films about erotic issues every teenage onanist has already settled. Meanwhile, Goddard and the others haven't made one good film. I was dumbstruck by Wajda's *Ashes and Diamonds*. What more could you pack in? Soviet tanks; veterans of the Spanish War; some little Jewish girl singing "The Weeping Willows Are Rustling" as people dance the polonaise; record players being dragged here and there; and Cybulski constantly toying with his pistol and then killing his victim, who falls at the exact moment when the sky explodes with fireworks in honor of the victory; good communists, bad communists; secret police investigations; chapels filled with corpses; roadside crosses; and terrifying Partisans. Wajda didn't understand that the book he based his film on, also called *Ashes and Diamonds*, wasn't anything special in Polish literature. Cybulski's problem is a real one. It's the Jesse James problem: to shoot or not to shoot. The way I figure, if Polański had made the film, there would have just been a bed, and on top of it, Cybulski and the girl. Outside the window, the drunken city would be celebrating. Then it would really be *Ashes and Diamonds*. There's only one other film I know that's as stupid: *Eighth Day*. But Cybulski in *Ashes and Diamonds* and Cybulski in *Eighth Day* are two completely different actors. If you watch *Ashes and Diamonds* and pay attention to how Cybulski plays with his pistol, you can't believe for a minute that this man has killed and wants to kill again. If you watch him in *Eighth Day*, you're apt to think he's a smart, decent young man, capable of real love and cognizant of its value. Cybulski saved the film. The second time I saw it, I just kept my eyes on him the whole time. My own private complexes have nothing to do with my opinion.

The most amusing man in Polish film had to be Henio Szlachet, who is already a legend today. It was Henio who first started called me "Hłaskower," to make my name more Jewish-sounding. He addressed the actor Kęstowicz as "my dear Mister Kęstower." When he called and invited me to Wrocław to do some work on the adaptation of *Next Stop—Paradise*, he said, "Hłaskower, I'm telling you: This isn't cinema, it's a cheap flick." The next day, he woke me up with the words, "This isn't a cheap flick, it's cinema." While we were out scouting locations one time, we caught a sunset. He pointed to a lake lying in a valley and said to me in a put-on Jewish accent, "Gib a look, you. Oy, how lonely, such a lake." He wanted to convey the living beauty of the landscape through vivid language.

Then there was the whole business with the cannon, which cemented Szlachet's reputation. As the director of photography in a picture about soldiers, he bought a defective cannon from the Polish Army to use as a prop. Afterward, accounting gave him a tough time about the budget numbers, and they wouldn't reimburse him for the purchase of the artillery. He was on the line for it himself, which is how Henryk Szlachet ended up owning a piece of mortar. I thought about him when I was in Israel, watching Alex Pfau shoot a documentary. A desperate producer was running after him, shouting, "Mister Pfau, I'm begging you: no monkey business!" The director didn't want to waste tape reshooting scenes. "Szlachetu" as Szlachet enjoys being called, speaks Polish just as well as Hostowiec, but everybody would beg him to put on a Jewish accent, and nobody could do it like him.

My older colleagues at the Writers' Union were constantly persuading me to go to the West for a little while, to Paris, of course. They told me to apply for a stipend from a special committee at the Writers' Union. I applied, and I got it. When I became a passport holder and had a contract with several publishers, including Julliard, Dutton Company, and Kiepenheuer und Witsch, I was set to travel. I requested my stipend. It turned out the stipend, given to me by the committee, had been withdrawn. They told me to go visit the Ministry of Culture. At the Ministry of Culture, they couldn't say anything except to confirm that the stipend had indeed been withdrawn. I asked to speak with the Minister of Culture; he received me quite affably and said that yes, the stipend had been withdrawn, but it wasn't his decision, since it had been given to me not by him personally, but by a special Stipend Committee through the Polish Writers' Union. The Minister of Culture regretted he couldn't do anything to help, and suggested I go see the Stipend Committee at the Writers' Union. The stipends fell under the aegis of the stipend fund at the Ministry of Culture, but they were disbursed by the union, and so on. Jan Wilczek, who'd formerly been Minister of Culture, was an amusing fellow. He always used to say he hated attending official funerals because, even with years of experience, he was afraid he'd slip at graveside and fall in. At least I can say this about Karol Kuryluk, who held the post at the time: he was pretty honest about lying. All the legends about him slipping and falling out of favor on my account are made up. He withdrew my stipend without knowing about my contracts with various publishers. I wasn't even given the right to buy a ticket with zlotys. I had to pay in dollars.

In '58 I received the Publishers' Prize. I received it for my two un-published books, as a sign of trust in my future. But a couple of days later I was already in Paris. My colleagues who said good-bye to me at the airport didn't think I'd be back. Not for one minute did I imag-ine I would stay gone. I had no illusions about things; I knew people were only interested in Poland as a suburb of Russia. If I myself didn't care about the young prose of, say, Bulgaria or Romania, then I wasn't ridiculous enough to demand that people forget about Camus and Faulkner and start taking an interest in Polish young prose. I wanted to see things, though. And since *The Graveyard* and *Next Stop—Para-dise* were still unpublished, and I was told I had the right to find an-other publisher, I wanted to publish my stories. Jerzy Giedroyc be-came my publisher.

I walked through Customs. The silver eagle took to the air. Houses like matchboxes, fields like chessboards—this is all cliché. Some old woman was flying with me, going to the States on an invitation from her sister. Throughout the long flight on the nearly empty plane, the old woman happily told me she was sick with cancer and was going overseas to die. I didn't believe her, but I tried to offer some consol-ing words. She showed me the doctor's note, where I read that such and such a person was ill with very advanced cancer. As a rule, doc-tors don't usually write such notes. However, the sister of my fellow traveler, obviously not very well off herself, had agreed to host the old woman under the condition that the visit not last very long. She also showed me her X-rays, which I couldn't really make heads or tails of. Obviously, she'd had a separate, falsified attestation to present to the American embassy, which said she was a person in the bloom of health. Otherwise, she wouldn't have gotten a visa. But flying at a speed of six hundred kilometers an hour on a luxury four-engine air-plane, and looking at her happy and radiant face, I thought about all those elderly people just crawling into their graves, unable to let go of their crappy habits and miserable plans. I didn't know she wasn't the only one who was setting off, going to die in a place far from Poland. I was twenty-four years old, and everybody took me for a has-been. She was probably seventy and traveling to start over in a country where she didn't know anything or anyone except for her sister. Thousands of kilometers separated her from the country where her entire life had played out. I had eight dollars on me; she had X-rays attesting that she was about to kick the bucket. So we talked. She was about as radiant as Snow White after seven abortions. I was grim and racked with doubts about how I'd manage for very long outside of Poland. I didn't know back then that the world is divided into two halves: in one of them it's impossible to live, and in the other it's impossible to survive. Sitting next to the old woman, I took a newspaper out of my pocket, and on the last page I read the following: "Two wardrobe doors for sale, glass. Awaiting best offer." I understood right then that there was more truth in those few words about the life I was leaving behind than in all the hundreds of pages of prose I'd written. And only then, on that airplane, did I realize: the emperor is naked. Feeling defeated and ridiculous, I entered a new world and a new life. On that note, I'll stop going on about the pursuit of happiness. As they say, it's almost pointless. But it's something to live for.

CHAPTER SEVEN

Hotel Victory

Once I got to Paris, I acted like a complete idiot. I don't know why I felt so hopelessly ridiculous and alone. When I walked the streets and looked at all the people sitting in cafés, laughing and drinking, I was sure I cut a miserable figure. Of course, it didn't even occur to me that I ought to go to some school and start studying French, if only so I could see for myself how I wasn't the only idiot living in Paris. I used to go to a place called Chez Vania, where Russian taxi drivers would drink Smirnoff and discuss their lost millions. Before taking a shot they'd say, "Eto vse cherez Evreiev." *It's all because of the Jews.* My Polish acquaintances used to ask me, "Have you been to the Louvre yet?" I still haven't been to the Louvre.

After *Kultura* published my book, *Trybuna Ludu* printed an article with the headline "Prima Ballerina for a Week." I won't quote the whole thing here, but it started like this: "A new name has appeared this week on the list of those connected with the international bandits engaged in weapons smuggling against the communists." I wrote a letter to the editors at *Trybuna Ludu*, explaining that since my books had been refused publication in Poland, I had the unqualified right to seek a publisher abroad. Meanwhile, I added, a reader or critic might judge the quality of my work, but not a censor. I asked them to print my letter alongside their own commentary, which I couldn't have cared less about. They never printed it, of course. Instead, all sorts of journalists showed up at my place. The dumbest ones were from the newspaper

L'Express. When they asked me what I saw as my role in literature, I answered, to bear witness. They asked what I was bearing witness to, and I said, I'm a witness in the trial against humanity. They asked if I had any intention of returning to Poland. Of course, I said: I wasn't so stupid as to deprive myself of the opportunity to see the only sort of thing I know how to write about—crime, despair, etc. In the next issue they really dug into my writing. One columnist wrote that while he valued my lyrical pessimism very highly, everything I said was untrue: before the war, Poles had emigrated for better wages, and today that's not the case at all. I was reminded of those glass wardrobe doors. There's no point in writing, I told the journalists. They asked if it was possible we'd truly understand each other one day. Soviet tanks on the streets of Paris, I said, would give us that common ground and plenty of time to talk about it, too. In prison, it's true, you work from morning until evening, but at night there's time to chat.

This was after the speech Khrushchev delivered at the Twentieth Congress. A few intellectuals left the Communist Party in France and Italy, but in the final calculation, Khrushchev obviously came out on top. His declaration and promise of de-Stalinization convinced people there was a possibility of change for the better. The principle remained the same, but the execution had been poor, that was all. In his speech, Khrushchev built up a credit of renewed trust toward the Eastern Bloc, the price of which was a few dozen embittered Western communists. The subsequent incidents in Poznan and Budapest didn't erode the trust. Quite the opposite: in some ways, they strengthened it, because on the surface, life couldn't have been so terrible if people had the courage to assert their rights. But people who'd escaped from behind the Iron Curtain told us it was really untenable. Even the supplications of the unfortunate prime minister of Hungary, who asked that nobody interfere with his execution since it exclusively concerned the people of Hungary, didn't arouse anger at and disbelief in the conditions in the Soviet Union.

I was able to think and write about all this once I was already on the other side, and these were my first impressions in the West. I stumbled into a terrible period: France, the object of admiration by Poles, a symbol of freedom and democracy, was going through a difficult time, changing leaders every minute. The Elysian Fields were surrounded by police and army units, reminding me of Ujazdowskie Avenue in '43. One day they'd stop me on the street and check my identification papers; the next day the police would be on strike. I remember sitting in the Gare Saint-Lazare station, waiting for the first morning train to Maisons-Laffitte, and I saw two young policemen bullying an old Algerian man. They were in their early twenties. He must have been about seventy. They punched him in the face, laughing and joking the whole time. The old man didn't even defend himself. Instead he thrust his face forward for the beating. I learned from the prisoners in our jails that defeated men don't avoid the whip. "It doesn't pay to anger your executioner," they said. "It's better to help him out." When I asked if it did any good, I got different answers, though everyone basically agreed it couldn't hurt. It was clear nothing was going to help. The whole art of living depended on the maximal elimination of things that might worsen the fate of the damned.

Could Jesus have known about this during his Sermon on the Mount, when he recommended turning one's cheek? Did he know his words urging mercy would become something of an unwritten rule in prison? And when he said it, was he anticipating his own fate? Did he already understand human nature so well that he could give advice to humanity to last us until the end of the world? This is what I thought about as I wandered through the streets of Paris.

I was all right with the fact that I'd never write again. The communists had robbed me of my only human characteristic: hatred. The life I saw around me was strange. The crowds on the Elysian Fields were strange to me; the Algerian man I saw being brutalized was a stranger to me; the Poles I met, who said we'd spoiled any chances we might have had behind the Iron Curtain—they were strangers to me. Nothing I read made any impression on me, and when I went to the movies in Paris, it was a much different experience than in Warsaw. At exhibitions of abstract painters I was bored as a dog; in Warsaw, we used to stop before every glob of paint and gaze pensively. As I was standing in front of a painting by Bernard Buffet, I thought about the Arsenal Exhibition in Warsaw in '55 when, for the first time, in place of tractors and bricklayers, our young painters began to paint onions, still lifes, and women. Meanwhile, I was walking around Paris and still thinking about the man trying to sell his glass wardrobe doors and waiting for the best offer. When I'd tell people about it here, they'd crack up laughing.

I had a little bit of money and I wanted to go to the States, so I went to the American embassy to request a tourist visa. On my Polish passport, though, I was restricted in my movements to "All the countries of Europe," so I went to the Polish embassy in Paris to request that they write in "All the countries of the world" instead. They welcomed me warmly and wrote what I wanted; I asked them to extend my passport.

"We'd like to help you," said the official taking care of me. "The Americans will require that your passport be valid for at least a year. As soon as your American visa is ready, come see us and your passport will be extended."

"Why can't you extend it now?" I said. "My passport is only valid until the fifteenth of October, 1958. Nobody's even around the office in October, are they?"

"The Americans have their consular regulations; we have ours."

"Can I be sure everything will work out?"

"Certainly. You'll receive your visa, we will see that your passport's extended, and you'll take your trip to the States."

"But how can I be sure you'll extend my passport?"

"You have my word of honor," the official said. We shook hands and I left. The official asked me to come back on Sunday, and meanwhile I went to the American embassy to write the obligatory statement saying I had no intention of violently overthrowing the government of the United States of America. I had to swear I wasn't mentally ill or a homosexual, give a list of the suicides in my family, and so on.

On Sunday, after wolfing down two or three cans of sardines and putting on a dark suit, I went to have dinner at the home of the official from the embassy. There was another person there who never told me his name, but from the looks of him, he wasn't a member of the inner circle of Cardinal Stefan Wyszyński, the ardent anticommunist. We began to drink; they asked me why I decided to publish my book in an enemy publishing house. I said every publisher is the enemy if you're a writer, because they delete obscene words, and if you want to wring an advance or an honorarium out of them, you've got to go on about your poor health and other problems. I suggested they ask that same question of the publishers in Poland; then they'd learn the reasons. All I knew is the Polish publishers turned me down.

The terrible drinking went on. The official held his drinks, but the operative conked out and we had to put him into a car. Taking hold of each other like old friends, we made plans to someday go to Poland and travel the forest trails the official had ranged in his Partisan fighting days. I don't know why he called me "Comrade General" the whole night. I explained to him as to a child that I was only a deserter from the reserves. I used the same lines I'd used before the military commission when they asked me if I was able to serve in the army.

"No," I told them.

"Why not?"

"Because I'm a nervous type."

"That's not an excuse."

"I stutter when I get nervous."

"That's not an excuse, either."

"How am I supposed to toss a grenade?"

"The grenades are high quality."

"Sure, but you've got to count to three before you toss them."

There was a scene at the end, as usual. The security agent was driven off, yelling, "Comrade General, I'm not like the others . . . ," and went to gather his thoughts in the Paris fog. The official and I decided we had urgent "family business" to attend to in the neighborhood of Place Pigalle. I'd never been to a proper bordello before. An old, pretty, gray-haired woman came out to greet us. Flabbergasted, I kissed her hand. My comrade was much more suave and sure of himself. Afterward, we parted with a slap on the back.

I ran into another acquaintance of mine from Poland. He called me up and asked me to come over. I went. He took me under the arm in silence and led me through his apartment. Without a word, he opened up his closet, where two suits and a pair of his wife's ugly dresses were hanging. He had probably bought them from the Jews near Saint Paul's. He also showed me his radio, his TV, his refrigerator.

"Remember how I used to live in Poland?" he asked.

"Yes," I said. "Don't worry. I'll never come back here or call again. That's what you wanted to tell me, right?"

"Yes," he said. "Think of me what you will."

"I'll do you one better. I won't even think of you."

"That would be best."

Next I went to Nice and got acquainted with the Côte d'Azur in the classic manner: I caught the clap. But I couldn't make myself understood to the porter at the hotel. When I pointed to the lower half of my body, he shook his head knowingly.

"*La femme?*" he said.

I waved my hands, trying to dispel this notion. There was a flash of understanding in his eyes.

"*Attendez,*" he said, and picked up the phone and began explaining something to the person on the other end. He gave me a key and showed me to my room. I followed him trustingly. Fifteen minutes later a black man with an athlete's build ran in and started shouting, "Hi, buddy boy!" He immediately started taking his clothes off. I tried to clear the matter up, but I had no luck. I had to pay him thirty francs for the visit, and I went to seek salvation on my own.

I spied the cupolas of an Orthodox church and had an idea for deliverance: I'd go to the priest and ask him to give me the address of a doctor. The clergyman listened to my story in a silence pregnant with disapproval and outrage. However, he agreed to go with me to a doctor and explain the source of my affliction. We walked along the streets of Nice, the priest upbraiding me, asking how it's possible that a young man could have so little respect for himself, and so on. Every one of his outbursts ended with the words, "Kak vam ne stydno, molodoi chelovek?" *Aren't you ashamed of yourself, young man?*

I walked with my head hung low. The priest stroked his beard and sermonized. We walked along the sunny streets. Suddenly the clergyman grabbed me by the arm and pointed to the doors of a certain restaurant.

"I met a girl here once," he whispered. "Gorgeous. Had an ass like a church bell."

After the doctor's visit we went to a Russian bar.

The owner was the strangest businessman I've ever met in my life. I asked how the beefsteak was.

"More like beefshit than beefsteak," he answered sneeringly.

"And the pancakes?"

"Not worth a damn, either."

"Fish?"

"Inedible."

"The steak tartare?"

"Poison."

I was trapped, but I ordered the beefsteak anyway and a bottle of mineral water. He gave me the steak and poured water in my glass. He started laughing again with a sneer.

"Even the water's phony," he said, and immediately explained. "It's all because of the Jews."

I met a gorgeous woman in that bar once. I was nursing a glass of whiskey, and I saw the young girl toss me a glance. I was self-assured. I ordered another whiskey and one for her, too. She gladly accepted it. She didn't speak English, but from her charming babble I was able to ascertain she thought I had pretty eyes, or nice hands, or maybe she was telling me I was very handsome.

"American?" she asked after a while.

"No."

"German?"

"No."

"English?"

"No."

"What then?"

"Polish," I answered victoriously.

An expression of terror and contempt overtook her face, to steal an expression from *Lady Hamilton, or The Most Beautiful Eyes in London*. She nervously grabbed her bag and ran out of the place. The owner looked at me and said gloomily, "It's all because of the Jews."

After that I went to Germany, where my friend Janek Rojewski and I frequented the nightspots. The singularity of the nightspots in Germany consists mainly of three attributes: the owners are Poles of the Jewish faith; the whores are daughters of the land of poets and thinkers; the clients are American soldiers. You would often hear people say in these places that Poles of the Jewish faith shouldn't be residing and making a living in Germany. This opinion has its truth. On the other hand, I'm not sure you can ask people who lived through six years in Auschwitz or Dachau to go and work road construction in Israel. They wouldn't withstand even two hours of work like that. But all the same, Poles of the Jewish faith working in Germany won't have a happy ending. I'm afraid one day the Germans will lose their patience, and the swastika will once again rear its ugly head.

An acquaintance of mine told me how to make money in Germany. He started selling radios and set up shop opposite a German fellow who had been running a similar store for ten years. The German paid his taxes and delivered the highest-quality goods to his clients. My acquaintance sold his goods 15 percent cheaper. After a while, the German went bankrupt, and the fellow I knew made big bucks. However, the wholesalers stopped selling to him because of the objections of other business owners, and my acquaintance racked up colossal debt. In Germany they don't send you to jail for debt if you're a business owner, because according to the calculations of the naive Germans, with business there's always the chance of recovering some money. The business was a front, and my friend was making crooked deals while he paid some poor soul twenty marks a day to sit behind the counter in the empty store, where the only thing on offer to the customers was a single vacuum cleaner and three cheap transistor radios. Not a single German would use the term "Jew," of course, and nor would I, consciously. However, they readily employ the phrase "damn Polish swine."

Rojewski and I left in a hurry. From Germany we traveled to Sicily, where we got ourselves into a real pickle. Rojewski had the habit of proposing to women every chance he got. When we arrived in Mondello at four o'clock in the afternoon, we read that a few days back, two families had gotten into a shoot-out at high noon. The shooting lasted a few hours. It was a family vendetta, and several people had been killed. Twenty years prior, some Sicilian had gone to America to make money, and before he left he promised his fiancée he'd send for her to come to the States and they'd get married. Which he never did, and the girl was left with a baby on her lap. Since then the families had been in a feud, which came to a head just as we were arriving. The romantic disposition of my friend Rojewski kept me in a state of high alert. *Nota bene*: Sicilians, who have a fondness for firearms, get worked up when you call them Italians. I saw some young men who were shooting their guns just like in the cowboy movies. They tossed a stone to the wind and fired.

We stayed with a fisherman there. On the wall, next to a picture of the Madonna with a candle burning in front of it, was a portrait of a young man in a black frame. I figured it was a family member, but one day I went to another house. Again, next to the Madonna was the same man. I thought the families were somehow related and they were both mourning the same person. But later on, when I was traveling to Taormina, I saw the man in the picture again, next to the Madonna. I asked who it was. The ne'er forgotten deceased turned out to be *Capitano* Salvatore Giuliano, killed ten years earlier by his own cousin, his *assistente*, as the Sicilians say. The career of the *assistente* didn't last long, but his rise was just as brilliant as his crash. He was poisoned in prison by people who were faithful to the *capitano*. The police, who'd ordered the *assistente* to kill his *capitano*, had put him in prison to protect him from revenge.

A few years later I was back in Sicily, and I made friends with a lot of people who'd been deported from the States. One of them told me that for many years he'd been a professional hit man. I got to know this gentleman and asked what kind of pay he commanded. After a minute, he said, "I never got more than three grand a head." He was telling me about his adventures, when suddenly he glanced at his watch and said he had to run. I got up to shake his right hand, and my shirt came open. My new pal saw the medallion I'd gotten from an American friend in Chicago: it was the Madonna, with the inscription *Our Lady of Mercy Pray for Me*. My pal kissed the medallion and walked away.

Our stay in Sicily was over. We had to get to Rome because I had in mind to go to the Polish embassy and get my passport extended. We put up at a hotel, and I went to the embassy.

"We have to ask Warsaw," they told me.

"They gave me their word of honor in Paris they'd extend my passport when I needed it."

"Wait two days."

I was back at the embassy in two days. They told me to keep waiting.

"I can't wait," I said. "My Italian visa expires in two days. I have to leave Italy. I've only got a German visa, and I can't get one from anywhere else because my passport expires in a few days."

"Go to Berlin and see the Polish Military Mission. They'll have an answer for you."

I went to Berlin. The person I spoke to there told me to return to Warsaw immediately.

"Why?" I asked. "I went to the West on my own money; I'm not here on any official mission; I'm not receiving any stipend."

"Return to Warsaw."

"My whole life you've been teaching me that we, the socialist people, are the freest people in the world," I said. "So why can somebody with an American passport travel to the West and stay there as long as he likes, while I can't? I don't want anything else for myself. But I do .want the same rights as any American or Brit."

"Am I to understand this as a refusal to return?"

"No," I told him. "But let me ask you something. If a Polish diplomat, a member of the party, gives me his word of honor, can I trust him?"

"Yes."

"The Polish consul in Paris gave me his word of honor that my passport would be extended. The consul is a party member."

"Will you return or not?"

"I'll return, but only when I want to."

"I'm giving you two days to think it over."

After two days we met again, not in the Polish Military Mission this time but in Café Kempinski. Before our meeting I'd told Janek Rojewski, who didn't have any ideas in his head back then about staying behind in the West, to come with me to the café and be a witness to the conversation. "You know what they'll write about me if I stay here," I told him. "Tell a few people we both hold in high esteem how it really went down."

Rojewski agreed.

We arrived at Café Kempinski. His Excellency was waiting for me. I introduced Janek.

"You need witnesses?" he asked.

"Yes," I said. "What's been decided in Warsaw?"

"You have to return. You'll stay two weeks in Warsaw, and then you can come back to the West again."

"What do I have to spend two weeks in Warsaw for?"

"Because there's a rumor going around that you intend to stay in the West."

"That's not my fault," I said. "I didn't spread the rumor. It's you folks who called me a spy in the papers. It's Bohdan Czeszko who wrote he didn't want to get his hands dirty by shaking mine. It's Sokorski who said I betrayed Poland."

"Return to Poland, spend some time in the city, and then come back."

"How do I know it'll really turn out that way?"

"I give you my word of honor."

"I've heard that before. In Paris."

Rojewski, who until then had been sitting quietly, suddenly fell into a rage and turned pale.

"Don't believe a single word of it," he said. "I've been to Russia. I know these people. They'll leave you to rot. Don't take their word or their promises. Either they extend your passport right here and now, or you don't go back."

I got up from the table.

"I won't say 'until next time,'" I told the diplomat. "We won't meet again."

I was wrong. Maybe we will meet again. The man I'd been speaking with was one of Europe's great specialists in intercepting defectors and sending them back to the East; a few months after our meeting, he sought asylum on moral grounds. It was granted. Nobody will ever throw him in jail for all the people he sent to their deaths. Nobody will ever take him to task for the people he destroyed, the people who spent years in prison. He'll never know hunger, because he's full of valuable information. He'll give interviews to the press, and afterward he'll probably receive some grant to go to America and see for himself that it isn't hell or a prison, but a beautiful and mighty nation. And he'll certainly write a book, in which he'll confess to making a mistake, just like Colonel Światło and Colonel Monat made mistakes. And he'll live a peaceful, pleasant life for as long as he's in the papers. But once the papers forget him, his former colleagues will remember him. That's how the career of Minister Tykociński will end.

Things weren't easy for me after I requested asylum and went through all the possible background checks in Germany. There's not much I can say about the Germans. While I was there, I had the opportunity to write a few screenplays, twice for a film, once for television. I've got nothing to say about the Germans. I wasn't afraid of them during the war, and I didn't spend any time thinking about them after it was over, but they started to really scare me after I spent some time there and saw how they live: peacefully, comfortably, and quietly. I remember a German cabbie telling me once, "The Americans betrayed us. In 1945, we had a great number of army divisions ready for battle. If we'd gone into Russia together, there wouldn't be all of this today." I left Germany because it reminded me too much of Poland: nobody wanted to know anything there, either. Some of the people I talked to were older, men in their fifties who drove around in Mercedes 300SLs. They'd been boys, maybe ten years old, during the war, and they didn't know anything about the tricks of the SS men. If they were ordered to kill, they killed. If they were ordered to live peacefully, they lived peacefully. I remember a German writer saying to me once, "Get out of here. You'll never write anything worthwhile about Germany or the Germans. I won't, either. The Germans are a subject for a locksmith, not a writer."

I lived in Munich for a while, where I met Jan Nowak, the director of the Polish division of Radio Free Europe. Director Nowak showed me a directive meant for internal circulation in the party. This is what Leon Kruczkowski had to say about me: "As we see, comrades, it's no long road from the first step in the clouds to the final step in the swamp of the imperialist secret service."* After that I went to Berlin, showed up at the Polish Military Mission, and asked for the right to return to my country. The person I talked to told me to fill out an application, warning me at the same time I'd be held legally account-able. I filled it out and I left.

I told myself, there's more to Poland than Putrament and Krucz-kowski and all those others. Poland is all those people who read my books and believed in me. So I'll go back there and stand before the judge as a spy. Let them try to prove I was in possession of top secret material, because you can't become a spy out of nothing. I'd say to them, "You all had the courage to spit on me; you had the courage to call me a spy; you ruined this country for me, the greatest country there is for a writer. My family is ashamed of me. So go ahead and fin-ish me off. I'm a lunatic, and I admit to nothing, no matter how you torture me. You had the courage to accuse me, now have the courage to convict me." Of course, I realized that nobody would believe I'd worked for enemy agents hostile to Poland. But if there's even one person among my readers who would believe it, then this book is written for him.

I didn't get a return visa. I left for Israel and decided to wait there for an answer while Warsaw made its decision. I went to the Polish consulate on Allenby Street, where they told me again that the deci-sion hadn't been made yet. I came across a lot of people of the Jewish faith who wanted to go back to Poland, but they weren't allowed in. The communists allow themselves to make mistakes, but they didn't extend that same right to the people who came to Israel only to dis-cover they had nothing in common with Judaism, with Jewish cus-toms, and with the government of Israel. These people left Poland during a time when a wave of anti-Semitism was sweeping through the country. Israel was the only place they could take refuge from

---

* This quotation is taken from the protocol of the XII Plenum of the Communist Party (October 15–18, 1958). The copy lists the date of November 1958 and is ac-companied by the notation "For party use only." The above fragment is found there on page 167. (MH)

the Poles. These people, predominantly older, couldn't bear the Israeli climate or the difficult work or the inhospitable nature of the
native Israelis. So they decided to return, but the commies wouldn't
let them. That's how they began to hate Poland and everything Polish.
And that's how Poles of the Jewish faith were humiliated and Poland
was brought to shame once again. Thanks to the commies, the cycle
of hatred came full circle, and this time it was forever.

I found a job as a construction worker. One day, in the Polish consulate, they told me that a certain Minister Bida would speak with me.
I was intrigued. A lot of people swore that Bida was the prototype of
Szczęsny, the hero of Igor Newerly's novel *A Souvenir from Cellulose*.
The Szczęsny I remembered was a warrior: he'd killed a Defa man
with his bare hands. Defa was the political police in Poland before the
war. Szczęsny was an authentic character. The old man sitting across
from me and staring intently at my passport was a bureaucrat who
had to strain himself just to give off the impression of being honest.
He asked me why I was working construction. I said I was broke. He
told me construction work wasn't fitting for a Polish writer. I asked
him why, but he didn't bother answering. He told me there was still a
chance I could return. I had to go back to Berlin and hold a press conference, where I would swear there's nowhere quite so great as Poland
to call home.

"You're asking me to take it all back? Everything I said?" I asked.
"To make fools of the people who gave me asylum and who wanted
to help me? Do I understand you correctly?"

Bida stared at me. Then he said:

"Consider for a minute whose satellites fly higher. You'll go to
Berlin, and in the same spot where you requested asylum, you'll announce that you made a mistake."

"I'll tell it to the courts in Poland."

"If you get the chance."

He gave me my passport, and I left. I thought to myself, "Things
aren't so good over in Poland if they don't have the nerve to throw me
in jail and beat me till I sing." Anyway, I didn't have anything to tell them.
For a while I kept going back to the consulate, and they kept telling me
they still didn't have an answer. I thought about serenading them with

chivalrous love ballads and knocking on their windows late at night, but I never followed through.

For a while I worked for the newspaper *Maariv*. I was hired by the paper for a month's stay in Israel with the understanding that I'd write a weekly column, and that they'd reimburse me for the trip. Immediately after I landed, I handed my ticket to the editor Philip Ben. Ben slipped the ticket into his pocket.

"Come to the office tomorrow; we'll reimburse you for the ticket."

"Better keep the money there," I said, "and I'll ask you for it on the eve of my departure. Is that all right?"

"Fine," Philip Ben said.

I began my career as a columnist: the first column I wrote was on a German film called *Rosemary*. I wrote about it because, however shabby it was artistically, it portrayed the real atmosphere of the times in Germany. And also because, back then, German films weren't being shown in Israel, and I thought, with its immense success in Germany and abroad, it would interest the Israeli reader. I wrote a few more columns. Finally, after a month, I went to the office.

"I'll be staying in Israel a little while longer. I don't have any reason to go back to Europe. I'd like to ask for the money," I told Ben.

"What money?"

"For the travel costs you promised me the paper would take care of."

"What travel costs?"

"The airplane ticket. According to the agreement."

"What agreement?"

"The one between us."

"Do you have a copy of this agreement?"

"No. It was an oral agreement, but that's as good as a written one."

I remember that scene well, because I never saw a guy have such a good time as Ben did then, when I told him that oral contracts have equal weight as written ones. Ben doubled over in laughter, and so did I. We were both laughing at my foolishness. I went out onto the street, still laughing. I'm sure Philip Ben was, too.

Next I went to the publisher who'd put out my book in Hebrew without even asking me for consent. When I asked him for a check, he told me to come back a week later. A week later, the secretary told me the publisher's mother was sick. Two weeks later, his own health began to fail. After the third week, he was called up to the army. Two months after that, he was bankrupt. I went to see a lawyer, who told me to bury the issue and forget it.

Those were tough times. I left my construction job because I was counting on returning home, and because Bida, that prototype for a literary hero, told me not to work construction. Even today I don't know why construction work is a shameful business for a Polish writer. It was actually excellent work. The people who worked there had belonged to the Stern Gang, and during break time they'd tell me stories of bombings, terror, and the death of Stern, whom Wańkowicz wrote such stupid things about. After '48 all of them were deemed *personae non gratae*. It was similar to what happened in Poland with the Home Army. The terrorists did their job, the terrorists battled bravely against everybody, and then they were relegated to the scrap heap.

I wasn't working construction anymore. Once Janek Rojewski, my pal and bosom buddy from childhood, became licensed as an architect, he couldn't be seen with the likes of me. And so began a period of hunger. After ten days without food, I started having hallucinations. I remember walking to the beach one evening and spotting some old woman putting down her binoculars and heading into the water. I filched the binoculars and went to the porter at a hotel where I'd once lived.

"Listen," I told him. "I've got a few days left in me. Give me a room. I just want to die in a bed. The binoculars and my shoes are yours."

I had a great pair of shoes I'd bought in Berlin at a store called Budapest. The porter sized me up like a pro.

"All right. The owner of the hotel is in America. I'll take the shoes and the binoculars now. You'll get room number one."

Room number one was right next to the shitter. At one point it had been a full bathroom, but the owner of the hotel realized he could make another room out of it. The shitter was separated by thin cardboard walls, and I went there to die. I was so sure I was going to die that I handed over my shoes and the binoculars, and then I lay on the bed in my clothes. I didn't even have the strength to undress. I didn't feel troubled, or depressed, none of those things you read about. I only knew I was going to die. The porter brought me a pitcher of water. Waking up from time to time, I'd drink the water and immediately fall back to sleep. I had hallucinations, but they were always cheerful, pleasant visions. When Dostoevsky writes about his heroes, he says they're sick people with extremely expressive and torturous dreams. I wasn't sick. I was healthy as a bull, and I was dying of hunger, at twenty-five years old, six feet tall, and a hundred and seventy-five pounds on the scale. Now and then the porter would come in, and he'd quietly approach the bed and lift up my eyelid. Then he'd walk out. I'll never forget his hand, lifting my eyelid with such a practiced movement. I saw a scene once like that in *The Asphalt Jungle*. A gangster approaches a fellow he's just shot and lifts the victim's eyelid. After that he goes back to gabbing with his friends, and nobody says a word about the dead man.

And then one day the porter woke me up. He gave me a cup of coffee strong enough to wake the dead and a roll with smoked meat. I fell asleep again, but he came back after an hour, pouring coffee into my mouth and talking for a long time. I couldn't understand a thing. Finally he said that the American consulate was looking for me. Somehow they had some money intended for me and I had to go pick it up. He brought a hot meal and fed it to me.

"All right," I said. "I've got to go pick it up. Let me have the shoes."

"What shoes?"

"My shoes!"

"But you gave those shoes to me."

"But I told you I was about to kick the bucket. And I didn't."

"That's got nothing to do with me," he said. "I've seen your kind before. I was sure you'd kick the bucket. I sold the shoes."

"Well, I can't go to the American embassy in my socks."

"How was I supposed to know? You said you were at the end of your rope. I did you a favor."

"But I'm alive."

"That's your problem. When you came here, I thought you were going to croak after three days. It was lucky the owner had gone to

America; otherwise, you'd have had to go lie on the beach."

Finally, the porter went and borrowed a pair of shoes from some missionary. The holy man's shoes pinched my feet, but somehow I crawled to the consulate. I got my check and had to go buy a pair of shoes. The salesman was an acquaintance of the porter at the hotel. While I was sitting in the store and trying on shoes, I noticed a man I'd never seen before. He was sitting across from me, mimicking me. He had a sunken face, wild eyes, and a two-week growth on his chin. When I put the shoe on my right foot, he did the same. When I got up to see how they felt, he got up, too.

"Misha," I said to my porter. "Tell that guy to fuck off. You've got to do it, because I don't know Hebrew."

The porter and the salesman looked at me, and the guy sitting opposite looked at me, too. And all four of us were quiet for a minute. But of course, there were only three of us. It was like a scene from a bad story or film. This isn't fiction, though. It's just an attempt to explain some things to a few people. I owe it to them.

For a while I lived with my friend Dyzio T., a young scientist and superlative drunk. One would think that the Holy Land, stomping ground of Jesus Christ, Barabbas, and King David, has seen everything. But Dyzio managed some new surprises. I remember once we were walking along Ben Yehudah Street. It must have been a hundred and four degrees outside, and Dyzio announced our next mission: downing a bottle. We walked into a bar. It was even hotter there, and the sweat was pouring off us with every glass. When we finished the bottle, Dyzio said, "You know, I really didn't want that vodka."

"Then why'd we drink the whole bottle?" I asked.

"It just seemed like the thing to do."

There was this terrible incident, too: After stepping into a bar on HaYarkon Street, I ordered a glass of cognac. A woman came over and sat down next to me. She wanted a round, too. I said I was broke and told the barman I'd only pay for myself. I ordered another drink, then a third. The young woman kept up with me. When I finally got the bill, the barman rang me up for six drinks.

"Nothing doing," I told him. "I warned you I was only paying for myself."

The barman gave me a clean bill. I reached for the ashtray to snuff out my cigarette, but the angry prostitute pushed the ashtray away.

"For customers like you, even the ashtray's beyond your means," she said.

"But you're not," I answered her, and put the cigarette out on her cheek.

And I was arrested. A few years later I read that my beloved Humphrey Bogart had gotten himself into a similar situation once. The judge asked him, "Sir, were you drunk?" and Bogart stared back at him with a look of high concentration on his face. Then he said, "Who the hell *isn't* at four in the morning?" When they let me out of jail, *Maariv* printed a picture of me standing between two policemen. The picture brought me sympathy and fame. After a while, when I married Sonja Ziemann, some savvy German journalists bought the picture and got it into all the tabloids with the caption "And you think you can change him?" The question was directed toward my wife.

It was hard to find work back then, especially if it was under the table. A huge number of immigrants had arrived from the Eastern Bloc. Many of them were old, and a third of them were doctors. Walking along the streets of Tel Aviv, you'd see placards with doctors' names hanging on every gate. It was hard to find manual labor in Tel Aviv and Haifa. My friends advised me to go to Eilat, since even if I didn't find work, they said I'd like it there, because Eilat's a lively place.

When I got off the plane, it was hard to tell right away if Eilat was an attractive place or not. I hadn't taken ten steps when a young man approached me.

"Are you Hłaskower?" he asked me.

"That's me."

"I've seen your picture in the paper," he said. "Come to such-and-such a bar tonight."

My new acquaintance was waiting for me there with two other people. One of them, I learned, had been a tank commander in '48, during the war. After receiving attack orders, he plowed through some Arab bank and with a couple of stiff shots smashed the reinforced safe and disposed of a few clerks. Then, cash in his pockets, he carried out his mission. The other one had been a successful contraband runner. He shot dead two Arabs during a street altercation in Jerusalem. He claimed they'd provoked him. Both found themselves in Israel after deserting the Soviet Army and committing a series of armed robberies and murders on German territory. Another man, a resident of the merry city of Eilat, took a seat at our table. As an NKVD officer, he'd killed every member of the Ukrainian family who'd betrayed his own family to the Germans. He fled through Poland and Czechoslovakia to Germany. But the most terrifying of all was yet another fellow, who came to the table and didn't say a word about himself, but whose story I read in the papers later. He was born in Poland and immigrated to Israel. A while later he learned that the German who had murdered his family was serving in the Foreign Legion. He fled from Israel to France without a passport, joined the Legion, and during the war in Indochina he killed the man who'd murdered his family. Then he deserted the Foreign Legion and returned to Israel as a stowaway on a ship. There were several charges against him. In Israel, he was charged with illegally crossing the border and serving in a foreign army. Meanwhile, France was calling for his extradition so he could be tried for deserting the Legion and settling his account with the SS man. We drank a few rounds, and another fellow joined us. The son of wealthy American parents, he'd had the bright idea to rob a bank. He was caught and sentenced to fifteen years. He escaped from prison and fled, via Mexico and South America, to Israel.

All of these men were in Eilat against their will. The police had sent them there for three or five years. All the people I met looked ten years older than they actually were. Their hair and their teeth fell out quickly. A few of them had become monstrously fat. Others had dried up, and their faces were worn like old leather. They'd take two salt tablets with each meal. In that climate, a man sweats out everything fast. During the day they'd drink massive amounts of beer; at night, cognac. Back then there wasn't even a movie theater in Eilat, but there were clubs where people played cards. These people's curse was that there were no women around. European women didn't want to go down there, because after two years they would have turned into old women, and as for the Sabras, they didn't have the least desire to associate with criminals.

When I was there, the temperature got up to one twenty, but they told me it could get even hotter sometimes. And they drank like sailors. The men who worked in the copper mines would get their checks on payday and go straight to the bar. They'd give the bartender their paycheck and tell him, "Let me know when it runs out." Room and board were free. A few of them saved their money so that as soon as they stopped being wards of the police they'd be able to start a new life. But it would always end the same way: they'd be depressed as hell about the fact that there were no girls, no movies, no entertainment. They'd go and gamble and then, after a while, they'd have nothing left and start to save again. At least there were no taxes.

I couldn't find any work in Eilat. The bus I came back on passed through Be'er Sheva, and I ended up staying for a few days with a friend of mine. I'd jumped into the heart of madness: it was just around that time that the so-called "black" Jews began to protest against the "whites." The blacks were in a bad place: they were Sephardim who maintained their Arab customs and were struggling both with their trades and with the language. They got lower-paying jobs than the Jews from Europe or the ones born in Israel. When I got off the bus in Be'er Sheva, things were hot. Furious blacks chased after me for two days with their knives, shouting "*vas-vas.*" They didn't speak Yiddish, of course, and the only word they knew in that language was *vas*—literally, *what.* They called all the white Jews, the Ashkenazim, "*vas-vas.*" They destroyed the post office and cut the telephone lines. The police finally got the situation under control, and things quieted down again. Similar incidents occurred in Haifa, too. Tired out from my forty-eight-hour chase through the streets of the city, with knife-wielding Sephardim at my heels, I gave up on finding work in Be'er Sheva and went back to Tel Aviv.

Once again I made my way to the Polish consulate. There was no visa for me. The Russians I talked to about all this visa business implored me not to go through with it. "The communists don't forgive," they told me. But I was deaf and blind: I wanted to return to Poland and stand before a judge, accused of espionage. That was my idea for how I wanted to spend my life. They had the courage to call me a spy, but they didn't have the courage to put their money where their mouths were. When I think about it today, cowardice seems like their only human trait.

Jurek, a friend of mine from Warsaw, found me work. And what a job it was; namely, in a fiberglass factory. Outside, the temperature would rise to a hundred and twenty degrees; inside, it was like a blast furnace. The worst of it were the bits of fiberglass floating in the air that would pierce right through our shirts and overalls and embed deep in our skin. We used talcum powder on the blisters, so we looked like the extras who played lepers in *Ben Hur*. After working the night shift, I'd go down to the beach in the morning and try to dry out my skin in the sun. It didn't help much, since once it stopped burning, it started to itch. Or maybe it was the other way around. I claimed it burned; my foreman claimed it itched. I worked under an assumed name in the factory because, as a "tourist," I didn't have the right to work. At night, I'd talk with my foreman, who came from Hungary. I told him all sorts of secrets about my pretend family life, my troubles with my wife and daughter. After a while, I was so into the role that I kept inventing new ups and downs in my marriage, and of course, I was doing all this under the name Jerzy Buchbinder-Press. People would listen and give me advice about what to do with my wife and daughter, and I kept thinking up new misadventures. That's how we spent our evenings. When I finally quit and found myself a different job, I couldn't get used to the fact that I didn't have a wife and daughter anymore, and I continued telling stories of family troubles. I think Jurek Press will forgive me if he ever reads this, but I don't know if his wife will: Hania never had a clue that for a while there she was married to two men.

I'll never be able to write any objective, meaningful commentary on Israel for the simple reason that the people there saved my life. When I didn't have what to eat, they gave me work at a factory, even though everybody knew I was working under false papers. Another time, they gave me a job in construction under the guise of a work program for the mentally ill. In my case, it was considered work therapy. I worked alongside schizophrenics and alcoholics. People who had just arrived from Poland helped me, even though their situation wasn't much better and they had the right to hate any and every ethnic Pole. Many of them came here just to discover that at heart they were Poles, not Jews, but the commies wouldn't let them return.

Herling-Grudziński, in *A World Apart*, writes about a performance by a sailor who sings the song "The Great Wide Sea." The performance takes place in a Soviet labor camp. Nevertheless, the people who sing along with the sailor experience a sense of nostalgia and longing for their country. It's a country they've been separated from, a country of terror, hunger, and despair. I observed a similar scene in Israel; there was a character who, as a rule, always introduced himself like this: "Captain Abkarov, retired officer of the Department of the Interior." He sang Lensky's aria from *Eugene Onegin* in a lyrical tenor. One resident of Eilat, sitting at night on the terrace of a restaurant in only a short-sleeved shirt, liked to sing: "So much, so very, very much of life has passed by, on land and sea, but we never forgot our Soviet homeland." My Polish friends usually sang songs from the repertoire of Mieczysław Fogg. Only the people who arrived from Germany never, ever sang. When I'd say to people, "Why did you come here?" they'd always give me the same answer: "Because they let us out."

Their assimilation in Israel wasn't easy. The Sabras weren't crazy about the newcomers from Eastern Europe. They were ashamed of the massacre of the Jews and their meekness during the war. When the Polish consulate put together an exhibit on the anniversary of the Warsaw Ghetto Uprising, I went to have a look with a pretty Sabra girl.

"Look, Esther," I said. "This is more or less what it was like."

She glanced for a second at the photographs of children who'd been shot and people who'd been marched to the gas, and then she said, "We're late. I want to see the new Monty Cliff movie."

In the movie theater across the street they were showing the film *Suddenly, Last Summer*, with Montgomery Clift and Elisheva Taylor. Taylor, as is well known, converted to the religion of Moses during the making of the film, before she married. She went from Elizabeth to Elisheva, which the Israeli press celebrated. I was walking through the city market where a man who sold women's undergarments was hawking bras in the bust sizes of beloved film stars. He was giving the following pitch:

"Lollobrigida yesh! Silvana Pampanini! Mansfield yesh!" *We've got Lollobrigida. Silvana Pampanini. We've got Mansfield.*

He paused for effect and stretched out a brassiere to its massive full size, yelling, "Elisheva Taylor, shesh lira, yesh. Ayzeh likvidatsia! Ayzeh likvidatsia!" *We've got Elisheva Taylor, six lira. What a sale! What a sale!*

Esther went to take a look at Elisheva's bust, and I stood for a minute in front of the photos. People who'd just come over from Europe, too, stopped to have a look. Strapping young men who modestly called themselves Sabras walked by indifferently. They themselves, filled with contempt for life and ready at any moment to die for Israel, weren't about to choke up for the helpless people who went without resistance to their deaths. The European immigrants didn't garner their sympathy. Being used to hard physical work, they disdained all those immigrants who tried to find jobs in stores, offices, or hospitals. In principle, there was only one way to garner the sympathy of the Sabras: through hard work. A man who was afraid of the sun and physical exertion couldn't expect that a true Israeli would ever call him *chevra-man*, or buddy boy.

But it wasn't as simple as that, as far as work was concerned. I remember going with a friend once to a job. He was a talented young journalist from Katowice. Our work was simple: we had to pour concrete thresholds. You started with a mold that weighed around 150 pounds, and you poured around twenty pounds of concrete into it. Then you put it to the side and waited for the concrete to dry. We started at five in the morning, and we had to stop by ten. My friend couldn't take the work.

I went to work without him and started loading the damn thresholds onto a truck. But I was working with Arabs, who were scared like hell of competition. The job was so terrible, though, that even the Sabras wouldn't try for it. All the same, the Arabs were afraid of every new man, since that was how they put bread on the table. Well, one of them let a concrete block drop on my hand, and at twelve in the afternoon I had to leave work and go to the hospital. The doctor asked me what happened, and I told him it was a work injury. He asked me where I worked. I told him I couldn't say, because I didn't have official papers and I didn't want to cause any trouble for my boss. The doctor looked at me and I was ready to run, but he ordered me back and silently examined my arm.

"Now it's you who's going to be in trouble with the law," I said.

Without looking up from the X-ray, he said to me, "It's clear you're not a Jew. Otherwise you wouldn't say such stupid things. Jews are always in trouble with the law, but it's hardly a result of their own initiative. Where are you from?"

"Poland."

"Interesting," he said. "I had a patient yesterday who'd been working for your secret police before he escaped. Here, the people he'd snitched on back home—they escaped earlier than he did—they got ahold of him and carved him up. Now he's got to run again. He'll end up somewhere where others will find him—others, who escaped even earlier than the ones who found him here. It'll never stop."

He examined my hand. Two months later I was back there again. This time, I'd hurt my hand myself because I hadn't wanted to wear protective gloves while operating a grinding machine. Again, while working under the table, of course. The doctor looked at my hand, and I wouldn't tell him where I was working, just like the first time. It was always like that, and somebody always helped me. Once, I had a job at a surveying company. The family of the fellow who found me the spot had been betrayed during the war by profiteers.

I'd run across the fields carrying my poles, and my boss would yell something at me from far away.

"I can't hear you," I'd yell back.

I waved my hand. From a quarter mile away, I ran up to him.

"Up you!" he shouted, trying to speak to me in Polish. "You didn't run the wire correctly."

"You're saying it wrong, sir. It's not 'up you,' but 'up yours,'" I told him cheerfully, and took off under the hot sun. That job had an extra appeal; namely, snakes. You had to wear tall boots to protect yourself from various reptiles and amphibians. An Englishman worked with me for a while. He used to kill the snakes with his bare hands.

"The fucking snake," he'd mutter, in English.

"What's he saying?" my boss asked me.

I cupped my hands up to my mouth and shouted the translation to him across the field.

"What's that?" my boss called back.

I ran across the field again, feeling the sweat pour down my body. I had to run, though. My boss was a curious man who needed to know immediately what the Englishman and I were talking about. So I ran.

"He said, 'The fucking snake,'" I yelled when I was a hundred yards away from my boss.

"You say he not to lift a muscle unless he's working," he shouted back.

"Tell him, not 'say he'!" I yelled.

"What the hell?"

I'd shout back, cupping my hand to my mouth and correcting his sentences. And so the days passed. In the evenings my boss was always in good humor. We usually worked fourteen hours a day. The boss woke us up at three in the morning, and we worked till dusk. One day, when we were doing some surveying outside of Tiberias, my boss came running across the field, brandishing a newspaper in his hand.

"They caught him!" he howled. "They caught him!"

"Who?" I asked.

"Eichmann," my boss said. Everyone ran in, and we all started to read the newspaper report about Eichmann's capture. I stood off to the side, smoking a cigarette. My boss looked at me threateningly.

"You won't pull any fucking tricks on me," he said. "You're a *sheygets*. Get back to work."

My boss's family had been murdered by my fellow Christians. He had every reason to wring my neck, but he never did. That's why everything I write about Israel can never be "apt invention." I owe too much to the people there. It's impossible for me to be objective: the very fact that I'm alive, I owe to them. That's something that matters to me, though not necessarily to others. People whose nation had been massacred by my fellow Christians saved my life, and that's not something I can be objective about.

I was living in the Hotel Victory back then, where the rules were primordially simple. When you walked in, you undressed in the corridor and gave your clothing and personal items to the porter, who locked them up. You entered the main hall in just your underclothes. You gave your things to the porter since a few of the hotel's clients made a living by their sticky fingers. The professional thieves never stole from one another, but one day a young upstart who wasn't familiar with criminal etiquette complicated things.

I'd been at the surveying firm, but then I started working at a film company. The company didn't have an office. They held court at Café Noga. The president was a guy named Zyskind, and Fishbayn was the VP. The shareholders of the company were Café Noga's waiters and regulars. When the firm couldn't pay for their coffee, they promised the waiter a share of future profits. The company flourished like that. I received my salary in alcohol. I worked as an actor, a scriptwriter, an adviser to President Zyskind on artistic matters, and obviously, I was a shareholder, too.

I used to sit in the café, completely sauced, drinking away my salary, constantly revising a screenplay. At first it was a film about Eichmann, then I ditched Eichmann for a drama about a Sabra girl who marries a rich American and longs to go back home. Then the president told me to come up with something funny, preferably with some swimming scenes, because then the girls in the movie could take off their clothes, and the public really goes for that. That turned into a story about the lives of fishermen in Eilat. From there, I rewrote it into a bloodcurdling tale of profiteers during the war who sell aspirin to the Jews, pretending it's potassium cyanide. Four days later we decided on a story about a unit of Israeli soldiers sitting smack in the middle of a minefield. That became a story about a good German who comes to Israel to atone for the guilt of his family. After making some necessary changes, it turned into a story about a girl who gets in a family way, leaves her kibbutz, and becomes a streetwalker.

When the talk was about money, things could get touchy. I wasn't supposed to know too much. The president and the vice president would retreat to the shitter and lock themselves in there, counting their future profits. When they'd resolved the issue, they'd come back to the sitting area. A few years after all of this, I was invited to London by one of the most famous directors in the whole world, who decided he wanted to become a producer as well. At one point during our meeting he excused himself and went off with his financial point man to the shitter. They talked for a half hour. It was another case where I wasn't supposed to know too much. It's too bad that a good film is always a child of chance, and never a question of intelligence and vision. When I was on-site for a film in Madrid, the producer, his secretary, his financial adviser, and I all worked together in one room. Also present were two agents representing the interests of their Hollywood clients. If, let's say, I was working on a certain scene that was supposed to feature actor X, actor Y's agent would protest, complaining that the scene was too long and it would make actor X too popular with the public. The director would get pissed, but he was dependent on dozens of idiots who represented the actors, producers, banks, etc. I don't think I can say how good films ever get made, and I doubt there's anybody who really can.

I was sitting in my swim trunks in the Hotel Victory one day, having a friendly conversation with some card sharks, when I noticed my once and future wife walking up to the hotel. Two years before, we'd had a nasty split-up. I had just finished shaving, and I still had my electric razor and a sorry excuse for a towel. I put them down on the table to greet this angelic woman, then turned around: my razor and the ratty towel were gone. Someone pinched the whole deal, taking advantage of my brief moment of euphoria. All I had left was my wife. I looked at her, hopeless romantic that I am, and made some quick calculations regarding my feelings. After coming to the conclusion that I had nothing against West German currency, I decided I'd marry Sonja a second time.

I left Israel and stopped thinking about the commies. I had more important issues to deal with. The German occupation, which ended so many years ago for everyone else, began all over again for me.

Glossary

While the following Glossary is not comprehensive, it represents an effort to include the most important characters—human and nonhuman alike—mentioned in this book, without being cumbersome or difficult to use. All under- and oversights are mine alone. —R.U.

Adenauer, Konrad (1876–1967), Chancellor of West Germany from 1949–63, and a founder of the Christian Democratic Union.

Admiral Ushakov, 1953 film by Soviet film director Mikhail Romm.

Andrzejewski, Jerzy (1909–83), Polish novelist and short story writer. His 1948 novel, *Ashes and Diamonds*, is considered one of the great works of postwar Europe; Andrzej Wajda based his 1958 film of the same name on it.

Arzhak, Nikolai (1925–88), pen name of Russian writer, translator, and dissident Yuli Daniel, who, along with Andrei Sinyavksi, was put on trial in 1965 for anti-Soviet activity.

Berman, Jakub (1901–84), Polish communist in charge of the Polish secret police from 1944–53.

Białoszewski, Miron (1922–83), Polish writer, author of nearly a dozen books of poetry.

Bierut, Bolesław (1892–1956), president of Poland after World War II, hard-line Stalinist and former security forces agent. He had many pseudonyms, including Tomasz, Jerzy, and Rutkowski. Born Bolesław Biernacki.

Borejsza, Jerzy (1905–52), brother of Józef Różański. Writer and communist propagandist, and founder of publishing house Czytelnik, one of the largest and most influential presses in communist Poland, and still in existence today. Born Beniamin Goldberg.

Borowski, Tadeusz (1922–51), Polish writer, poet, and journalist. He was a prisoner at Auschwitz and later wrote a collection of short stories based on his experiences. Entitled *This Way to the Gas Chambers, Ladies and Gentlemen*, it has become a European classic. After the war he became an ardent communist, but eventually became disenchanted with the regime and committed suicide.

Bossak, Jerzy (1910–89), Polish documentary filmmaker and journalist.

Brandys, Kazimierz (1916–2000), Polish writer, essayist, and screenwriter. An editor at *Nowa Kultura* from 1956–60, he also wrote many novels, among them *Samson*, which was among the first works in Poland to deal with the Holocaust. He quit the Communist Party in protest of the treatment of philosopher Leszek Kołakowski in 1966 and in 1978 left Poland permanently, settling in Paris, where he died.

Brodzki, Stanisław "Staszek" (1916–90), Polish journalist and cultural editor of *Trybuna Ludu* from 1948–57. Served as president of the Association of Polish Journalists from 1956–57.

Broniewski, Władysław (1897–1962), Polish poet, translator, and revolutionary writer. He fought in the Polish-Bolshevik War. A revolutionary lyricist and immensely talented writer, he was one of the most beloved poets of his generation.

Brycht, Andrzej (1935–98), Polish journalist, writer, and poet, and member of the "Contemporaries," a literary movement in the late 1950s in which Hłasko and Marek Nowakowski were often grouped as well. Works include *Time without Maria: Poems* and *Dancing in Hitler's Quarters*.

Brzozowski, Stanisław (1878–1911), Polish writer, philosopher, publicist, and literary and theater critic. One of the most influential Polish philosophers of all time, known for his concept of the "philosophy of labor."

Čapek, Karel (1890–1938), Czech writer, novelist, and dramatist known for his work in science fiction, and for introducing the word "robot" into modern languages. He was an outspoken critic of Nazism and fascism.

Chapaev, Vasily (1887–1919), a celebrated Red Army commander during the Russian Civil War, and a Soviet national hero. Chapaev is the subject of a 1923 novel by Dmitry Furmanov and a 1934 film by the Vasilyev brothers.

Cherkasov, Nikolai (1903–66), Soviet actor and recipient of the 1941 Stalin Prize, known most famously for playing the title roles in Sergei Eisenstein's films *Alexander Nevsky* and *Ivan the Terrible*.

Chessman, Caryl (1921–60), American criminal who gained celebrity after being convicted on multiple rape, robbery, and kidnapping charges. Sentenced to death, he was granted several stays of execution. The final one arrived minutes too late: the telephone rang outside the San Quentin gas chamber with news of another stay of execution after the room had already filled with fumes.

Cotton, Jerry, a fictional character in crime novels written by various authors and popular throughout German-speaking countries. Debuted in 1954, Jerry Cotton was an FBI agent in New York City.

Crooked Circle Club (1952–62), a gathering place for intellectuals and freethinkers to engage in discussion that was often otherwise taboo or suspect. Named after the street where its meetings took place, Ulica Krzywego Koło [Crooked Circle Street].

Cybulski, Zbigniew "Zbyszek" (1927–67), legendary Polish actor best known for playing nonconformist rebels on the Polish silver screen after the war. Cybulski and Bogumił Kobiela were two of the founders of the alternative and independent student-professional Bim-Bom Theater in Gdańsk, established around 1954. Died after slipping and falling under a speeding train at the Wrocław train station.

Czeszko, Bohdan (1923–88), Polish screenwriter, author, and member of the Polish Sejm from 1965–80. His novel *A Generation* was the basis for Andrzej Wajda's first film, of the same name. Czeszko also wrote the screenplay for the film.

Dygat, Stanisław "Staś" (1914–78), Polish writer and journalist best known for his 1946 novel, *Lake Constance*.

Dymsza, Adolf (1900–1975), one of the most popular Polish film and theater actors and cabaret performers, through the forties, fifties, and sixties, known for his comedic and lighthearted style. Born Adolf Bagiński.

Dzerzhinsky, Felix (1877–1926), Russian founder and first director of the Cheka, the Soviet secret police. Under "Iron Felix," tens of thousands of citizens and soldiers were executed or tortured to death without trial. Enjoyed the admiration of both Lenin and Stalin for his revolutionary fervor and ideals.

Express Wieczorny, popular Warsaw daily founded in 1948. It was in this newspaper that Wiech's stories appeared.

Fejgin, Anatol (1909–2002), Polish communist who gained infamy as a high-ranking official in the secret police.

Fogg, Mieczysław (1901–90), one of the most popular Polish singers of the twentieth century. He gave more than 16,000 concerts over the course of his career. Born Mieczysław Fogiel.

Ford, Aleksander (1908–80), Polish film director and professor at the National Film School in Lodz. Roman Polański and Andrzej Wajda were among his students. He left Poland after the 1968 anti-Semitic campaign and finally settled in Florida, where he eventually committed suicide after a long decline in his career. In addition to *Eighth Day of the Week*, his films included *The Street Legion* and *Majdanek: Cemetery of Europe*; his final film, *The Martyr*, produced in 1975, is based on the life of Dr. Janusz Korczak. Born Mosze Lifszyc.

Frykowski, Wojciech (1936–69), Polish actor and writer. One of five people killed by followers of Charles Manson at Roman Polański's Beverly Hills home.

Gałczyński, Konstanty (1905–53), Polish poet who became known for his absurdist short satirical pieces called *The Green Goose Theater*.

Giedroyc, Jerzy (1906–2000), legendary Polish writer and activist. Founder of the influential Paris-based émigré journal *Kultura*. The journal was one of the leading forums for prominent Polish intellectuals.

Gombrowicz, Witold (1904–69), Polish novelist and dramatist who found himself stranded in South America at the outbreak of World War II; he would never go back to Poland. Though many of his works were banned in Poland during his lifetime, he is one of the foremost Polish writers of the twentieth century. His works include *Ferdydurke, Pornografia*, and *Trans-Atlantyk*.

Grzybowska Square, in the old Jewish quarter in Warsaw.

Guzy, Piotr (1922–), Polish writer who emigrated to London in 1957 after being investigated by the secret police; later worked for BBC and Radio Free Europe.

Herling-Grudziński, Gustaw (1919–2000), Polish writer, journalist, and soldier. Best known in the West for his personal account of life in the Soviet gulag, *A World Apart*, published in 1951.

Hersey, John (1914–93), American writer and journalist, and one of the founders of "New Journalism." *The Wall*, published in 1950, is a fictional account of the rise and fall of the Warsaw Ghetto.

Hertz, Paweł (1918–2001), Polish poet, essayist, literary critic, translator, and publisher.

Hofmokl-Ostrowski, Zygmunt (1873–1963), renowned Vienna-born Polish lawyer.

Irzykowski, Karol (1873–1944), Polish writer, film theoretician, literary critic, and chess player. Though little known outside of Poland, his 1903 experimental novel, *Pałuba*, is hailed there as a forerunner to modernism.

Iwaszkiewicz, Jarosław (1894–1980), Polish poet, dramatist, and writer who served in various official posts as a liaison for the arts. He has been widely criticized for opportunism under the communist regime, including for attacking Miłosz after the latter defected.

Jasiński, Jakub (1759–94), Polish-Lithuanian general and poet who fell in the Kościuszko Uprising of 1794 against Imperialist Russian and Royal Prussian forces.

Jedlicki, Witold (1929–95), Polish activist and intellectual. Member of the Crooked Circle Club and active in the Solidarity Movement.

Kaczmarek, Czesław (1895–1963), Polish Catholic bishop arrested and tortured by the secret police. Brought to trial in 1953, he was convicted on trumped-up charges of collaborating with a Vatican-Washington conspiracy, and even of collaborating with the Nazis. Sentenced to seventeen to twenty-two years in prison, he was freed in 1955 and rehabilitated.

Kadochnikov, Pavel (1915–88), actor and cult figure in Russian cinema. He frequently played patriotic roles.

Kameralna and Krokodyl, two fashionable Warsaw restaurants/banquet halls. Kameralna was located on Foksal Street; Krokodyl was in the Old City. Writers, journalists, and the upper classes frequently gathered there.

Kariera [*Career*], Polish literary journal.

Kasperczak, Janusz (1927–2002), Polish boxer, Olympian, and first postwar European champion.

Koestler, Arthur (1905–83), Hungarian novelist, essayist, and journalist; his novel *Darkness at Noon* was one of the most influential anti-Soviet books ever written. It is widely considered one of the greatest novels of the twentieth century.

Kolyma, region in northeast Russia, host to many of the Soviet Union's harshest gulag labor camps.

Konopnicka, Maria Wasiłowska (1842–1910), Polish poet, novelist, journalist, translator, children's writer, and advocate for women's rights.

Konwicki, Tadeusz (1926–), Polish writer and celebrated film director. His underground novel *A Minor Apocalypse* is probably most known in the West.

Korchagin, Pavel, the central character in the classic 1936 novel of socialist realism, *How the Steel Was Tempered*, by Nikolai Ostrovsky.

Korczak, Janusz (1878–1942), Polish children's author, pediatrician, and pedagogue. After spending many years as director of an orphanage, Korczak refused to part with his children and in 1942 accompanied them on a death train to Treblinka from the Warsaw Ghetto. His children's books often take the form of fairy tale and include *King Matt the First* and *Kaytek the Wizard*. Born Henryk Goldszmit.

Kott, Jan (1914–2001), Polish critic and theoretician of theater. An ardent Stalinist early in life, Kott later changed his views, resigned from the party in 1957, and left Poland in 1965, defecting three years later. His most well-known work is *Shakespeare, Our Contemporary*, published in 1964.

Kraszewski, Józef (1812–87), Polish writer, historian, and journalist. Author of many works of historical fiction, he wrote more than 200 novels in his lifetime.

Krokodyl (see Kameralna).

Kruczkowski, Leon (1900–1962), Polish writer and publicist who came to hold various government posts in the communist government, including Deputy Minister of Culture and Art from 1945–48.

Kryvitsky, Walter (1899–1941), a defector to the West from the Soviet Union who first revealed the Nazi-Soviet nonaggression pact. His book, *I Was an Agent of Stalin*, was published in 1939. Two years later, he was found dead in a hotel room in Washington, D.C., most likely murdered by the Soviets. Born Samuel Ginsberg.

Krzeczkowski, Henryk (1921–85), Polish writer, translator, and publicist. Born Herman Gerner.

Kubiak, Tadeusz (1924–79), Polish poet and satirist, also the author of many radio plays for children.

Kultura [Culture], a leading Polish émigré journal published first in Rome, then in Paris, from 1947–2000.

Kuryluk, Karol (1910–67), Polish journalist, editor, activist, politician, and diplomat. Honored by Yad Vashem for his role in saving Jews during the Holocaust, Kuryluk was a well-respected writer and later served as Minister of Culture from 1956–58.

Lasota, Eligiusz (1929–2001), Polish journalist and editor of *Po Prostu* from 1953–57; later a representative in the Polish Sejm, 1957–61.

Łoś, Stefan (1901–55), Polish journalist, author of youth fiction, and vaudeville writer. Former president of the Polish Writers' Union.

Lubyanka, headquarters of the Soviet secret police on the eponymous Lubyanka Square, in Moscow.

Lysenko, Trofim (1898–1976), Ukrainian Soviet agronomist and chief biologist under Stalin, whose research, now largely viewed as fraudulent, led to massive famine and hardship.

Maariv, Israeli daily founded in 1948.

Mach, Wilhelm (1917–65), Polish writer, essayist, and literary critic. From 1950–58 he was the editor of *Nowa Kultura*, a literary journal. He committed suicide in 1965.

Mandalian, Andrzej (1926–2011), Polish poet, screenwriter, and translator. Wrote many works of socialist realist fiction in the Stalinist period, then joined the opposition in the 1970s; translated the memoirs of Russian gulag survivor Yevgenia Ginzburg. His works include the poetry collections *Everyday Words* and *Landscape with Comet*.

Mazurkiewicz, Władysław "Władzio" (1911–57), Polish serial killer from Kraków. Known as the "Gentleman Killer," he was convicted and executed after confessing to the murder of at least thirty women.

Michałowska, Mira (1914–2007), Polish writer, journalist, satirist, and acclaimed translator of, among others, Ernest Hemingway and E. L. Doctorow. Also wrote in English and published a series of short stories and letters in *The New Yorker, The Atlantic Monthly*, and *Harper's*, under the pseudonyms Mira Michal and Mira Zlotowska.

Mickiewicz, Adam (1798–1855), Polish national Bard. *Pan Tadeusz*, published in 1834, is the Polish national epic. Other major works include *Forefathers' Eve* and *Konrad Wallenrod*. Exiled from Poland in 1823 for anti–Imperial Russia activity, he spent the rest of his life in Russia, Italy, and France, and died in Constantinople while organizing a Jewish legion to fight against Russia.

Miłosz, Czesław (1911–2004), Polish poet, prose writer, and translator, and recipient of the Nobel Prize in Literature in 1980. *The Captive Mind*, his 1953 nonfiction book, is considered a classic investigation of the intellectual under a repressive regime.

Minkiewicz, Jadwiga "Kropka," (1911–2007), "Dot," so-called because of her diminutive stature. Actress and wife of Polish writer and journalist Janusz Minkiewicz.

Minkiewicz, Janusz (1914–81), Russian-born Polish writer, poet, and noted translator from Russian to Polish.

Monat, Colonel Paweł (1921–?), Polish officer who operated in intelligence in Korea for three years. In 1955, he was assigned as Polish military attaché in Washington, D.C., and later in Warsaw. He defected to the West with his family in 1959 and wrote an article in the June 27, 1960, issue of *Life* magazine. His book, *Spy in the U.S.*, was published in 1952 by Harper & Row. The date of his death, if he is indeed dead, is not publicly known.

Monte Cassino, site of a battle in southern Italy between Axis powers and Allied forces in 1944. The Allied forces eventually broke through the German lines, but at an extremely high cost. "Czerwone maki na Monte Cassino" ["The Red Poppies of Monte Cassino"] is one of the best-known Polish military songs of World War II, composed on the eve of battle.

Morozov, Pavel (1918–32), dedicated young communist allegedly murdered by his family for informing on his father for forging documents and selling them to the detriment of the communist state. The story propagated by the authorities, who made "Pavlik" Morozov into a folk hero, has come under serious doubt since the fall of the Soviet Union.

Mortkowicz, Jakub (1876–1931), Polish publisher and bookseller. Many of his editions became classics, highly treasured for their production quality as well as their contents. He committed suicide in 1931.

Mostowski Palace, eighteenth-century mansion in Warsaw. Destroyed in World War II and afterward rebuilt, it served as the headquarters for the Commission on Internal Affairs and the Police.

Mycielski, Zygmunt (1907–87), Polish composer and music critic.

Newerly, Igor (1903–87), great Polish novelist and educator. A friend of Janusz Korczak, he preserved the latter's diary when Korczak was sent to the death camps with his orphans. In 1964, he began serving the first of two consecutive terms as president of the Warsaw branch of the Polish Writers' Union. His 1952 novel, *A Souvenir from Cellulose*, is considered a masterpiece.

Nowak-Jeziorański, Jan (1914–2005), Polish journalist and politician. A war hero outside of Poland for his work as a courier between the

Home Army and the Polish government in exile during World War II, he later became the head of the Polish section of Radio Free Europe.

Nowakowski, Marek (1935–), celebrated Polish writer and member of the "Contemporaries," a literary movement in the late 1950s in which Hłasko and Andrzej Brycht were often grouped as well. Works include *This Old Thief* and *Death of a Turtle*.

Nowe Drogi [*New Paths*], ideological and theoretical monthly publication of the Central Committee of the Polish United Workers' Party, published from 1947–89.

Obory, writers' colony located outside of Warsaw.

Odrodzenie [*Renaissance*], first Polish weekly established after the war. It lasted from 1944–50 and printed stories by some of Poland's leading literary figures. In 1950 the magazine merged with *Kuźnica* [*Forge*], a magazine with a more markedly Marxist bent.

Okęcie, neighborhood in Warsaw.

Pawlikowski, Adam (1925–76), Polish actor, writer, and composer. His first film role was in Andrzej Wajda's *Canal* in 1957.

Petelski, Czesław (1922–96), Polish screenwriter and film director.

Po Prostu [*Simply Speaking*], a weekly magazine published in Warsaw from 1947–57. A magnet for young intellectuals, many prominent writers worked there early in their careers.

Polański, Roman (1933–), celebrated Polish-French film producer, writer, and actor. His films include *Rosemary's Baby* (1968), *Chinatown* (1974), and *The Pianist* (2002).

Production novel, term given to Soviet propaganda novels that regularly featured great feats of construction for the goal of building a better socialist society.

Prus, Bolesław (1847–1912), one of the great Polish novelists of all time. His character Ignacy Rzecki is the hero of the 1890 novel *The Doll* [*Lalka*]. Rzecki is an idealist who is an oddity in his times. Born Aleksander Głowacki.

Prutkowski, Józef (1915–81), Polish satirist and writer. Born Józef Nacht.

Przekrój [*Cross-Section*], oldest Polish weekly newsmagazine, established in 1945 by Marian Eile.

Putrament, Jerzy (1910–86), Polish writer and editor. Author of *Noah's Ark*, among others. Character of *Gamma* in Czesław Miłosz's *The Captive Mind*.

RGO (Rada Główna Opiekuńcza), Council of Economic Protection, a charitable organization active in Poland until 1945. The organization distributed coupons, something akin to food stamps, and Hłasko and others used these coupons in lieu of poker chips.

Różański, Józef "Jacek" (1907–81), brother of Jerzy Borejsza. Worked as interrogator and eventually a colonel in the Stalinist Ministry of Public Security. One of the most brutal secret police interrogators in Poland. Born Józef Goldberg.

Rudnicki, Adolf (1912–90), Polish essayist and novelist, best known for his 1932 novel, *The Rats*. Rudnicki, who was Jewish, took part in the Warsaw Uprising of 1944; his later work focused on the Holocaust and Jewish resistance. Born Aron Hirschhorn.

Runyon, Damon (1880–1946), New York writer and journalist whose stories were famous for their colorful characters, and involved the world of gambling, horses, and crime. The musical *Guys and Dolls* was based on his stories.

Rybakov, Anatoly (1911–98), Russian writer and anti-Stalinist. His most well-known work, *Children of the Arbat*, first appeared in samizdat in the Soviet Union in the 1960s but was not officially published until 1987.

Sandauer, Artur (1913–89), renowned Polish-Jewish literary critic, essayist, and translator, and longtime professor at the University of Warsaw.

Spychalski, Marian (1906–80), Polish architect, military commander, and communist politican. De jure head of state of Poland from 1968–70.

Stadelheim Prison, in Munich's Giesing district, one of the largest and most notorious prisons in Germany.

Stempowski, Jerzy (1893–1969), Polish essayist and literary critic. Wrote under the pseudonym Paweł Hostowiec. Author of over fifteen collections of essays and works of criticism.

Strzelec, the Polish Rifleman Association, was a Polish paramilitary organization founded in Lwów in 1910. Józef Piłsudski was the leader of the organization at one point.

Światło, Józef (1915–94), Polish official in the secret police who worked under Fejgin and earned the nickname "Butcher." He defected to the West in 1953 and later worked for the CIA and Radio Free Europe.

Szpilki [*Pins* or *Stilettos*], a satirical illustrated weekly founded in 1935 by Zbigniew Mitzner and Eryk Lipiński. In addition to caricatures and cartoons, it included contributions by such prominent writers as Julian Tuwim, Antoni Słonimski, and Konstanty Gałczyński.

Sztandar Młodych [*Youth Standard*], a daily youth newspaper, published from 1950–97.

Tertz, Abram (1925–97), pen name of Russian writer and dissident Andrei Sinyavski. Most famous for his 1960 novel, *The Trial Begins*. In 1966, Sinyavski and fellow writer Yuli Daniel were put on trial for anti-Soviet activity, a process that resonated around the world and ignited the Soviet dissident movement.

Toeplitz, Krzysztof (1933–2010), Polish journalist, writer, and screenwriter.

Trybuna Ludu [*People's Tribune*], a major Polish party line newspaper, similar to Russia's *Pravda*.

Tukhachevsky, Mikhail (1893–1937), commander in chief of the Red Army from 1925–28. He commanded the Soviet invasion of Poland in 1920, was defeated by Józef Piłsudski outside of Warsaw, and later was killed in Stalin's purges.

Tyrmand, Leopold "Poldek" (1920–85), Polish novelist and essayist who emigrated to the United States in 1964. He was famous for his writings on jazz and was instrumental in introducing the music to Poland. In the US his essays appeared in *The New Yorker* and the *New York Times Magazine*, among others.

UB (Urząd Bezpieczeństwa), Ministry of Public Security, which was responsible for intelligence and counterintelligence.

Uris, Leon (1924–2003), American novelist whose works include *Mila 18*, which chronicles the destruction of Polish Jewry. Mila 18 was the address of the bunkers/headquarters of the Jewish Resistance in Warsaw.

Vlasov's Army, also known as the Russian Liberation Army, under the command of General Andrei Vlasov, united various anti-communist factions to fight as one against the Red Army. For a period, it was subordinate to the Nazi High Command.

Vyshinsky, Andrei (1883–1954), Soviet politician, political philosopher, and jurist. Served as prosecutor general of the Soviet Union from 1935–38, and was thus largely responsible for prosecuting the accused during Stalin's Great Purge. He later served as foreign minister.

Wańkowicz, Melchior (1892–1974), Polish journalist and writer.

Werfel, Roman (1906–2003), Polish communist apparatchik and editor of *Nowe Drogi* from 1952–59. Former member of the Politburo.

Wiechecki, Stefan (1896–1979), Polish satirical writer and journalist, mostly remembered today for his humorous feuilletons, in which he chronicled the everyday life of Warsaw and its unique dialect. Wrote under the pseudonym Wiech and was known lovingly as The Great Wiech.

Wilczur-Garztecki, Juliusz (1920–), Polish writer, literary critic, and translator. Indeed, he did work for the secret police.

Willys, an American truck manufacturer best known for its Jeeps, many of which were used during World War II.

work order [*nakaz pracy*], compulsory job assignment. Recent graduates of universities and graduate schools would be assigned to a specific job, often in rural areas. Many young people wasted away in towns and villages where their expertise was neither wanted or appreciated, nor particularly useful.

Wyszyński, Cardinal Stefan (1901–81), Polish cardinal and prelate of Poland. Wyszyński was well known for his opposition to Nazism and communism and was imprisoned in 1953 for protesting against a new wave of persecutions.

Yezhov, Nikolai (1895–1940), head of the Soviet secret police from 1936–38. He personally tortured and saw to the execution of Genrikh Yagoda, his predecessor at the secret police, in 1936, based on trumped-up charges of espionage. Yezhov eventually met an almost identical fate in 1940.

Zelenay, Tadeusz (1913–61), Polish poet, writer, and translator who took part in the Warsaw Uprising. Works include *A Sentimental Spring* and *The Yellow Window*.

Żeromski, Stefan (1864–1925), prominent Polish novelist and dramatist, sometimes called "the conscience of Polish literature." His works include *The Spring to Come* and *The Labors of Sisyphus*.

Żuławski, Juliusz "Julek" (1910–99), Polish writer, editor, and translator; editor at *Nowa Kultura* from 1950–51.